# Study Guide

Volume II - From 1865 to Present

to accompany

Garraty

# The American Nation:
A History of the United States

Eighth Edition

Billy B. Hathorn
*Laredo Community College*

HarperCollins*CollegePublishers*

# Study Guide

Volume II - From 1865 to Present

to accompany

Garraty

# The American Nation:
## A History of the United States

Eighth Edition

Study Guide, Volume II - From 1865 to Present to accompany Garraty's THE AMERICAN NATION: A HISTORY OF THE UNITED STATES, Eighth Edition

**Copyright © 1995 by HarperCollins College Publishers**

All rights reserved. Printed in the United States of America. No part of this book may be used or reproduced in any manner whatsoever without written permission with the following exception: testing material may be copied for classroom testing. For information, address HarperCollins College Publishers, 10 East 53rd Street, New York, NY 10022.

ISBN: 0-673-99228-4

95 96 97 98  9 8 7 6 5 4 3 2

# Contents

Preface .................................................................................................... vi

Chapter 16: Reconstruction and the South .................................................... 1

Chapter 17: In the Wake of War ................................................................. 15

Chapter 18: An Industrial Giant .................................................................. 30

Chapter 19: American Society in the Industrial Age ....................................... 46

Chapter 20: Intellectual and Cultural Trends ................................................ 59

Chapter 21: Politics: Local, State, and National ............................................ 72

Chapter 22: From Isolation to Empire .......................................................... 87

Chapter 23: The Age of Reform ................................................................ 105

Chapter 24: Woodrow Wilson and the Great War ......................................... 122

Chapter 25: Postwar Society and Culture: Change and Adjustment ................ 139

Chapter 26: The New Era: 1921-1933 ........................................................ 154

Chapter 27: The New Deal: 1933-1941 ...................................................... 170

Chapter 28: War and Peace ..................................................................... 188

Chapter 29: The American Century ........................................................... 205

Chapter 30: The Best of Times, the Worst of Times ..................................... 224

Chapter 31: Society in Flux ...................................................................... 246

Chapter 32: Our Times ............................................................................ 261

Answers ................................................................................................ 283

# Preface

This Study Guide is intended to help you review and deepen your understanding of the material in the textbook *The American Nation*, Volume II, Eighth Edition, by John A. Garraty.

Each chapter of the Study Guide follows the same format. Each chapter begins with *Learning Objectives* which introduce the key themes of the chapter and suggest what you will know and be able to do after studying the chapter. These objectives are followed by an *Overview* of the chapter. This is a summary of the chapter's content. Next is an interactive section called *People, Places, and Things*. Here you will have space to write definitions of key concepts and terminology, descriptions of significant events, and identifications of important personalities that are contained in the chapter. In several chapters there are *Map Exercises* requiring you to identify historically significant places both by name and by location on an outline map. Following these exercises is a set of *Self-Test* questions, both multiple-choice and essay, that will help you check your comprehension of the chapter material and your attainment of the Learning Objectives.

At the end of each Study Guide chapter is a section titled *Critical Thinking Exercise*. The purpose of these exercises is to help you develop selected critical thinking skills, especially those that are crucial to the study of history: Classifying information, comparing and contrasting relationships, cause and effect relationships.

You can attain maximum benefit from the Study Guide by using the following procedure:

- Read the Learning Objectives
- Quickly read the Overview
- Read the textbook chapter
- Complete the People, Places, and Things exercises
- Rehearse for the Self-Test by rereading the Learning Objectives and Overview carefully. Double check any misunderstandings, information gaps, or confusion with the appropriate section of the textbook.
- Take the Self-Test
- Complete the Map and Critical Thinking Exercises
- Reread the Learning Objectives. You should be confident of your ability to do as your instructor asks.

Answers to the Map Exercises, Self-Test: Multiple Choice, and Critical Thinking Exercises are in the Answers section at the back of the Study Guide.

Billy B. Hathorn

CHAPTER 16

# Reconstruction and the South

## Learning Objectives

*After reading Chapter 16 you should be able to:*

1. Compare and contrast the provisions of Presidential and Congressional Reconstruction.
2. Describe the problems and accomplishments of the Radical Reconstruction governments in the postwar South.
3. Explain why sharecropping and the crop-lien system came to dominate southern agriculture after the Civil War.
4. Explain why Radical Reconstruction governments faltered and were replaced by conservative Democratic party governments by 1877.
5. List the provisions of the Fourteenth and Fifteenth constitutional amendments.
6. Discuss how and why whites rebelled against the "Black Republican" coalition.
7. Understand how the disputed 1876 presidential election was resolved.

## Overview

### Presidential Reconstruction

Lincoln's assassination doomed the South's best hope for a mild peace after the most devastating war in United States history. Jefferson Davis was captured in Georgia but never brought to trial on charges of treason and murder. Only one Confederate was executed for war crimes, Major Henry Wirz, commandant of Andersonville prison.

The political question of readmitting the southern states proved to be extremely complex. Massachusetts Senator Charles Sumner and Pennsylvania Congressman Thaddeus Stevens claimed that the Union could not be legally dissolved and insisted that the Confederacy had "committed suicide" and should be regarded as "conquered provinces." Lincoln urged a milder approach, the "ten percent plan," which reflected the president's lack of vindictiveness and the wisdom of seeking consensus to restore government in the southern states. Regimes were authorized under Lincoln's plan in Tennessee, Louisiana, and Arkansas.

Radicals in Congress opposed the plan because it allowed the President to set policy toward the recaptured regions. Their Wade-Davis bill required a majority in each former Confederate state to take loyalty oaths. It barred Confederate officials from voting in elections for state constitutional conventions. Lincoln pocket-vetoed Wade-Davis, and there matters stood until Andrew Johnson became president.

Johnson drew his political strength from the poor whites and farmers of eastern Tennessee who approved his distaste for the aristocratic class. Radicals, cautious about Johnson's states' rights views, were disappointed when the president issued an amnesty proclamation similar to Lincoln's. By the time Congress convened in 1865, the South had organized governments, ratified the Thirteenth Amendment, and elected members of Congress.

**Republican Radicals**

The Republican factions offered different approaches to Reconstruction. Sumner's group demanded total civil and political equality for blacks. Stevens's forces drew a distinction between the "natural rights" of the Declaration of Independence and "social equality" of former slaves. They were willing to accept less than they preferred to gain support among Republican moderates. Moderates wanted to protect slaves from exploitation and guarantee their basic rights, but they rejected political equality. Some Republicans favored black voting rights because adoption of the Thirteenth Amendment meant that the South would gain new seats in Congress because the Three-fifths Compromise had become invalid.

Southerners, moreover, provoked northern resentment by their choices of congressmen. Georgia elected Confederate Vice-President Alexander Stephens to the Senate though he was in federal prison awaiting trial for treason. The Black Codes enacted by southern governments to control the former slaves also alarmed many northerners. The codes granted some freedoms for blacks but prevented them from bearing arms and restricted occupational opportunities. Congress hence named a joint committee headed by Senator William P. Fessenden of Maine to study the question of Reconstruction. The hearings strengthened the Radicals, who pushed through legislation expanding and extending the Freedmen's Bureau to assist the former slaves in making the transition from slavery to freedom. For the first time in history, Congress overrode a presidential veto to legislate a Civil Rights Act designed to enforce the Thirteenth Amendment. Johnson's veto of the Freedmen's Bureau and the Civil Rights Act ultimately drove the moderates into the Radical camp.

**The Fourteenth Amendment**

In June 1866, Congress submitted the Fourteenth Amendment to the states, which broadened the definition of citizenship to include blacks and guaranteed due process and "equal protection" of the laws. Although it did not specifically outlaw segregation, the amendment struck at the discriminatory Black Codes and authorized reducing congressional representation to any state that denied the vote to black males. It repudiated the Confederate debt. As a states' righter opposed to centralization of power, Johnson tried to make opposition to the Fourteenth Amendment the focus of his "swing around the circle" in the 1866 mid-term Congressional elections. He failed dismally, as Radicals gained a "veto-proof" Congress and control of the northern state governments.

## The Reconstruction Acts

The ten southern states that initially rejected the Fourteenth Amendment were divided by Congress in the First Reconstruction Act of 1867 into five military districts, each controlled by a major general with near dictatorial powers. By ratifying the amendment, Tennessee was spared military rule.

To end martial law, the states were required to adopt constitutions that guaranteed blacks the right to vote and disfranchised many former Confederates. Subsequent Reconstruction Acts empowered the military to register voters and to supervise the election of delegates to constitutional conventions. The ten states were required to ratify the Fourteenth Amendment.

## Congress Takes Charge

The Radical Congress, determined to prevent the seating of "unreconstructed" southern congressmen, proceeded to increase its control over the judicial and executive branches. Laws passed between 1866 and 1868 increased the authority of Congress over the army, the constitutional amendment process, and over Cabinet members and lesser appointive officers.

Congress proceeded to remove President Johnson through the Tenure of Office Act, which forbade the president from dismissing officials who had been appointed with Senate consent without first obtaining Senate approval to remove. Johnson tested the law by dismissing Secretary of War Edwin Stanton, a Lincoln appointee who sympathized with the Radicals. After impeachment by the House, Johnson was tried before the Senate in a partisan, vindictive manner. Because seven Republican senators voted to acquit Johnson, the Senate failed by one vote to convict and remove the president from office. Had Johnson been removed, executive independence would have been seriously weakened.

## The Fifteenth Amendment

Though President Johnson had considerable support in his former party, Democratic delegates chose former New York Governor Horatio Seymour to face the Republican nominee, General Ulysses S. Grant. Grant won in the electoral college, but without the vote of southern freedmen, he would not have obtained a majority of the popular vote. Therefore, in a bid to gain greater strength among blacks, both North and South, the Republicans succeeded in sending the Fifteenth Amendment to the states for ratification. It forbade discrimination in voting on account of race or previous condition of servitude but omitted any reference to the denial of the vote on the basis of sex. By 1870, the amendment had obtained the approval of the needed three-fourths of the states, including the ex-Confederacy.

## "Black Republican" Reconstruction: Scalawags and Carpetbaggers

The real rulers of the "black Republican" governments were whites: (1) the scalawags, the southerners who cooperated with the Republicans because they accepted defeat in the war and hoped to advance their own interests, and (2) the carpetbaggers, northerners who went to the South as idealists eager to help the freed slaves, as government employees, or more commonly as settlers hoping to make a fresh start.

The former slaves voted overwhelmingly Republican, and a few managed to gain public office. None was elected governor, and fewer than 20 served in Congress. The blacks who held office tended to be better educated and more prosperous; a considerable number had been free before the war. Some black officeholders performed well, whereas others, particularly a group in South Carolina, were incompetent and dishonest.

Corruption was not confined to the South; the New York City "Tweed Ring" made off with probably more money than all the southern thieves, black and white, combined. Moreover, Reconstruction governments in the South expanded the region's railroad network, rebuilt levees, and expanded social services, including segregated public education, hospitals, and asylums.

## The Ravaged Land

The destruction of the South complicated the rebuilding of its political system. The freedmen learned that "freedom" meant the opportunity to provide for their own living, not merely relief from the drudgery of work. Congressman Stevens proposed the confiscation of 394 million acres from the wealthiest 70,000 southern planters. A few freedmen were settled on poor-quality federal land in the South under the Homestead Act. Many freedmen chose not to work like slaves and devoted more time to leisure and less to farm labor. Such life-style changes contributed to allegations of laziness and shiftlessness among the freedmen.

## Sharecropping and the Crop Lien System

The sharecropping system involved the breakup of large estates into smaller parcels of land. A black family was settled on each unit. The planter provided housing, farm implements, draft animals, and other supplies, and the freedman's family provided the labor. The crop was divided usually on a 50-50 basis. Under this system few blacks could accumulate enough money to own their farm lands.

Sharecropping also trapped many whites into a system of perpetual poverty. Such poverty was caused by the lack of capital to finance sharecropping. Because landowners had to borrow against October's harvest to pay for April's seed, the crop-lien system developed. To protect their investments, lenders insisted that the grower concentrate on marketable cash crops: sugar, tobacco, and particularly cotton. Though the South made important gains in manufacturing, the sharecropping and crop-lien system held back the economic development of the region, which continued to lag behind the North.

## The White Backlash

Southern white Republicans, mostly of Whig ancestry, used the Union League of America to control the pivotal black vote. Dissident southerners, hoping to check the Union League, turned to terrorist societies, of which the Ku Klux Klan became the most notorious. Originally a social club, the Klan by 1868 organized night riders to intimidate the freedmen from exercising their voting rights. Congress struck at the Klan with three Force Acts that placed elections under federal supervision and punished those interfering with any citizen's exercise of the franchise.

Nevertheless, the Klan worked to destroy Radical regimes in the South by weakening the will of both white Republicans and blacks, many of whom gave up trying to exercise their rights. As blacks increasingly sat out elections, "conservative" Democratic parties regained control of each southern state from the previous Radical rule. Northerners, meanwhile, grew tired of Reconstruction and reconciled themselves to the return of white control in the former Confederacy.

## Grant As President

The expansion of industry in the North and the rapid development of the West seemed more important to many than the plight of the freedmen. Some Republicans were alarmed that Ulysses Grant had not lived up to expectations as president. He seemed unable to deal with economic and social problems or to cope with government corruption. Though personally honest, Grant is remembered for having presided over one of the most corrupt administrations.

The Whiskey Ring implicated his private secretary, Orville Babcock, and cost the government millions in taxes. Secretary of War William Belknap's management of the Bureau of Indian Affairs was called into question. Dissatisfaction with the scandals and Grant's failure to obtain civil service led to formation in 1872 of the Liberal Republican party, consisting of editors, college presidents, economists, and some businessmen and politicians. Both the Liberal Republicans and Democrats nominated *New York Tribune* editor Horace Greeley to oppose Grant. Because the news of the scandals had not yet publicly surfaced, Grant easily won reelection. In 1874, the Democrats took control of the House for the first time since the Civil War. Republican strength in the South steadily declined thereafter.

## The Disputed Election of 1876

Grant declined to seek a third term, and the Republicans turned to Ohio Governor Rutherford B. Hayes, a former Union general with a spotless reputation. The Democrats chose New York Governor Samuel Tilden, who had prosecuted the Tweed Ring.

The election was characterized by fraud on both sides though neither Hayes nor Tilden was personally responsible for such chicanery. The electoral vote stood at 184 for Tilden and 165 for Hayes, with 20 disputed votes from Florida, Louisiana, and South Carolina. To win, Hayes had to garner all 20 votes. This feat came about through the decision of an Electoral Commission established by Congress to resolve the impasse.

The 15-man commission, divided 7-7 between the parties with one independent, was created because the Democratic House and Republican Senate did not trust the other to do the job of counting the votes. When the independent was elected as a United States senator, his position was assumed by a Republican Supreme Court justice. The vote was 8-7 to give all disputed electoral votes to Hayes, a move which gave Hayes a one-vote victory margin. Most modern authorities contend that the worst-case scenario for the Democrats should have still enabled Tilden to carry Florida and win, 188-181.

**The Compromise of 1877**

Forces for compromise had been struggling to resolve the election impasse. In return for acceptance of his 185-184 "victory," Hayes agreed to remove the last federal troops from Louisiana and South Carolina. He appointed former Confederate General David M. Key of Tennessee, as postmaster general, the Cabinet post with authority over patronage. Despite the hopes of some former Whigs that a two-party system would again prevail in the South, the region remained Democratic. The historian C. Vann Woodward contends that the compromise, more than any statute or constitutional amendment, impacted the freedmen by providing for a return to expediency and concession.

## People, Places, and Things

*Define the following concepts:*

pocket veto _____

_____

amnesty _____

_____

impeachment _____

_____

sharecropping _____

_____

crop-lien system _____

_____

*Describe the following:*

ten percent plan _____

_____

Wade-Davis bill _____

_____

Thirteenth Amendment _____

_____

Black Codes _____

_____

Freedmen's Bureau _____

_____

Civil Rights Act _____

_____

"swing around the circle" _____

_____

Fourteenth Amendment _____

_____

Reconstruction Acts _____

_____

Tenure of Office Act _____

_____

Fifteenth Amendment _____

_____

Force Acts _____

_____

Compromise of 1877 _____

_____

*Identify the following people:*

Thaddeus Stevens _____

_____

Charles Sumner _____

_____

Andrew Johnson _____

_____

Radical Republicans _____

_____

scalawags _____

_____

carpetbaggers _____

_____

Ku Klux Klan _____

_____

Ulysses S. Grant _____

_____

Liberal Republicans _____

_____

Horace Greeley _____

_____

Rutherford B. Hayes _____

_____

Electoral Commission _____

_____

David M. Key _____

_____

## Self-Test

**Multiple-Choice Questions**

1. Reconstruction involved bitter controversies over all of the following issues *except*:
   A. Southern recognition of emancipation
   B. Readmission procedures for southern states
   C. Control of governments in the southern states
   D. Civil and political rights for former slaves

2. President Lincoln's ten percent plan for Reconstruction required southern states to do all of the following *except*:
   A. Adopt a republican form of government
   B. Accept the abolition of slavery
   C. Provide education for former slaves
   D. Guarantee blacks the right to vote

3. The Wade-Davis bill required southern states to:
   A. Guarantee black social equality
   B. Repudiate the Confederate debt
   C. Guarantee universal manhood suffrage
   D. Gradually abolish slavery

4. Andrew Johnson was made Lincoln's running mate in 1864 for the political benefits that would result from his:
   A. Being a Radical Republican leader
   B. Patient, compromising manner
   C. Being a Democrat from a border slave state
   D. Having been a southern slaveowner

5. Radical Republicans in Congress did *not* object to that part of President Johnson's Reconstruction policy that:
   A. Barred former Confederates from holding public office
   B. Would increase the number of Democrats in Congress
   C. Required southerners to repudiate the Confederate debt
   D. Allowed southern states to use special legal codes to control freedmen

6. President Johnson vetoed all of the following *except*:
   A. Civil Rights Act
   B. Freedmen's bill
   C. Wade-Davis bill
   D. Reconstruction Act

7. The Fourteenth Amendment guaranteed:
   A. Citizenship to former slaves
   B. Land ownership for former slaves
   C. Freedom to slaves
   D. The right to vote for the freedmen

8. The Fourteenth Amendment provided for all of the following *except*:
   A. Required former Confederate officials to pay their war debts
   B. Prohibited former Confederate officials from voting
   C. Guaranteed former slaves due process of law
   D. Guaranteed all citizens equal protection of the laws

9. President Johnson believed that citizenship and voting rights of former slaves were the concern of:
   A. The federal government
   B. State governments
   C. The executive branch
   D. Congress

10. The South was divided into five military districts under provisions of the:
    A. Tenure of Office Act
    B. Civil Rights Act
    C. Reconstruction Act
    D. Force Acts

11. The impeachment charges against President Johnson were most immediately provoked by his:
    A. Partisan "swing around the circle"
    B. Readmission of Confederate states
    C. Dismissal of Secretary of War Stanton
    D. Advice that southern states not ratify the Fourteenth Amendment

12. The Fifteenth Amendment was an attempt to gain _____ for former slaves:
    A. Land ownership
    B. The franchise
    C. Educational opportunities
    D. Citizenship

13. The Radical Reconstruction governments in the South were usually controlled by:
    A. Scalawags
    B. Carpetbaggers
    C. Former slaves
    D. Democrats

14. The Radical Reconstruction governments did all of the following *except*:
    A. Clean up corruption
    B. Raise taxes
    C. Initiate public schooling
    D. Finance railroad construction

15. After the Civil War:
    A. The South's general economic condition declined
    B. The planter elite no longer controlled land ownership
    C. The sharecropping system of labor management declined
    D. Most former slaves became small landowners

16. All of the following refer to the southern economy during Reconstruction *except*:
    A. Former slaves disliked working for wages
    B. Money was scarce
    C. Cotton production declined
    D. The South's share of manufacturing increased

17. The Liberal Republican party of 1872 advocated all the following *except*:
    A. Lower tariffs
    B. Sound money
    C. Universal suffrage
    D. Honest government

18. The disputed votes in the 1876 presidential election were assigned to candidates by:
    A. The Joint Committee on Reconstruction
    B. A special Electoral Commission
    C. The Supreme Court
    D. The Electoral College

19. After his inauguration in 1877, President Hayes:
    A. Demanded that the South ratify the Fifteenth Amendment
    B. Blocked pensions for Civil War veterans
    C. Withdrew remaining occupying troops from the South
    D. Pardoned former President Grant for involvement in corruption

20. Arrange the following events in sequence: (a) Wade-Davis bill, (b) Reconstruction Act, (c) Fifteenth Amendment, (d) Compromise of 1877
    A. a, b, d, c
    B. a, b, c, d
    C. c, d, b, a
    D. b, a, c, d

## Essay Questions

1. Compare and contrast provisions of the ten percent plan, Wade-Davis bill, Johnson's amnesty plan, and the Radical plan for Reconstruction. Why was the Radical plan finally adopted?

2. Define the problems faced by Radical Reconstruction governments. List the major accomplishments of these governments.

3. Explain why sharecropping and the crop-lien system dominated the landowner-merchant-labor relationship in the southern economy.

4. Explain why advocates of Radical Reconstruction failed to accomplish many of their goals.

5. List key provisions of the Fourteenth and Fifteenth Amendments and describe the historical context in which they were proposed and ratified.

# Critical Thinking Exercise

## Facts, Inferences, and Judgments

Being able to distinguish among a statement of fact, an inference, or a judgment is an important skill to critical thinking. It involves knowing what can be proven directly, what is a legitimate implication derived from the facts, and what can be concluded from the historical record.

Historians interweave statements of fact, inferences they derive from the facts, and statements of their judgment into a seamless historical narrative. Active and analytical readers, or critical thinkers, should be able to distinguish among these types of communication:

A *fact* reports information that can be directly observed, or can be verified or checked for accuracy.

> Example: "Until the adult male population of the entire area reached 5,000, it was to be ruled by a governor and three judges. . . ."

An *inference* is a conclusion based on factual information, yet goes beyond the facts to make a more general statement about something.

> Example: "The western lands. . . became a force for unity once they had been ceded to the national government."

A *judgment* expresses an evaluation based on certain criteria which may or may not be expressed.

> Example: "Seldom has a legislative body acted more wisely."

Place an "F" before each factual statement in the following narrative, an "I" before each inference, or a "J" before each judgment.

____ 1. The real rulers of the black Republican governments were white scalawags and carpetbaggers.

____ 2. Scalawags were by far the more numerous of the two.

____ 3. A few scalawags were prewar politicians or well-to-do planters.

____ 4. Most scalawags had supported the Whig party before the secession crisis.

____ 5. That blacks should fail to dominate southern governments is certainly understandable.

____6. Blacks lacked experience in politics and were mostly poor and uneducated.

____7. Not all black legislators and administrators were paragons of virtue.

____8. In South Carolina, despite black Republican control of the legislature, members divided into factions and failed to press for laws that would improve the lot of poor black farmers.

____9. One Arkansas black took $9,000 from the state to repair a bridge that had cost $500 to build.

____10. However, the corruption must be seen in perspective.

____11. Graft and callous disregard of the public interest characterized government in all regions and at every level during the decade after Appomattox.

____12. The New York City Tweed Ring probably made off with more money than all the southern thieves, black and white, combined.

____13. The evidence does not justify southern corruption.

____14. The evidence suggests that the unique features of Reconstruction politics do not explain it either.

____15. In fact, Radical southern governments accomplished much.

____16. Tax rates zoomed, but the money financed the repair and expansion of the South's dilapidated railroad network, rebuilt crumbling levees, and expanded social services.

____17. Much state money was spent on economic development: land reclamation, repairing and expanding war-ravaged railroads, and maintaining levees.

CHAPTER 17

# In the Wake of War

## Learning Objectives

*After reading Chapter 17, you should be able to:*

1. Understand how the accelerating tide of materialism among Americans in the late nineteenth century fostered "Social Darwinism."
2. Discuss the similarities between the major political parties in the 1870s and 1880s.
3. Explain Booker T. Washington's "Atlanta Compromise."
4. Identify the Plains Indian tribes, their locations, and common cultures.
5. Analyze the major Indian wars in the West.
6. Discuss the impact of mining and land policy on the West.
7. Identify the major transcontinental railroads, their routes, and methods of financing.
8. Analyze the development and decline of the cattle kingdom.

## Overview

### The American Commonwealth

The political history of the late nineteenth century bore little relationship to the meaningful issues of the day. The English author James Bryce, in *The American Commonwealth*, claimed that the politicians neglected to solve the problems spurred by rapid industrialization.

### "Root, Hog, or Die"

In the post-Reconstruction era, many Americans embraced laissez-faire, the notion that government should not interfere in economic matters. Charles Darwin spurred the belief in inevitable progress governed by the natural selection of individual organisms best adapted to survive in a particular environment.

This "survival of the fittest" ideology was further espoused by Yale professor William Graham Sumner, who told students "It's root, hog, or die," when asked if he favored any government aid to industries. Rhetoric aside, entrepreneurs did not hesitate to accept government aid, whether railroad subsidies or protective tariffs.

## The Shape of Politics

Congress dominated the government between the administrations of Andrew Johnson and Theodore Roosevelt but was held in overall low esteem. The Senate was perceived as a "rich man's club," whereas the House of Representatives gained notoriety for disorder and inefficiency. Partisan divisions were sectional—stemming from the outcome of the Civil War. The parties were often balanced in Congress, but the Republicans won all but two presidential elections between 1860 and 1908. Business usually favored Republicans, though steel magnate Andrew Carnegie and banker J. P. Morgan admired Grover Cleveland, the only Democrat to occupy the White House between James Buchanan and Woodrow Wilson.

## Issues of the Gilded Age

These four issues dominated the post-Reconstruction era:

(1) Veterans' pensions,
(2) The tariff,
(3) Currency reform,
(4) Civil service.

By "waving the bloody shirt," Republican politicians blamed Democrats for the Civil War and the Lincoln assassination and supported the Grand Army of the Republic's call for Union pensions. Both parties supported a high or moderately high tariff, but Cleveland worked to lower rates even in the election year of 1888. Business sought tariff protection, but consumers disliked paying more for imported goods. Tariff debates often turned into occasions for logrolling, lobbying, and politicking.

Currency issues revolved about free silver and greenbacks, the paper money issued by the Union government during the war. Steps were taken to increase or decrease the amount of money in circulation, but the net economic effect was negligible. Civil service was proposed as government grew larger and more complex. The number of federal employees rose from 53,000 in 1871 to 256,000 by the turn of the century.

## Blacks After Reconstruction

President Rutherford Hayes told blacks that their interests would be protected when southern whites regained control of their state governments so that whites would have no desire to continue harassing former slaves, a policy Frederick Douglass termed "sickly conciliation." For a while, blacks were not totally disenfranchised in the postwar South, but by 1900 few blacks were permitted to vote, a result of poll taxes, literacy tests, and the once white-only Democratic primary.

In 1883, the Supreme Court struck down the Civil Rights Act of 1875 on grounds that the Fourteenth Amendment protected blacks from discrimination by the states, but not by individuals. In *Plessy v. Ferguson* (1896), the court affirmed a policy that would stand for 58 years: segregation was legal so long as separate facilities were of equal quality.

## Booker T. Washington and the Atlanta Compromise

In his 1895 "Atlanta Compromise," Washington urged whites to assist black "self-help" endeavors. He advised blacks to accept segregation and second-class citizenship while concentrating on learning useful skills. After blacks improved themselves accordingly, they would be accepted as equals by whites, Washington predicted. Though he chose accommodation, Washington worked against restrictive measures and organized the black voters in the North.

More radical than Washington was T. Thomas Fortune, the founder of the Afro-American League, who called on blacks to demand civil rights, better schools, fair wages, and an end to discrimination.

## The West After the Civil War

The West was populated after the war by many foreign-born residents coming from Mexico, China, and Europe. Besides its great open spaces, the West contained several bustling cities, the most significant being San Francisco (population 250,000), home of Levi Strauss and Wells, Fargo. The western economy was based on agriculture, mining, commercial ventures, and the early stages of industrialization. The West epitomized the "every man for himself" psychology.

California was particularly affected by the steady flow of Chinese laborers, more of whom came to the United States under the Burlingame Treaty of 1868. The Chinese provided much of the labor needed to build the western link of the transcontinental railroad from Sacramento to Promontory Point, Utah.

## The Plains Indians

For 250 years Indians had been driven back steadily by the whites, but they still occupied roughly half of the United States by 1860. The Plains tribes lived by hunting the buffalo, millions of which ranged over the plains. From the whites, the Indians obtained the horse, the cavalry sword, the rifle, liquor, and diseases. Over time, the buffalo herds diminished and warfare increased. The United States government treated each tribe as a separate sovereign nation in the policy of "concentration" employed in the 1851 tribal council called at Horse Creek near Fort Laramie, Wyoming, by Thomas Fitzpatrick. Each Indian tribe was persuaded to accept limits to its hunting grounds.

## Indian Wars

Warfare erupted on the Plains when federal troops were pulled from the West to fight against the Confederacy. In 1864, a party of Colorado militia led by Colonel J. M. Chivington came upon an unsuspecting Cheyenne community at Sand Creek and killed an estimated 450 people. General Nelson A. Miles termed this Chivington Massacre the "foulest and most unjustifiable crime in the annals of America." In turn, the Indians slaughtered dozens of isolated white families. In 1866, the Sioux under Red Cloud massacred Captain W. J. Fetterman's band of 82 soldiers, who were constructing the Bozeman Trail through Sioux hunting grounds.

In 1867, the government announced that the Plains Indians would be confined to two small reservations, one in the Black Hills of South Dakota and the other in Oklahoma. When gold was discovered in the Black Hills, miners entered reservation lands, and the Sioux again went on the warpath. Led by Crazy Horse, Sitting Bull, and Rain-in-the-Face, 2,500 Sioux annihilated a 264-man force led by General George Custer at the Little Bighorn River in Montana. Nevertheless, the Indians ran short of rations that autumn and returned to the reservation.

## The Destruction of Tribal Life

The slaughter of the buffalo signaled the destruction of tribal life on the Plains. By the 1880s the buffalo neared extinction, and tribes in the mountains and deserts gave up their fight. The Dawes Severalty Act of 1887 split up tribal lands into individual allotments in a vain attempt by Congress to convert the Indians into small agricultural capitalists. By 1934, the government resumed the previous policy of encouraging tribal ownership and recognizing distinct Indian cultures.

## Exploiting Mineral Wealth in the West

Gold and silver discoveries spurred the growth of mining towns, which sprang up overnight. Claims were staked out along every stream and gully. Soon the boom collapsed, as the prospectors encountered mainly backbreaking labor and disappointment. Law enforcement was a constant problem, as such mining towns as Virginia City, Nevada, and Deadwood, South Dakota, attracted rascals, pickpockets, and gamblers from throughout the world. Virginia City was built on the riches of the Comstock Lode and the Ophir vein, and Deadwood was born in the Black Hills strike. The mines about Deadwood were ultimately controlled by Homestake Mining, a company still in production. Similarly, Anaconda Mining dominated the area about Butte, Montana.

## The Land Bonanza

The 160 acres of land permitted under the Homestead Act of 1862 was insufficient for raising livestock or commercial agriculture in the West. The Timber Culture Act of 1873, helpful to farmers in Kansas, Nebraska, and the Dakotas, allowed individuals to claim an additional 160 acres of land if they agreed to plant a quarter of it in trees within ten years. The Timber and Stone Act of 1878 allowed anyone, including lumber companies, to acquire a quarter section of forest land for $2.50 per acre.

Frontier farmers grappled with many problems as they pushed across the plains with their families. Despite the rich soil, the farmers faced periodic drought, floods, grasshopper plagues, blizzards, and fires. Only the most hardy could endure.


**Western Railroad Building**

Government subsidized the laying of railroads across the West through loans and land grants, the first of which was awarded in 1850 to the Illinois Central. Most of the grants went to four transcontinental railroads: Union Pacific-Central Pacific from Omaha to Sacramento; the Atchison, Topeka, and Santa Fe from Kansas City to San Francisco; the Southern Pacific from San Francisco to New Orleans; and the Northern Pacific joining Duluth with Portland, Oregon.

The Pacific Railway Act established the pattern for land grants, with builders of the Union Pacific and Central Pacific allocated five square miles of public land on each side of the railway for each mile of track laid. The Union Pacific created a construction company, Credit Mobilier, to lay its western rail line. Credit Mobilier stock was partly owned by a group of congressmen and other government officials. When scandal resulted, the House censured Representative Oakes Ames of Massachusetts, who had sold the stock to colleagues at below-market prices. The loans made to the Union and Central Pacific ranged from $16,000 to $48,000 per mile, depending on the terrain. In competing for the subsidies, the two companies built redundant miles of inferior-grade track. The one transcontinental railroad built without such grants was James Hill's high-quality Great Northern, connecting St. Paul with the Pacific.


**The Cattle Kingdom**

Columbus brought the first cattle to America on his second voyage in 1493. By 1866, a number of Texans drove large herds northward toward Sedalia, Missouri, railhead of the Missouri Pacific, but the route was hampered by the wooded terrain and the presence of Indian reservations. The next year drovers led herds north by a more westerly route along the Chisholm Trail to Abilene, Kansas. At the same time Charles Goodnight and Oliver Loving drove 2,000 head in a great arc west to New Mexico Territory and into Colorado.

The "long drive," which involved guiding herds of up to 3,000 across a thousand miles of country, produced the American cowboy, exalted in song, story, and on film. The young cowboys patronized dance halls, saloons, and gambling dens. Contrary to popular legend, they did not terrorize towns and honest citizens. Historian Robert Dykstra surveyed the major "cattle towns" of Abilene, Wichita, Ellsworth, Dodge City, and Caldwell and found that there were only 45 total homicides in all five towns between 1870 and 1885.

### Open-Range Ranching

Cattlemen found that the hardy Texas stock could flourish on the prairie grasses of the Great Plains. The grasses offered cattlemen a bonanza almost as valuable as the gold mines. Open-range ranching required ownership of only a few acres along some watercourse. In this semiarid region, control of water enabled a rancher to dominate the surrounding area. Outfits such as the Nebraska Land and Cattle Company and the Union Cattle Company of Wyoming soon dominated the business, much as large companies had consolidated mining holdings.

Major John Wesley Powell, later director of the United States Geological Survey, proposed that western lands be divided into three classes: irrigable lands, timber lands, and "pasturage" lands. On pasturage lands the "farm unit" should be 2,560 acres (four sections), Powell urged.

### Barbed-Wire Warfare

The Desert Land Act of 1877 allowed anyone to obtain 640 acres in the arid states for $1.25 an acre provided that the owner irrigated part of it within three years. Over 2.6 million acres were taken up under this law, but in most cases no sincere effort was made to irrigate the land.

Ranchers formed cattlemen's associations to halt thievery and protect their water rights. To keep other ranchers' cattle from those sections of the public domain they considered their own, the associations fenced huge areas. Barbed wire, invented in 1874 by Joseph F. Glidden of Illinois, hence contributed to the disappearance of the open range. Walter Prescott Webb wrote that the "advent of barbed wire brought about the disappearance of the open, free range and converted the range country into the big-pasture country."

The range-cattle kingdom was further undermined by blizzards, which preceded and followed the summer drought of 1886.

## People, Places, and Things

*Define the following concepts:*

graduated income tax _____

_____

laissez-faire _____

_____

"survival of the fittest"_____

_____

"rich man's club" _____

_____

"waving the bloody shirt" _____

_____

greenbacks _____

_____

"concentration" _____

_____

severalty _____

_____

logrolling _____

_____

*Describe the following:*

Grand Army of the Republic _____

_____

Rutherford B. Hayes _____

_____

*Plessy v. Ferguson* _____

_____

Atlanta Compromise _____

_____

Burlingame Treaty _____
_____

Horse Creek _____
_____

Sand Creek Massacre _____
_____

Fetterman Massacre _____
_____

Black Hills _____
_____

Little Bighorn _____
_____

Pacific Railway Act _____
_____

*The Great Plains* _____
_____

"bonanza" farms _____
_____

*Identify the following people:*

Booker T. Washington _____
_____

22

Nelson A. Miles _____

_____

George A. Custer _____

_____

Joseph McCoy _____

_____

Joseph Glidden _____

_____

Oakes Ames _____

_____

Charles Goodnight _____

_____

Nelson A. Miles _____

_____

Grover Cleveland _____

_____

## Map Exercise

Refer to the map below. Place the appropriate letter that represents the Indian tribe that lived in various regions of the West. Consult a historical atlas as needed.

_____ 1. Apache

_____ 2. Arapaho

_____ 3. Blackfoot

_____ 4. Cheyenne

_____ 5. Comanche

_____ 6. Crow

_____ 7. Kiowa

_____ 8. Nez Perce

_____ 9. Sioux

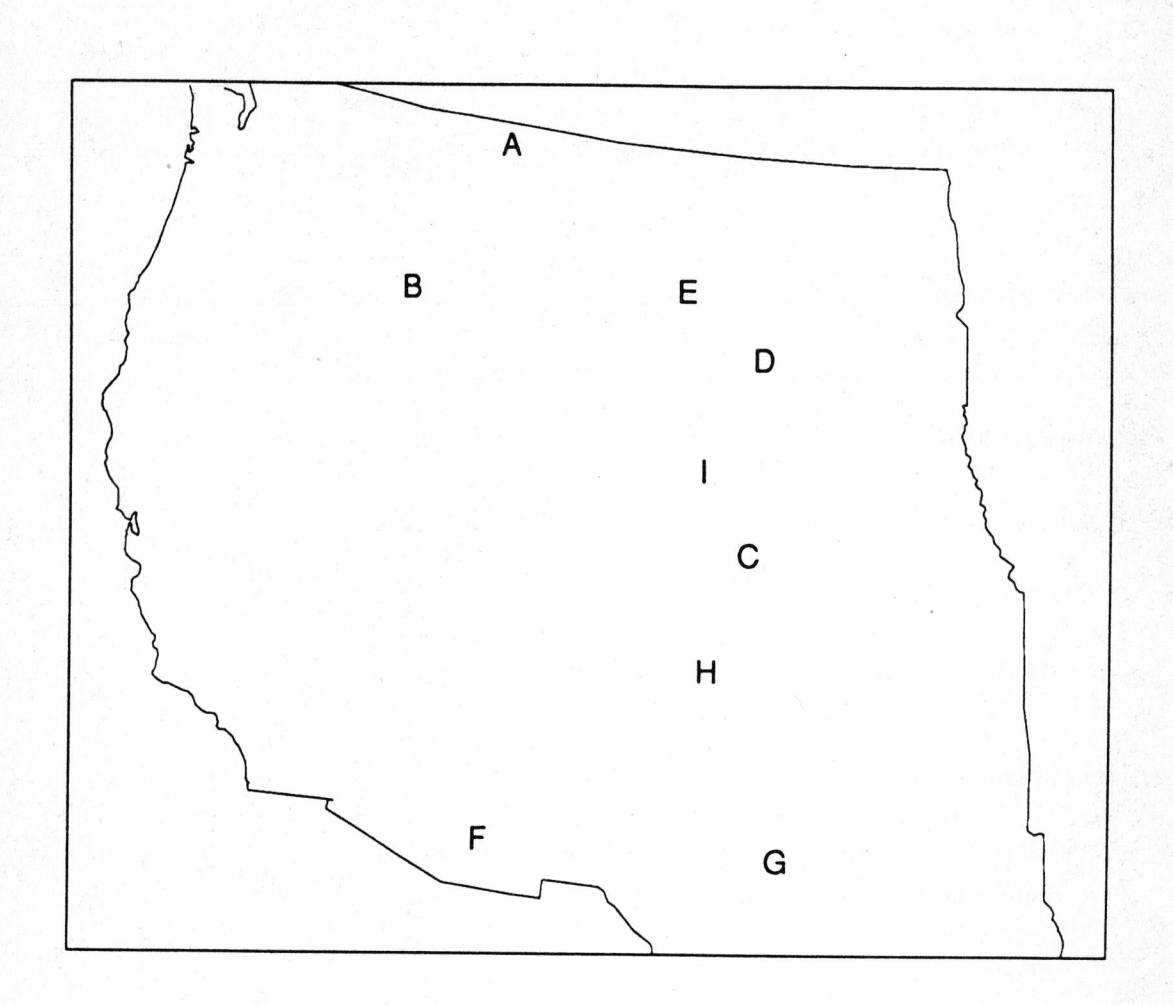

24

# Self-Test

## Multiple-Choice Questions

1. Mark Twain's *Roughing It* was based on his experiences in:
   A. Deadwood
   B. San Francisco
   C. The Fraser River country
   D. Virginia City, Nevada

2. The cattle trails began in:
   A. Western Kansas
   B. South Texas
   C. North Louisiana
   D. Eastern Oklahoma

3. The infamous figure in the Sand Creek massacre was:
   A. J. M. Chivington
   B. W. J. Fetterman
   C. Nelson A. Miles
   D. Crazy Horse

4. All of the following were Sioux chiefs *except*:
   A. Crazy Horse
   B. Red Cloud
   C. Geronimo
   D. Sitting Bull

5. Which law abolished Indian tribal organization and divided reservations for the benefit of individuals?
   A. Desert Land Act
   B. Timber Culture Act
   C. Dawes Severalty Act
   D. Homestead Act

6. The Yale professor who promoted Social Darwinism was:
   A. Oakes Ames
   B. William Graham Sumner
   C. Walter Prescott Webb
   D. George Hearst

7. In *The American Commonwealth* James Bryce:
   A. Stressed laissez-faire
   B. Took issue with the classical teachings of Adam Smith
   C. Decried the failure of politicians to confront the issues
   D. Justified Social Darwinism in business

8. Which of the following was *not* an issue in the Gilded Age:
   A. "Waving the bloody shirt" of rebellion
   B. High tariff rates
   C. Graduated income tax
   D. Civil service

9. In the Civil Rights Cases the Supreme Court:
   A. Upheld *Plessy v. Ferguson*
   B. Ruled that the Fourteenth Amendment protects civil rights against invasion by the states but not individuals
   C. Forbade segregation in public accommodations
   D. Declared that the Constitution is "color-blind"

10. In the Atlanta Compromise, Booker T. Washington:
    A. Demanded passage of a federal law permitting blacks to vote
    B. Called for desegregation of public accommodations
    C. Urged his fellow blacks to improve their personal economic well-being before seeking full political and social equality
    D. Challenged *Plessy v. Ferguson*

11. Immigrants who helped to build the Central Pacific from Sacramento to Promontory Point were mainly:
    A. Irish
    B. Mexican
    C. German
    D. Chinese

12. The principal Indian reservations were located in:
    A. South Dakota and Oklahoma
    B. Colorado and Wyoming
    C. Montana and North Dakota
    D. Kansas and Nebraska

13. Plains Indians adapted all of the following from the white man *except*:
    A. The desire to farm
    B. The horse
    C. The rifle
    D. Alcohol

14. Thomas Fitzpatrick:
    A. Persuaded the Plains Indians to accept limits to their hunting grounds
    B. Staged a massacre of the Cheyenne in 1864
    C. Was part of the Central Pacific "Big Four"
    D. Urged the division of western lands into three categories according to usage

15. The cattle trail that reached Abilene, Kansas, was named:
    A. Chisholm
    B. Sedalia
    C. Goodnight-Loving
    D. Sioux

16. The most decisive blow to the Plains Indians came through:
    A. Neglect of farming
    B. Blizzards and droughts
    C. Decline of bison herds
    D. The American army

17. The editor of the *New York Age* who advocated immediate civil rights for blacks was:
    A. T. Thomas Fortune
    B. Booker T. Washington
    C. James Bryce
    D. Rodman Paul

18. Which railroad garnered the first federal land grant?
    A. Union Pacific
    B. Central Pacific
    C. Illinois Central
    D. Great Northern

19. The most populous city of the postwar West was:
    A. Denver
    B. Los Angeles
    C. Seattle
    D. San Francisco

20. Which president once operated ranches in the Dakota territory?
    A. Benjamin Harrison
    B. Grover Cleveland
    C. Theodore Roosevelt
    D. Rutherford Hayes

**Essay Questions**

1. Discuss four key political issues of the Gilded Age in light of James Bryce's criticism of the American political leadership.

2. Explain how the Plains Indians were finally subdued to the reservations.

3. Discuss the short-lived mining boom in the West, life in the mining camps, and the eventual domination of the mines by eastern capitalists.

4. Explain how and why the Civil Rights Cases of 1883 and *Plessy v. Ferguson* differed from Supreme Court decisions regarding racial issues since 1954.

5. Discuss the construction of the first transcontinental railroad, tracing the route, companies involved, government policies, and abuse of taxpayers.

## Critical Thinking Exercise

Circle the response in each of the following which is *unrelated* to the other three selections.

1. Massacre
   Bison
   Army
   Faro

2. Claims
   Irrigation
   Prospectors
   Assay

3. Comstock
   Atchison
   Deadwood
   Homestake

4. Semiarid
   Desert
   Humid
   Drought

5. Discrimination
   Separatism
   Citizenship
   Repression

6. Grasshoppers
   Blizzards
   Fire
   Harvest

7. Scalping
   Soldiers
   Reservation
   Warriors

8. Comanche
   Cherokee
   Crow
   Cheyenne

9. Miners
   Drovers
   Mavericks
   Fencing

10. Laissez-faire
    Subsidies
    Social Darwinism
    Supply and demand

CHAPTER 18

# An Industrial Giant

## Learning Objectives

*After reading Chapter 18, you should be able to:*

1. Evaluate the rapid growth of railroads toward the end of the nineteenth century.
2. Explain the role of Thomas Edison in American technology.
3. Describe the impact of Andrew Carnegie in the establishment of the steel industry.
4. Understand how John D. Rockefeller acquired his domination of the petroleum industry.
5. Evaluate traditional support for free enterprise along with the call for government regulation of business.
6. Explain the ideas of Henry George, Edward Bellamy, and Henry Lloyd.
7. Understand the premise of Marxian socialism.
8. Understand conditions that gave rise to the need for labor unions.
9. Recount the major labor strikes toward the end of the nineteenth century.

## Overview

### Industrial Growth

Between the end of the Civil War and the beginning of the twentieth century, the United States was transformed into a world industrial power at a pace not previously seen in history. Great Britain and Germany, the most prosperous European nations, lagged behind the United States. The gross national product increased by 44 percent between 1874 and 1883.

In the name of progress, business glorified material wealth. Such attitudes produced a generation of Robber Barons who engaged in such corrupt practices as stock manipulation, bribery, and restraint of trade, a euphemism for monopoly. Many immigrants viewed America as a land of opportunity though some mired in grinding poverty had to struggle for survival in dreary, unhealthy living conditions.

Expanded industry affected nearly everyone, making available packaged cereals and canned foods. The perfection of the typewriter revolutionized the performance of office work. George B. Eastman pioneered the development of massproduced film and the simple but efficient Kodak camera.

## Railroads: The First Big Business

With high fixed costs, railroads needed to carry as much traffic as possible in order to net a profit. Therefore, feeder lines were constructed to draw business to the main lines. Among the first railroads was Cornelius Vanderbilt's New York Central, which ultimately operated between New York City and the principal Midwestern cities. Thomas Scott's Pennsylvania Railroad linked Philadelphia and Pittsburgh to Cincinnati, Indianapolis, St. Louis, and Chicago. The Baltimore and Ohio gained access to Chicago, which became the nation's railroad hub.

In the Southwest, Jay Gould consolidated the Kansas Pacific, Union Pacific, and Missouri Pacific. In the Northwest, Henry Villard and James J. Hill built their respective Northern Pacific and Great Northern. Most southern trunk lines in the South, such as the Louisville and Nashville, were controlled by northern capitalists.

Railroads charged what the market would bear—more for manufactured goods and less for bulky products like wheat or coal. The railroads stimulated the economy, particularly in rural areas with undeveloped resources. Inventions such as the air brake, steel track, and Pullman sleeping car vastly improved later rail technology. To speed the settlement of new regions, the land-grant railroads sold land cheaply and on easy terms. They offered reduced rates to travelers interested in buying farms.

## Iron, Oil, and Electricity

The giant steel industry that emerged after the Civil War was a result of the process perfected independently by Henry Bessemer of Great Britain and William Kelly of Kentucky. Steel could be mass-produced in locations near the iron-ore fields of Lake Superior and the coal deposits about Pittsburgh. Petroleum production, pioneered in the drilling of a well in Pennsylvania by Edwin L. Drake, provided lubricants and kerosene, decades before gasoline was needed to power the internal combustion engine.

Alexander Graham Bell's telephone offered competition to Western Union telegraph. By 1900, American Telephone and Telegraph operated 800,000 phones nationwide. At Menlo Park, New Jersey, Thomas Edison built the prototype of the modern research laboratory from which came patents on the phonograph, motion picture projector, storage battery, mimeograph, and incandescent light bulb. In 1882, Edison opened a power station in New York to demonstrate that electricity could be a substitute for steam power in factories. By the early years of the new century almost 6 billion kilowatt-hours of electricity were being produced annually.

## Competition and Monopoly: The Railroads

Classical economists maintained that railroad competition advanced the public interest by keeping prices low and assuring the most efficient producer of the largest profit. Amid such competition, the railroads offered rebates, passes, and even drawbacks (rebates on the business of the shippers' competitors) to large shippers. Small shippers, therefore, suffered rate discrimination and found that they sometimes paid two to three times the price per mile for sending goods in contrast to their larger rivals. Charles Francis Adams, Jr., maintained that a person trying to run a railroad honestly would be akin to Don Quixote tilting at windmills.

Railroads constantly reorganized to improve efficiency or just to survive. Reorganizations brought most of the large systems under the control of such financiers as J. P. Morgan. Critics sometimes referred to reorganizations as "Morganizations."

## Competition and Monopoly: Steel

His competitors built new steel plants in good times, but Andrew Carnegie expanded in bad times, when it cost considerably less to do so. Carnegie could hence buy out competitors during business panics. He also grasped the importance of technology by employing top-flight specialists and chemists to keep setting new records in steel production. In 1875 he built the J. Edgar Thomson Steel Works, named after a president of the Pennsylvania Railroad. After he mastered the industry, Carnegie retired to devote himself to philanthropy. In 1901, Morgan bought out Carnegie Steel and created U.S. Steel (since USX), the world's first billion-dollar corporation.

## Competition and Monopoly: Oil

Oil-refining centers were based in Cleveland, Pittsburgh, Baltimore, and New York. Standard Oil in Cleveland, founded by 31-year-old John D. Rockefeller emerged as the giant in the industry. Rockefeller exploited technical advances and persuaded or coerced competitors to sell out. By 1879, he controlled over 90 percent of the nation's oil-refining capacity along with a network of pipelines and petroleum reserves. A meticulous organizer, Rockefeller made certain there was no waste in the economies of large-scale production.

After achieving his monopoly, Rockefeller organized the Standard Oil trust in order to evade Ohio laws that forbade his company from operating in other states. Therefore, his board of nine trustees could manage Rockefeller holdings across state lines. The Rockefeller trust was intended to centralize and streamline the operation of his far-flung petroleum holdings.

## Competition and Monopoly: Utilities and Retailing

Telephone and electric lighting companies established monopolies to offset costly duplication of equipment and loss of service efficiency. Edison realized little profit from his invention of the electric light; he complained that his patents were mainly "invitations to lawsuits." In 1892, Edison merged with its main competitor, Thomson-Houston Electric, to form General Electric. Thereafter, GE and Westinghouse dominated utilities.

Department stores also expanded, particularly the firms of John Wanamaker in Philadelphia, Alexander Stewart in New York, and Marshall Field in Chicago. Similarly, three giant firms, Equitable Life, New York Life, and Mutual Life, dominated the life insurance business. Equitable offered a new group policy, the tontine, which stressed living rather than dying and added an element of gambling to insurance.

## Americans React to Big Business

Americans saw no contradiction between free enterprise and government regulation of business. Instead, there was the fear that monopolists were destroying economic opportunity and threatening democratic institutions. Talk persisted of the likelihood of a future autocracy or revolutionary socialism.

Former President Hayes in 1890 denounced the "evils of the money piling tendency" which he claimed rewarded the wealthy too generously. Business leaders defended the concentration of wealth; Carnegie said that the rich should use their money so as to "produce the most beneficial results for the community."

Many clergymen denounced unrestrained competition, which they considered un-Christian. The American Economic Association denounced laissez-faire and declared state aid "an indispensable condition of human progress."

## Reformers: George, Bellamy, Lloyd

Henry George in *Progress and Poverty* attacked the maldistribution of wealth in the United States, arguing that only a single tax on land could prevent the disparity between rich and poor from growing larger. Though George lost his race for mayour of New York City, single-tax clubs sprang up nationwide. Edward Bellamy's utopian novel *Looking Backward 2000-1887* described a future socialistic America in which all citizens shared equally. Bellamy maintained that such a state would arrive without violence or revolution. A third assault on monopoly was Henry D. Lloyd's *Wealth Against Commonwealth*, which excoriated Standard Oil and the advocates of Social Darwinism.

## Reformers: The Marxists

Marxian ideas, which claim that the state should own all the means of production, reached America in the 1870s. Laurence Gronlund in *The Cooperative Commonwealth* viewed competition as "established anarchy," middlemen as "parasites," and speculators as "vampires." Daniel De Leon, a follower of George, Bellamy, the Knights of Labor, and Marx, claimed that workers could not improve their lot until they joined his revolutionary Socialist Labor party.

## The Government Reacts to Big Business: Railroad Regulation

Regulation of the railroads was strongly endorsed by the National Grange of the Patrons of Husbandry, founded in 1867 by Oliver Kelley. Granger-dominated state legislatures sought to outlaw freight rate discrimination. Railroads claimed that they were being deprived of property without due process. In *Munn v. Illinois*, the Supreme Court upheld the constitutionality of an act requiring a grain elevator owner to comply with a state warehouse act. Rail regulation by the states, inefficient from the start, was further hampered in 1886, when the Supreme Court declared unconstitutional an Illinois law that forbade long- and short-haul inequities.

In 1887, the Interstate Commerce Act declared that railroad rates should be reasonable and just. Moreover, rebates and other competitive practices were declared unlawful. However, the ICC could not fix rates, only take the railroads to court when it considered rates unreasonably high. While the ICC challenged laissez-faire, it did not undertake a radical assault on private property, as its critics feared.

### The Government Reacts to Big Business: The Sherman Antitrust Act

The Sherman Act declared illegal any combination "in the form of a trust or otherwise" that was "in restraint of trade or commerce among the several states, or with foreign nations." Persons forming such combinations were subject to $5,000 fines and a year in jail. The loosely-worded act allowed questionable business combinations to continue. Critics said that the law was designed more to quiet public clamor for action against the trusts than in breaking up any of the new combinations. Andrew Carnegie even confessed that he could not remember anybody ever mentioning the Sherman Act to him as he participated in the formation of U.S. Steel Corporation.

The Supreme Court emasculated the law in *United States v. E. C. Knight Company*, which held that the American Sugar Refining Company had not violated the law by taking over its competitors. Although the trust controlled 98 percent of all U.S. sugar refining, the court held it was not restraining trade.

### Labor Organizes

Early labor leaders tended to be visionaries out of touch with the practical needs of the workers. The Knights of Labor, headed by Uriah Stephens and Terence Powderly, urged that workers "own and operate" mines, factories and railroads. The Knights rejected the traditional grouping of workers by crafts and admitted blacks, women, immigrants, skilled, and unskilled, and endorsed the eight-hour day.

In 1886, a striker was killed at a plant in Chicago. Anarchists called a protest meeting at Haymarket Square. When police intervened, someone threw a bomb into their ranks, killing seven officers.

### The American Federation of Labor

The Knights of Labor suffered in public perception due to the Haymarket tragedy even though the union was not responsible for the riot. The new AFL, founded as a craft union by Samuel Gompers, understood that most workers would remain wage earners and emphasized a sense of common purpose, pride, and companionship. The AFL relied heavily on strikes, which were used to win concessions from employers and to attract recruits. Gompers's approach to labor problems produced solid gains, with membership rising from 125,000 at its founding in 1886 to more than 1,000,000 by 1901.

**Labor Militancy Rebuffed**

Employers frequently discharged workers who tried to organize unions and failed to provide rudimentary protections against injury on the job. Many employers considered workers who joined unions to be "disloyal," but they still treated labor as a commodity to be purchased as cheaply as possible.

When labor disputes developed, they were often violent. In 1877, President Hayes dispatched troops to halt a general rail strike that began on the Baltimore and Ohio. In 1892, violent strikes broke out among Idaho silver miners and at Carnegie's Homestead, Pennsylvania, steel plant. At Homestead, strikers seeking higher wages attacked 300 private guards hired to protect strikebreakers. Seven guards were killed, and thereafter an anarchist, Alexander Berkman, tried to assassinate Henry Clay Frick, the manager of the plant. The attack brought much sympathy to Frick and unjustly discredited the workers.

The most important strike occurred in 1894, when Pullman Palace Car workers walked out in protest against wage cuts. The workers were organized by Eugene Debs of the American Railway Union. President Cleveland dispatched troops to ensure movement of the mails. When Debs defied a federal injunction to end the walkout, he was jailed for contempt, and the strike was broken.

**Whither America, Whither Democracy?**

Each year more of the nation's wealth seemed to fall into fewer hands. As with the railroads, other industries appeared to be dominated by bankers. The firm of J. P. Morgan controlled railroad, steel, electric, agricultural machinery, rubber and shipping companies, two life insurance companies, and several banks. Centralization increased efficiency and living standards rose, but some questioned how ordinary people would be affected when a few tycoons with huge fortunes commanded extraordinary influence through Congress and the courts.

## People, Places, and Things

*Define the following concepts:*

Bonsack machine _____

_____

air brake _____
_____

feeder lines _____
_____

long-haul/short-haul inequity _____
_____

rebates _____
_____

trust _____
_____

"Morganizations" _____
_____

"unearned increment" _____
_____

utopian _____
_____

"Granger laws" _____
_____

injunction _____
_____

collective bargaining _____
_____

*Describe the following:*

New York Central _____

_____

Great Northern _____

_____

Louisville and Nashville _____

_____

Kelly-Bessemer process _____

_____

Mesabi range _____

_____

Western Union _____

_____

Menlo Park _____

_____

Standard Oil _____

_____

General Electric _____

_____

U.S. Steel _____

_____

*Progress and Poverty* _____

_____

*Wealth Against Commonwealth* _____

_____

National Grange of the Patrons of Husbandry _____

_____

Interstate Commerce Commission _____

_____

Knights of Labor _____

_____

Homestead strike _____

_____

Pullman strike _____

_____

*Identify the following people:*

Thomas A. Scott _____

_____

Jay Gould _____

_____

George Pullman _____

_____

George Westinghouse _____

_____

Edwin L. Drake _____

_____

Thomas A. Edison _____

_____

Alexander Graham Bell _____

_____

J. Pierpont Morgan _____

_____

Andrew Carnegie _____

_____

John D. Rockefeller _____

_____

John Wanamaker _____

_____

Edward Bellamy _____

_____

Terence V. Powderly _____

_____

Samuel Gompers _____

_____

Henry Clay Frick _____

_____

## Map Exercise

Refer to the map on the following page. Place the appropriate letter that represents the route followed by the respective railroad. Consult a historical atlas if necessary.

_____1.   Atchison, Topeka, and Santa Fe

_____2.   Baltimore and Ohio

_____3.   Central Pacific

_____4.   Chesapeake and Ohio

_____5.   Chicago, Burlington and Quincy

_____6.   Erie

_____7.   Great Northern

_____8.   Illinois Central

_____9.   New York Central

_____10.  Northern Pacific

_____11.  Pennsylvania

_____12.  Southern Pacific

_____13.  Union Pacific

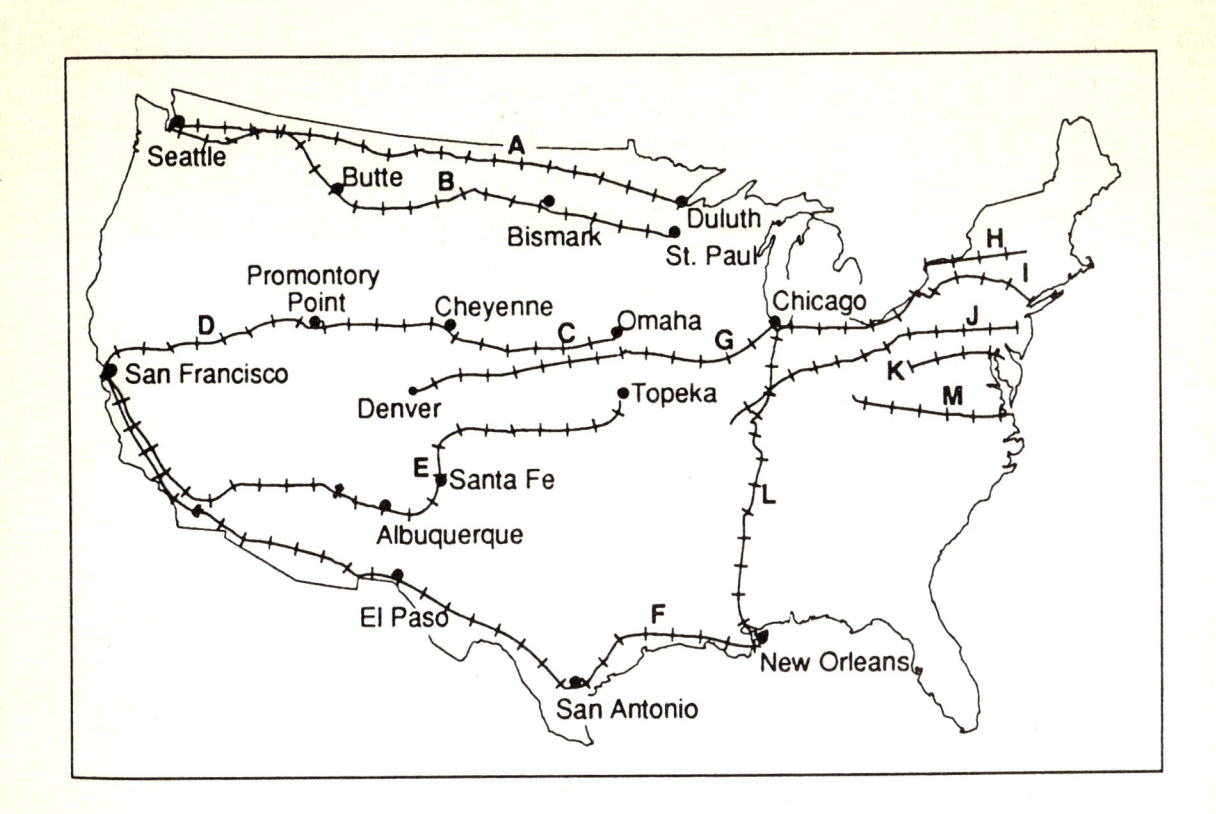

## Self-Test

**Multiple-Choice Questions**

1. *Munn v. Illinois*:
    A. Upheld the right of organized labor to bargain collectively
    B. Ruled that only Congress could regulate interstate commerce
    C. Permitted legislatures to regulate rail and warehouse rates within the state
    D. Discontinued rail subsidies

2. Rail improvements in the late nineteenth century included all of the following *except*:
    A. Air brake
    B. Standard-gauge track
    C. Automatic block signal
    D. Alternating current

3. The company that gained a monopoly over the telegraph was:
   A. General Electric
   B. Western Union
   C. Western Electric
   D. American Telephone and Telegraph

4. The first oil well drilled in the United States was in:
   A. Pennsylvania
   B. Ohio
   C. Texas
   D. New York

5. All of the following were invented by Thomas Edison *except* the:
   A. Incandescent light bulb
   B. Motion picture projector
   C. Phonograph
   D. Steel furnace

6. Laissez-faire refers to:
   A. Providing grants and subsidies to those who cannot survive Social Darwinism
   B. Efforts to reform the political process
   C. The desire that government should permit the laws of supply and demand to operate with minimal interference
   D. Policies to keep trusts from becoming monopolies

7. The Haymarket Riot:
   A. Was caused by actions of the Knights of Labor
   B. Resulted when someone threw a bomb into the ranks of the police at a mass meeting in Chicago
   C. Caused the decline of the American Railway Union
   D. Demonstrated broad support unions had gained by 1886

8. Which of these statements is *false?*
   A. The 1877 rail strike brought train traffic to a standstill in 14 states, prompting President Hayes to send in federal troops.
   B. The assassination of Henry Clay Frick ended labor unrest at the Homestead plant.
   C. Eugene Debs was jailed for disobeying an injunction issued in the Pullman strike.
   D. The goal of most strikers in the Haymarket affair was the eight-hour day.

9. An anarchist:
    A. Favors socialism
    B. Opposes organized government
    C. Opposes labor violence
    D. Objects to government intervention in the economy

10. A future cooperative society was predicted in a novel by:
    A. Henry Demarest Lloyd
    B. Henry George
    C. Alexander Berkman
    D. Edward Bellamy

11. Ultimately, which union was the most succcessful in the late nineteenth century?
    A. American Railway
    B. Knights of Labor
    C. American Federation of Labor
    D. National Labor Union

12. Daniel De Leon preferred what system of government?
    A. Marxian socialism
    B. British-style socialism
    C. Trade unionism
    D. Representative democracy

13. The first corporation to have a capitalization of over $1 billion was:
    A. Standard Oil of Ohio
    B. General Electric
    C. U.S. Steel
    D. American Sugar Refining Company

14. In which southern state did a steel industry develop due to the proximity of limestone, coal, and iron ore there?
    A. Texas
    B. Florida
    C. Alabama
    D. Tennessee

15. The *United States v. E. C. Knight Company* case determined that what firm was not automatically a monopoly in violation of the Sherman Act?
    A. Standard Oil of Ohio
    B. Carnegie Steel
    C. American Sugar Refining Company
    D. Marshall Field Department Store

16. Henry George saw the path to social justice as best obtainable through what method?
    A. A graduated federal income tax
    B. Democratic socialism
    C. Free enterprise
    D. A tax on land

17. The Standard Oil trust was primarily formed to:
    A. Evade Ohio laws regarding business activity in other states
    B. Gain monopoly status for the Rockefeller interests in the oil business
    C. Lower interest rates
    D. Avoid taxation

18. Laurence Gronlund's *Cooperative Commonwealth* condemns:
    A. Capitalism
    B. Socialism
    C. Communism
    D. Utopianism

19. All of the following refer to the Sherman Act *except*:
    A. It was vaguely worded and not strictly enforced
    B. It led to a rapid decline in the formation of new trusts after 1890
    C. It forbade combinations "in the form of trusts" and "in restraint of trade among the several states or with foreign nations"
    D. It carried fines of up to $5,000 and a year in jail for violation

20. Which of the following was *not* among the railroad builders of the late nineteenth century?
    A. Henry Villard
    B. Uriah S. Stephens
    C. James J. Hill
    D. Cornelius Vanderbilt

**Essay Questions**

1. Explain how railroads, steel, and petroleum companies tended to form monopolies in the late nineteenth century to dominate their respective markets.

2. What was the common thread linking Henry George, Edward Bellamy, and Henry D. Lloyd? Discuss their principal theories.

3. Explain how business and management prevailed in virtually every major labor altercation of the late nineteenth century.

4. Why did Congress pass the Interstate Commerce Act and the Sherman Antitrust Act? Discuss the provisions of each law and show how the laws were undermined.

5. Why did most Americans reject the proposals of Laurence Gronlund and Daniel De Leon?

## Critical Thinking Exercise

Each of these statements sets forth an opinion regarding economic thought. Designate each statement by either an "L" for laissez-faire, "R" for regulated capitalism, or "S" for socialism.

____1. The state ought to own all the means of production.

____2. The trend toward monopoly can best be addressed through government agencies that watch out for the interests of smaller companies facing continuing squeeze from big business.

____3. The best way to reduce railroad rates is to permit intense competition within the industry.

____4. The Interstate Commerce Commission has outlived any function it may have once had and should be abolished forthwith.

____5. "There is no good reason why labor cannot, through cooperation, own and operate mines, factories and railroads."

____6. "If I wanted a boiler iron, I would go out on the market and buy it where I could get it cheapest, and if I wanted to employ men, I would do the same."

____7. Workers must preserve the benefits of the eight-hour day, mine safety laws, and collective bargaining rights.

____8. Rising standards of living prove that the public benefited from the growth of industrial giants.

____9. The trend toward industrial consolidation will continue until one monster trust dominates the economy. Then all will realize that nationalization is essential.

____10. Granger laws established "reasonable" maximum rates over railroads and warehouses.

CHAPTER 19

# American Society in the Industrial Age

## Learning Objectives

*After reading Chapter 19, you should be able to:*

1. Discuss the life-styles of middle-class families and wage earners in the late nineteenth century.
2. Differentiate between "old" and "new" immigration.
3. Explain the interest in sports and recreation in the late nineteenth century.
4. Describe urban ghetto life in the late 1900s.
5. Show how cities modernized as the century ended.
6. Explain the role of settlement houses in urban America.
7. Evaluate the response of the churches to the challenges of the industrial society.

## Overview

### Middle-Class Life

The American middle class in the late nineteenth century included the professions, shopkeepers, small manufacturers, skilled craftsmen, and established farmers. A family with an annual income of $1,000 was considered quite well off, and many middle-class families employed servants. While the men concentrated on the workplace, women supervised the household and the rearing of children, who were taught proper manners.

### Wage Earners

The number of industrial workers grew rapidly from 1860 through 1890, and the standard of living particularly improved for such occupations as railroad engineers and conductors, machinists, and iron molders. Yet, unskilled laborers could barely maintain their families. Ordinary rail laborers were paid from $1 to $1.25 per day, and many squandered their wages on liquor and cigars. Mechanization contributed to monotonous working conditions and undermined the artisans' pride in their labor. Industrialization led to a decline in personal contact between employer and employee and led to swings of the business cycle, with full employment sometimes followed by depression.

**Working Women**

Thousands of women left the home to take low-paying jobs in industry and department stores. Educated middle-class women dominated the new profession of nursing and soon replaced men as teachers in most elementary schools. They also replaced men as clerks, secretaries, and operators of typewriters in government and business offices.

**Farmers**

The number of farmers and the volume of agricultural production continued to rise in the late nineteenth century, but the overall status of most farmers declined. Compared to middle class city dwellers, farmers seemed provincial and behind the times. Waves of radicalism swept through the farm country, giving rise to demands for social and economic experiments advocated by the Grange and the Populist party. In the South the crop-lien system kept many in economic bondage. Plains farmers overcame a succession of mostly natural hardships. Hamlin Garland in the anthology *Main-Travelled Roads* depicted the hardships, rewards, and disappointments of farm life, particularly for women, who had to perform endless chores amid near isolated conditions.

**Working-Class Family Life**

Family income varied among workers who received similar hourly wages, depending on the steadiness of employment and the number of family members holding jobs. Although some spent nearly all their income on food, others saved considerable sums on incomes of no more than $500 a year. Hence the standard of living of the middle class was affected by health, intelligence, the wife's ability as a homemaker, the degree of the family's commitment to middle-class values, and pure luck.

**Working-Class Attitudes**

The political, social, and economic attitudes of workers varied according to individual perspectives. Some workers favored laws to prohibit strikes; others urged nationalization of land and transportation; some preferred a graduated income tax. As the rich grew richer and the poor grew poorer, ordinary workers were still usually better off. Most did not call for radical changes in the economic system, though the gap between the most wealthy and the ordinary citizens was widening.

## Mobility: Social, Economic, and Educational

Considerable geographic mobility existed in urban areas a century ago, mobility that in most cases was accompanied by some economic or social improvement. The public education system encouraged the upwardly mobile, and more than 15 million attended school by the year 1900. In rural areas, however, school was held only when most of the youngsters were not needed in the fields. Industrialization created demands for vocational and technical training as well. In 1880, Calvin M. Woodward opened the Manual Training School in St. Louis; similar institutions offered courses in carpentry, sewing, and other crafts. Most people were motivated by the rags-to-riches myth and continued to subscribe to the middle-class values of hard work and thrift no matter how hopeless their economic situations may have seemed to have been.

## The "New" Immigration

Between 1866 and 1915, some 25 million foreigners entered the United States. The launching of the *Great Eastern* in 1858 had opened a new era in transatlantic travel. Competition among the steamship lines drove down the cost of passage. Immigrants, most of whom entered through New York City, arrived thereafter in record numbers. The only groups excluded were idiots, lunatics, persons liable to become public charges and, after 1882, the Chinese. Under the *padrone* system, unskilled Italian and Greek laborers were brought to the United States to work under contract for various companies. After 1890, there was a noticeable shift in the pattern of immigration. Newer arrivals were coming from southern and eastern Europe, rather than the traditional immigration from northern and western Europe.

## The Old Immigrants and the New

The southern and eastern Europeans had more difficulty assimilating into American culture. The immigrants held on to their close family and kinship ties and appeared clannish to native Americans. Sometimes immigrants feuded among themselves, as did German and Irish Catholics. Social Darwinists found this new immigration alarming and urged that southern and eastern Europeans, whom they considered physiologically inferior to Anglo-Saxons, be excluded from the United States. Some workers, fearing competition from immigrants, also feared the influx of foreigners. Employers sometimes grew fearful of the perceived radicalism of many new arrivals, particularly in light of the Haymarket bombing. Nativists formed the American Protective Association in 1887 to resist the "Catholic menace." Some immigrants believed that they had been kept out of the best jobs and could not climb the social ladder. Anti-immigrant attitudes reached a climax when Congress passed a literacy test bill in 1897, but the outgoing president, Grover Cleveland, vetoed the measure.

**The Expanding City and Its Problems**

Immigrant populations tended to settle in ethnically segregated neighborhoods in the large eastern cities. Many immigrants maintained their traditional culture and continued to speak their native languages. Some Americans blamed the slowly assimilating immigrants for a plethora of urban problems in the late nineteenth century, including crowded conditions, lack of sanitation, crime, and rampant poverty.

**The Urban Infrastructure**

The rapid growth of the cities put pressure on municipal officials to maintain sewer and water facilities, fire and police protection, street repair and maintenance, garbage collection, and health and zoning regulations. Immigrants were often jammed together without benefit of bathroom facilities or ventilation. Jacob Riis captured the horror of crowded tenements in *How the Other Half Lives*. The rich, meanwhile, retired to mansions in Boston's Beacon Hill and Back Bay and San Francisco's Nob Hill, isolated from the poorer parts of town.

**The Citie Modernize**

After the relationship between polluted water and disease was fully understood, communities improved their water and sewage systems. Public-spirited groups in the cities joined forces to plant trees, clean up littered areas, and develop recreational areas. Gradually, the facilities of urban living were improved. Streets were paved, first with cobblestone, then with quieter asphalt, and lighting brightened the cities after dark. The electric trolley changed the character of urban living by increasing the radius of the municipality to six miles or more. Previously, a city had been limited by the walking distance of its dwellers. The combined activities of trolley operators, real estate developers, and builders made home ownership possible for people of modest means and spurred suburban growth. Advances in bridge design also aided the flow of city populations. The Brooklyn Bridge, completed in 1883 at a cost of $15 million, carried 33 million people over the East River between Manhattan and Brooklyn. Such architects as Louis Sullivan emphasized the function of buildings, rather than the rules and precedents of the past.

**Leisure Activities: More Fun and Games**

Cities like New York, with its Metropolitan Museum of Art, remained unsurpassed as centers of artistic and intellectual life. Boston, likewise, sponsored an outstanding symphony. For working men, the saloon was a kind of club, a place to meet friends and consume alcohol, which was forbidden on most work premises. More attention was focused on such sports as tennis, golf, horseracing, and bicycling. Professional boxing gained fans from the working class when John L. Sullivan, who explained that he was committed to "hammering his opponent into unconsciousness," became heavyweight champion. Professional baseball teams appeared after 1869, when the Cincinnati Red Stockings offered some players up to $1,400 per season. In 1891, James Naismith developed the rules of basketball. Football evolved from English rugby in the late nineteenth century and was originally played almost entirely by upper- and middle-class collegians. The modern character of football came through the work of Walter Camp, the athletic director at Yale who named the first All America team in 1889.

## The Churches Respond to Industrial Society

Churches traditionally stressed individual responsibility, thrift, and hard work for one's behavior, a view often rebuffed in poorer sections of large cities. In New York, many Protestant congregations abandoned depressed areas of Lower Manhattan in order to serve middle-class and upper-class worshippers. Some Protestants considered immigrant poverty to be an act of God brought on by sinful man. After the Protestants left the inner cities, Catholicism remained behind to distribute alms and maintain orphanages and other forms of social welfare. The clergy was initially critical of organized labor, but the 1891 papal encyclical *Rerum novarum*, which criticized the excesses of capitalism, moved Catholicism to support unions and improved working conditions of laborers.

Dwight L. Moody, a Protestant evangelist likened to George Whitefield in the eighteenth century, sought to persuade slum residents to cast aside their sinful ways. The evangelists helped to establish the Salvation Army and the Young Men's Christian Association.

Some clergymen preached a "Social Gospel" which emphasized improving living conditions on earth, perhaps at the expense of saving souls for the heareafter. Such Social Gospelers as Washington Gladden advocated civil service reform, a ban on child labor, corporate regulations, and heavy taxation on incomes and inheritance. Most Social Gospelers supported capitalism, but a few, including William D. P. Bliss, became socialists. Charles Sheldon's *In His Steps* described how a mythical town could change its ways when a group of leading citizens decided to live truly Christian lives, asking themselves, "What would Jesus do?"

## The Settlement Houses

Settlement houses assisted immigrants in adapting to new communities by finding jobs, shelter, and other necessary assistance. The prototype of the settlement house was London's Toynbee Hall. In 1889, the socialist Jane Addams founded Chicago's Hull House, the most famous of the American settlement houses. The majority of settlement house workers were young women out of college, many of whom, while bounding in idealistic hopes, were absorbed in practical problems of slum dwellers.

The nurse Lillian Wald, in *The House on Henry Street* explained how settlement workers lived in the neighborhood and identified with it socially. Wald agitated for tenement house laws, regulation of the labor of children and women, better schools, playgrounds, child nutrition, and day care.

In 1898, the first Catholic-run settlement house opened in New York. Two years later the Brownson House in Los Angeles, catering to Mexican immigrants, opened its doors.

Beacon Hill _____

_____

*How the Other Half Lives* _____

_____

Brooklyn Bridge _____

_____

Cincinnati Red Stockings _____

_____

Young Men's Christian Association _____

_____

*Rerum novarum* _____

_____

*Applied Christianity* _____

_____

Toynbee Hall _____

_____

Hull House _____

_____

*Identify the following people:*

Hamlin Garland_____

_____

Louis Sullivan _____

_____

John L. Sullivan _____

_____

James Naismith _____

_____

Walter Camp _____

_____

Dwight L. Moody _____

_____

Lillian Wald _____

_____

## Self-Test

**Multiple-Choice Questions**

1. "Old" immigrants may have come from all of the following countries *except*:
   A. France
   B. Germany
   C. Sweden
   D. Italy

2. The first immigrants legally excluded from the United States were the:
   A. Chinese
   B. French
   C. Italians
   D. Russians

3. What President in 1897 vetoed a bill to establish literacy tests for immigrants?
   A. Chester Arthur
   B. Grover Cleveland
   C. Benjamin Harrison
   D. Theodore Roosevelt

4. The "Social Gospel" accented:
   A. Salvation by faith in Jesus
   B. Improving living conditions in the slums
   C. Vigorous revival movements to invigorate the ghettos
   D. The perfection of life in a heavenly utopia

5. Henry E. Huntington built:
   A. The Brooklyn Bridge
   B. Hull House
   C. The Pacific Electric Railway
   D. The Metropolitan Museum of Art

6. The right of labor to organize collectively was affirmed in the encyclical:
   A. *How the Other Half Lives*
   B. *The House on Henry Street*
   C. *Rerum novarum*
   D. *Applied Christianity*

7. Which of the following is *mispaired*:
   A. Jane Addams—Hull House
   B. Jacob Riis—*How the Other Half Lives*
   C. Kenneth Jackson—*The Crabgrass Frontier*
   D. William Bliss—evangelical Christianity

8. Football was *first* popular among:
   A. High school students
   B. Collegians
   C. Adults
   D. Young children

9. Traditional churches in the late nineteenth century usually attributed the poverty of laborers to:
   A. Lack of economic opportunity in the cities
   B. Unfair corporate practices
   C. The workers' lack of initiative and thrift
   D. Socialism

10. Washington Gladden opposed:
    A. Factory inspection laws
    B. The "Social Gospel"
    C. Regulation of public utilities
    D. The view that supply and demand should control wages

11. Workers in settlement houses tended to be:
    A. Male wage earners
    B. Immigrants
    C. Women college graduates
    D. Retired persons

12. The designer of the Brooklyn Bridge was:
    A. John Roebling
    B. Louis Sullivan
    C. Charles G. Finney
    D. Alexander T. Stewart

13. The leading Christian evangelist of the late nineteenth century was:
    A. Dwight L. Moody
    B. George Whitefield
    C. Washington Gladden
    D. Kenneth T. Jackson

14. Daniel H. Burnham is associated with:
    A. A vocational school in St. Louis
    B. A school of nursing in New York
    C. A Boston museum
    D. The design for the 1893 Chicago World's Fair

15. "New" immigrants would *not* have come from:
    A. Russia
    B. Scotland
    C. Turkey
    D. Italy

16. Social Gospelers would have opposed:
    A. Regulation of corporations
    B. Taxation on incomes and inheritance
    C. Literacy tests for immigrants
    D. Child labor legislation

17. The Brooklyn Bridge connects the borough of Brooklyn with:
    A. New Jersey
    B. Queens
    C. The Bronx
    D. Manhattan

18. Streetcars increased the radius of a typical city to:
    A. One mile
    B. Two miles
    C. Six miles
    D. Twelve miles

19. In time, women occupied most of the following jobs *except* for:
    A. Typists
    B. Elementary school teachers
    C. Unskilled factory workers
    D. Store clerks

20. Who described Americans of the late nineteenth century as "the most materialistic and money-making people ever known"?
    A. Lillian Wald
    B. Hamlin Garland
    C. Pope Leo XIII
    D. Walt Whitman

## Essay Questions

1. Explain how and why women displaced men in specific occupations in the late nineteenth century.

2. Discuss daily life among "typical" middle-class American families of the late nineteenth century, with specific reference to job, household, children, and values.

3. Contrast "Old Immigration" with "New Immigration." Mention specific countries from which immigrants came and discuss the problems of assimilation.

4. Explain how and why the "Social Gospel" contrasted with traditional Protestantism and Catholicism.

5. Discuss the burgeoning interest in sports and recreation in the late nineteenth century, with reference to team sports and such activities as tennis, golf, or bicycling.

## Critical Thinking Exercise

Each of the following statements refers to nineteenth century religion. Place a "P" beside those that reflect traditional Protestant doctrine and an "SG" beside those referring to dissenting Social Gospelers, which paralleled the thinking of *Rerum novarum* as well.

\_\_\_\_1.  Faith in God, thrift, and hard work will sustain the poor in transcending the material difficulties of life.

\_\_\_\_2.  Before people can lead pure lives, they need food, shelter, and the opportunity to develop their talents.

\_\_\_\_3.  Due to the excesses of capitalism, workers have the right to form unions.

\_\_\_\_4.  Slum conditions create the sins and crimes of cities.

\_\_\_\_5.  There is no substitute for personal responsibility in meeting social problems.

\_\_\_\_6.  The realities of life in industrial cities dictate the need for Christians to apply the teachings of Jesus to seek reforms like factory inspection laws and utility regulation.

\_\_\_\_7.  Man is "bad" because the institutions of society have made him so.

\_\_\_\_8.  The ultimate state of human perfection will be found only in the hereafter; therefore, society is limited in controlling individual behavior.

\_\_\_\_9.  People must be persuaded to cast aside their sinful ways in the interest of themselves and overall society.

\_\_\_10.  "No man in this land suffers from poverty . . . unless it be his sin."

\_\_\_11.  "I *am* my brother's keeper."

\_\_\_12.  "The effectual, fervent prayer of a righteous man availeth much."

\_\_\_13.  "Ye must be born again."

\_\_\_14.  It has become increasingly apparent that the wealth and authority of the state must be used to check the rapid growth of blighted areas.

\_\_\_15.  The inherent greed of unchecked capitalism will enslave us all.

CHAPTER 20

# Intellectual and Cultural Trends

## Learning Objectives

*After reading Chapter 20, you should be able to:*

1. Evaluate how and why Americans pursued knowledge, with special emphasis on the Chautauqua.
2. Recognize the major nineteenth century newspapers and magazines and their publishers.
3. List the major colleges and universities and explain their specializations and reasons for growth.
4. Explain advances in science and social sciences.
5. Analyze the tenets of "progressive education."
6. Explain how evolutionary teachings affected law.
7. Discuss the writings of such realistic authors as William Dean Howells, Mark Twain, Henry James, Theodore Dreiser, and Stephen Crane.
8. Differentiate between the realistic and romantic schools of art and recognize the works of Thomas Eakins, Winslow Homer, James Whistler, and others.
9. Evaluate William James's theory of pragmatism in philosophy.

## Overview

### The Pursuit of Knowledge

The industrialization and materialism of the late nineteenth century had a profound effect on education and literature. Darwin's theory of evolution moreover impacted philosophy, law, and history. As society became more complex, calls for specialized training and higher education increased. Such desire for knowledge was reflected in the Chautauqua, originally a two-week summer course for Sunday school teachers at Lake Chautauqua, New York. The Chautauqua featured speakers on national tour who discussed a multiplicity of subjects.

The first newspaper publisher to reach a mass audience was Joseph Pulitzer, owner of the *New York World* and *St. Louis Post-Dispatch*. Pulitzer, who sold a million papers daily by 1900, stressed news about crime, scandal, catastrophe, society, and the theater. Pulitzer's methods were copied by his rival, William Randolph Hearst, whose *New York Journal* outdid even the *World* in sensationalism.

## Magazine Journalism

In 1865, there were about 700 magazines in the United States; by 1900, more than 5,000. *The Atlantic Monthly*, *Harper's*, *The Nation*, and *The Century* featured current affairs, fiction, poetry, history, and biographies. In 1889, Edward W. Bok became editor of *Ladies' Home Journal*, which focused on child care, gardening, interior decorating, and commissioned public figures to discuss important questions. Bok printed reproductions of art masterpieces and crusaded for women's suffrage and other reforms.

## Colleges and Universities

Although fewer than 2 percent of college-age individuals were enrolled in higher education at the turn of the century, new institutions were established by the states and through the federal land-grant program under the Morrill Act. Philanthropists endowed older institutions and founded new ones. In 1869, Harvard's new president, Charles W. Eliot, transformed teaching methods through the introduction of the elective system, the elimination of required courses, and expanded offerings in science, economics, and languages.

Johns Hopkins University in Baltimore, modeled after German universities, specialized in graduate education and produced such scholars as Woodrow Wilson in political science, John Dewey in philosophy and Frederick Jackson Turner in history. The University of Chicago, established in 1892 through the Rockefeller fortune, stressed quality instruction, small class sizes, and academic freedom.

New women's colleges—Vassar, Wellesley, Smith, Mount Holyoke, Bryn Mawr, Barnard, and Radcliffe—were collectively referred to as the Seven Sisters. Academic freedom was sometimes undermined by business philanthropists, trustees of the institutions, and state politicians who considered the colleges as part of the patronage system.

## Scientific Advances

Yale professor Josiah Gibbs created an entirely new science—physical chemistry—and formulated how complex substances respond to changes in temperature and pressure. Gibbs's work contributed to advances in metallurgy and in the manufacture of plastics and drugs.

Albert Michelson of the University of Chicago made the first accurate measurement of the speed of light, research that enabled Albert Einstein to offer the theory of relativity. In 1907, Michelson became the first American scientist to win a Nobel prize.

## The New Social Sciences

Social scientists of the late nineteenth century applied the theory of evolution to nearly every aspect of human relations, seeking objective truths in fields that by nature are subjective.

The classical economists were challenged by a group of scholars led by Richard T. Ely of Johns Hopkins, who opposed laissez-faire and extolled the value of the state as indispensable to progress.

Traditional sociologists had maintained that society could be changed only by the force of evolution, which moved with cosmic slowness. Thereafter such scholars as Lester Frank Ward urged the improvement of society by "cold calculation" and triumph over the "law of competition."

The new political scientists rejected the emphasis by John C. Calhoun on states' rights and stressed the significance of parties, pressure groups, and, in the case of Woodrow Wilson, the power of congressional committees. Wilson viewed politics as a dynamic process and offered no objection to the expansion of state power.

**Progressive Education**

Dynamic social changes prompted educators to de-emphasize the three R's, strict discipline, and rote learning. Settlement house workers found that slum children needed training in handicrafts and hygiene as much as academic studies. They argued for the establishment of playgrounds, nurseries, and kindergartens. "We are impatient with the schools which lay all stress on reading and writing," declared the socialist Jane Addams.

John Dewey outlined the "progressive" theory of education, which focuses on the needs of the child, rather than the academic discipline. In *The School and Society*, Dewey insisted that information be related to what the child already knows and urged that the school become an active instrument of social reform.

**Law and History**

Jurisprudence, by nature conservative and rooted in tradition, also felt the pressure of evolutionary thought. Oliver Wendell Holmes, Jr., argued that judges should not limit themselves to the written law but should stress the "necessities of the times." Holmes's views were often in the minority during his years on the Supreme Court, but in the long run the Court adopted much of his reasoning.

Historians had long claimed that the roots of democracy came from the ancient tribes of northern Europe. This "Teutonic origins" theory, since discredited, provided ammunition for those who wanted to restrict immigration. Frederick Jackson Turner, the leading historian of the late nineteenth century, argued that the westward movement had fostered nationalism, individualism, and democracy. Turner went so far as to claim that nearly everything unique to America could be traced to the frontier experience.

## Realism in Literature

The romantic era of literature—epitomized by Longfellow, Lew Wallace, and Frances H. Burnett—slowly gave way to the Age of Realism. The realist school focused upon the complexities and problems associated with industrialism and slum life. Realist authors created multidimensional characters, depicted persons of every social class, and used dialect and slang to enhance their subjects.

## Mark Twain

The first great American realist author was Samuel L. Clemens, known by the pen name Mark Twain. Twain possessed a keen reportorial eye, a zest for living, a sense of humor, and the ability to love humanity yet be repelled by vanity and perversity. Twain's novels included *The Gilded Age,* a satire of the unscrupulous Colonel Beriah Sellers; *Huckleberry Finn*, a realistic portrait of the mischievous title character and the loyal slave Jim; *The Innocents Abroad*, a look at Americans traveling in Europe, and *Life on the Mississippi*, an acclaimed account of the world of the river pilot.

## William Dean Howells

Howells's novels focused on the social problems stemming from industrialization. *The Rise of Silas Lapham* dealt with ethical conflicts faced by businessmen in a competitive society. In *A Hazard of New Fortunes*, Howells attempted to portray realistically the range of metropolitan life. As a literary critic, Howells introduced Americans to Tolstoy, Dostoyevski, Ibsen, and Zola and encouraged such young novelists as Stephen Crane, Theodore Dreiser, Frank Norris, and Hamlin Garland.

Crane embodied the Darwinian school of literature known as naturalism. The naturalists believed that the human being was a helpless creature whose fate was determined by his environment. *Maggie: A Girl of the Streets* describes the seduction and eventual suicide of a young woman in the slums. *The Red Badge of Courage* captured the pain and humor of war. Dreiser's *Sister Carrie* is a naturalistic novel that treated sex so forthrightly that it was withdrawn after publication. In *McTeague*, Frank Norris told the story of a brutal dentist who murdered his wife with his bare fists.

## Henry James

Henry James, who was born to wealth, spent much of his life in Europe, writing novels, short stories, and plays. His works, which never received widespread popularity, stressed the clash of American and European cultures. He examined wealthy, sensitive, yet often corrupt persons in high society. James dealt with such social issues as feminism and the problems faced by artists in the modern world. *The American* told the story of a wealthy American in Paris in love with a French noblewoman who rejected him because of her family's disapproval. *The Portrait of a Lady* describes the disgust of an intelligent woman married to a charming but morally corrupt man.

## Realism in Art

Foremost among American artists was Thomas Eakins of Philadelphia, who glorified in the ordinary, never touching up a painting to please the sitter. Some of his finest paintings, such as *The Gross Clinic*, are illustrations of surgical procedures. *The Swimming Hole*, a glimpse of six men bathing, is a stark portrayal of nakedness

Winslow Homer of Boston, a master of watercolor, painted a variety of pictures in a realistic vein. He roamed America and painted scenes of southern farm life, Adirondack campers, and seascapes.

James A. McNeill Whistler, whose portrait of his mother is perhaps the most famous ever painted by an American, left the United States and lived abroad. An eccentric, Whistler painted both romantic and realistic works. Another expatriate artist, Mary Cassatt, a sister of the president of the Pennsylvania Railroad, was active in the impressionist movement. Her work was more French than American and was little appreciated in the United States.

## The Pragmatic Approach

Evolutionary thought challenged the biblical account of creation and the idea that the human race had been formed in God's image. Although many intellectuals embraced Darwinism, millions continued to uphold the literal truth of the Bible. If the Genesis account of creation could not be taken literally, the Bible remained a repository of wisdom and inspiration.

Darwin's impact on philosophy was especially significant. If one accepted evolution, logic dictated the belief that scientific laws were impermanent. Such thinking was called pragmatism by its founder, Charles S. Peirce.

Pragmatism was explained in less technical language by William James, the brother of Henry James. In *Principles of Psychology*, James may be said to have established that discipline as a modern science. To James, the environment was not in itself the determining factor of human behavior; instead, free will, the desire to triumph, and the relativity of truth were more important. Pragmatism bred insecurity among average citizens, who rejected a teaching in which there could be no reliance on eternal values in the absence of absolute truth.

# People, Places, and Things

*Define the following concepts:*

"soft social sciences" _____

_____

*padrone* system _____

_____

"Seven Sisters" _____

_____

"Teutonic origins" of democracy _____

_____

realism _____

_____

naturalism _____

_____

impressionism _____

_____

pragmatism _____

_____

*Describe the following:*

Chautauqua _____

_____

Associated Press _____

_____

*Harper's* _____

_____

*Ladies' Home Journal* _____

_____

University of Chicago _____

_____

*The Gilded Age* _____

_____

*Huckleberry Finn* _____

_____

*Sister Carrie* _____

_____

*The Portrait of a Lady* _____

_____

*Principles of Psychology* _____

_____

*Gulf Stream* _____

_____

*Identify the following people:*

Edward W. Scripps _____

_____

Joseph Pulitzer _____

_____

William Randolph Hearst _____

_____

Charles W. Eliot _____

_____

John Dewey _____

_____

Mark Twain _____

_____

William Dean Howells _____

_____

Henry James _____

_____

Thomas Eakins _____

_____

Winslow Homer _____

_____

James Whistler _____

_____

Mary Cassatt _____

_____

William James _____

_____

## Self-Test

### Multiple-Choice Questions

1. American higher learning in the late nineteenth century adopted what German method of instruction?
   A. The lecture
   B. The seminar
   C. The Chautauqua
   D. The dissertation

2. What was the first university to concern itself with graduate studies?
   A. University of Michigan
   B. Harvard
   C. Johns Hopkins
   D. University of Chicago

3. Which of these novels was *not* written by Samuel Clemens?
   A. *The Innocents Abroad*
   B. *Huckleberry Finn*
   C. *The Gilded Age*
   D. *The Rise of Silas Lapham*

4. Who introduced the elective system to higher education?
   A. Edward Bok
   B. Charles Eliot
   C. Thomas Eakins
   D. Daniel Coit Gilman

5. The scholar who defined the frontier as the principal force in shaping American life was:
   A. Albert Michelson
   B. William Rainey
   C. Frederick Jackson Turner
   D. Woodrow Wilson

6. According to Woodrow Wilson, which of these was the most influential in American government?
   A. The president
   B. Political parties
   C. Interest groups
   D. Congressional committees

7. The Chautauqua refers to:
   A. Realism in the arts
   B. A program of continuing education
   C. The Christian response to Darwinism
   D. A school of literary criticism

8. The philosophy that denies absolute truth is:
   A. Psychology
   B. Realism
   C. Romanticism
   D. Pragmatism

9. Which of the following was *not* associated with Johns Hopkins?
   A. Charles W. Eliot
   B. Woodrow Wilson
   C. John Dewey
   D. Richard T. Ely

10. *Dynamic Sociology* was:
    A. An attack on the teachings of Herbert Spencer
    B. Justification for Social Darwinism
    C. Published in *Popular Science Monthly* by William James
    D. An account of how environment contributes to individual behavior

11. "Progressive" educators are *least* likely to support:
    A. Rote learning
    B. Reciting the Pledge of Allegiance to the flag
    C. Instruction in civic duties
    D. Emphasis on hygiene

12. Oliver Wendell Holmes, Jr., stressed which of these concepts of law?
    A. Written statute
    B. Strict interpretation of the Constitution
    C. That changing times require adjustments in the law
    D. Reliance on precedent

13. Which of these authors is *mispaired* with his work?
    A. Henry James—*The Portrait of a Lady*
    B. Mark Twain—*A Connecticut Yankee in King Arthur's Court*
    C. William Dean Howells—*A Hazard of New Fortunes*
    D. Theodore Dreiser—*Maggie: A Girl of the Streets*

14. The first newspaper to surpass the 1-million mark in circulation was the:
    A. *New York Times*
    B. *New York World*
    C. *St. Louis Post-Dispatch*
    D. *New York Journal*

15. Who was the first American scientist to win a Nobel Prize?
    A. Albert Michelson
    B. Johns Hopkins
    C. Herbert Spencer
    D. Josian Gibbs

16. The artist associated with French impressionism was:
    A. Thomas Eakins
    B. James Whistler
    C. Winslow Homer
    D. Mary Cassatt

17. Which invention made possible the formation of the Associated Press?
    A. Telephone
    B. Linotype
    C. Telegraph
    D. Web press

18. The first newspaper chain was begun by:
    A. Edward W. Scripps
    B. William Randolph Hearst
    C. Joseph Pulitzer
    D. Charles W. Eliot

19. William James expanded on the ideas of:
    A. Herbert Spencer
    B. William Dean Howells
    C. Charles S. Peirce
    D. Benjamin Franklin

20. The Morrill Act provided funds for:
    A. The arts
    B. Scientific research
    C. Higher education
    D. Social science research

**Essay Questions**

1. Explain how newspapers and magazines contributed to the pursuit of knowledge in the late nineteenth century. Mention specific publications and their fields of specialization.

2. Explain the increase in the number of colleges and universities in the late nineteenth century. Mention specific institutions and educators and their respective fields of specialization.

3. Evaluate the advantages and disadvantages of "progressive education" from the point of view of a century ago and subsequent developments in education. Mention John Dewey's leadership in the field.

4. Explain how evolutionary thinking revolutionized sociology psychology, philosophy, and law. Mention specific individuals who dominated these disciplines a century ago.

5. Discuss pragmatism in light of scientific developments and religion. Stress William James's role in the discipline.

## Critical Thinking Exercise

Label each of the following statements as primarily "P" for "progressive education" or "T" for more traditional education.

____1. Education should not neglect rote learning of multiplication tables and rules of grammar.

____2. Education is the cornerstone of social progress and reform.

___3. Education should teach youngsters how to think as much as it instructs them in specific categories of knowledge.

___4. A study of American history should emphasize topics of current awareness and interest, rather than obscure points from the distant past.

___5. Field trips are ideal for stimulating student interest in a variety of matters.

___6. Education must center on the child, and new information should be directly related to what the child already knows.

___7. Education in America should concentrate on four basic subjects: mathematics, physical sciences, English and foreign languages, and history and its related fields of geography and government.

___8. Education should not neglect the teaching of moral values based on the Judeo-Christian ethic of western civilization.

___9. Education should teach youngsters how to use their leisure time more effectively and how to serve public needs.

___10. The value of particular topics of study need not be judged on the basis of immediate practical application.

___11. Colleges of education staffed by professional educators are best suited to prepare classroom teachers.

___12. Clear language and thought, not professional jargon, are essential to the development of an orderly mind.

# Chapter 21

# Politics: Local, State, and National

## Learning Objectives

*After reading Chapter 21, you should be able to:*

1. Explain the lack of political activism within the two major parties during the late nineteenth century.
2. Understand how political allegiances cut across sectional, partisan, ethnic, and economic lines.
3. Discuss changes in city government that occurred in the late nineteenth century.
4. Evaluate the presidencies of Rutherford Hayes, James Garfield, Chester Arthur, Grover Cleveland, and Benjamin Harrison as to style, policies, and effectiveness.
5. Name and evaluate a few of the congressional leaders in the late nineteenth century, including James G. Blaine and Thomas Reed.
6. Explain how discontent on the farm led to formation of the Alliance and Populist movements.
7. Understand why some advocated the use of silver as a basis for currency in the late nineteenth century.
8. Discuss the "watershed" election of 1896, in reference to candidates, parties, campaign techniques, outcome, and significance.

## Overview

### Political Strategy and Tactics

The Democratic and Republican parties, seeking to appeal to as wide a segment of voters as possible, have frequently avoided clear-cut stands on controversial questions. Such equivocations reached abnormal proportions in the late nineteenth century because the parties were nearly evenly divided.

Both parties stumbled over the tariff, which softened the impact of foreign competition on industrial areas but raised prices for consumers, many of whom were perpetually scrapped for cash.

**Political Decision Making: Ethnic and Religious Issues**

In order to establish winning electoral coalitions, the parties had to take into consideration the voters' ethnic backgrounds, religious affiliation, rural-urban factors, how they felt about the Civil War, and other aspects of their lives that had no relationship to national political issues. Southerners, Catholics, and German- and Irish-Americans trended Democratic; northerners, Protestants, and persons of Scandinavian descent, Republican. Often, such local and state issues as public education and prohibition interacted with religious, partisan, and ethnic factors.

Massachusetts Senator George Hoar extolled his fellow Republicans as "the men who do the work of piety and charity in our churches . . . who administer our school systems . . . who own and till their own farms . . . who perform skilled labor . . . who went to the war . . . who paid the debt, and kept the currency sound, and saved the nation's honor." Democrats, Hoar claimed, were "the old slaveowner and slave-driver, the saloon-keeper, the ballot-box-stuffer, the Kuklux, the criminal class of the great cities, and men who cannot read or write."

**City Government**

The movement of the middle class to the suburbs left a power vacuum in large cities which was filled by political "bosses," with their informal but powerful "machines." Immigrants who flocked to the cities were largely of peasant stock and unacquainted with principles of representative democracy. Political bosses marched the masses to the polls in servile obedience and reciprocated by finding jobs for the immigrants, distributing food, and aiding those jailed for minor offenses. The bosses helped to educate politically the immigrants so that they could make the transition from the near medieval society of their origins to the modern industrial world.

The most notorious boss, William Marcy Tweed, looted New York City taxpayers in a multiplicity of ways between 1869 and 1871. A corrupt manipulator, Richard Croker, ran New York's Tammany Hall Democratic organization from the mid-1880s to the end of the century. Some leading citizens shared in the urban corruption, particularly tenement owners who crowded renters into buildings and utility companies who sought franchises. Urban reformers resented the boss system because it gave power to "proletarian mobs" of "illiterate peasants."

**Republicans and Democrats**

Though Democrats held a lock on the "Solid South," New England and the West were Republican, the outcome of presidential elections was determined by such states as New York (with Connecticut and New Jersey), Ohio, Indiana, and Illinois. Opinion in these states was closely divided. All but three presidential candidates nominated between 1868 and 1900 came from those four states, and each of the three lost the election.

Lying, character assassination, and bribery undermined the body politic of the day. Drifters were often paid in cash or a few drinks to vote the party ticket. Sometimes the dead rose from the grave to cast ballots.

## The Men in the White House

Rutherford Hayes's Civil War record helped him to gain the governorship of Ohio in 1868. In 1876, the Republicans nominated him for president because of his reputation for honesty and moderation. Hayes saw himself as a caretaker president who thought Congress should assume the main responsibility for national problems. Though a protectionist in principle, Hayes played down the tariff question. He endorsed civil service reform, vetoed bills to expand currency, and approved the resumption of greenbacks in 1879.

Hayes's successor, James A. Garfield, was assassinated after four months in office. Like Hayes, Garfield was an Ohioan and a Union veteran who had avoided political controversy. Garfield's assassination resulted when two factions, the "Stalwarts" and the "Half-Breeds," argued over patronage. Garfield infuriated the Stalwarts by investigating a post office scandal and by appointing a Half-Breed collector for the Port of New York.

In July 1881, the Stalwart lawyer Charles Guiteau shot Garfield in the Washington rail station. He died in September, and Chester A. Arthur, the Stalwart who had been New York customs collector until Hayes removed him for partisan activities in 1878, moved up to the presidency. Personally honest and an excellent administrator, Arthur signed into law the Pendleton Act, which "classified" about 10 percent of government jobs and created a bipartisan Civil Service Commission. He tried to build up a personal following in the Republican party by distributing favors, but he was not nominated in 1884 because both factions distrusted him.

New York's Democratic governor, Grover Cleveland, won the 1884 election by defeating the Republican former House Speaker James G. Blaine of Maine. Cleveland's favorable attitude toward public administration endeared him to civil service reformers, and his conservatism pleased business. Blaine's reputation had been soiled by publication of the "Mulligan letters," which connected him to the corrupt granting of congressional favors to the Little Rock and Fort Smith Railroad in Arkansas. It was revealed during the campaign that Cleveland, a bachelor at the time of his election, had fathered a child out of wedlock. Nevertheless, Cleveland prevailed in a close election thanks to the support of disgruntled eastern Republicans known as "Mugwumps." Unlike his predecessors, Cleveland called for a lower tariff.

When seeking reelection, Cleveland led in popular votes, but the electoral majority went to the Indiana corporation lawyer, Benjamin Harrison, grandson of the ninth president. Described as a "human iceberg," Harrison was too reserved to make a good politician. He supported protective tariffs, conservative economic policies, and veterans' pensions. He appointed Theodore Roosevelt to the Civil Service Commission but proceeded to undercut him systematically.

Under Harrison, Congress spent for the first time in a period of peace more than $1 billion in a single session. The Republicans lost control cf Congress in the elections of 1890, and two years later Cleveland was swept back into power, defeating Harrison by a comfortable margin.

**Congressional Leaders**

The most outstanding congressional leader was perhaps James Blaine, who served in both the House and Senate from Maine. Blaine favored sound money but was open to suggestions for increasing the volume of currency. He supported the protective tariff, favored reciprocity agreements to increase trade, and was tolerant toward the defeated South. Almost alone among politicians of his era, Blaine was interested in foreign affairs, a factor leading Garfield and Harrison to appoint him secretary of state, but he could not overcome the impact of questions about his character.

Roscoe Conkling dominated New York politics in the 1870s but squandered his energies in bitter feuds, particularly the attempt to block civil service. Congressman William McKinley of Ohio was a man of simple honesty who believed in protective tariffs. John Sherman of Ohio, brother of the Civil War general, held national office without interruption from 1855 to 1898. Sherman mastered financial matters but compromised for political advantage. Thomas Reed of Maine was a sharp-tongued, vindictive orator who coined the famous definition of a statesman as a "politician who is dead." When he became Speaker of the House, Reed was nicknamed "Czar" because of his autocratic ways of expediting business.

**Agricultural Discontent**

Farmers suffered in the post-Civil War period as prices for their crops dropped sharply. The price of wheat dipped from $1.50 per bushel in 1865 to 60 cents in 1895; cotton fell from 30 cents a pound in 1866 to 6 cents in the 1890s. Farmers claimed that the tariff and the domestic marketing system that enabled middlemen to gobble up a share of agriculture profits worsened their predicament. Despite a few years of boom in agriculture, the long-term trend was discouraging to family farmers, many of whom lost their holdings and returned East.

**The Populist Movement**

The agricultural depression triggered a new outburst of farm radicalism, the Southern Alliance, which started in Lampasas County, Texas, in 1877. Alliance co-ops bought fertilizer, and other supplies in bulk and sold them to members. They sought to market their crops cooperatively but could not raise capital from banks. Other Alliance movements sprang up in the Midwest, but there was not national organization due to the partisan divisions of the northern and southern farmers. Alliance candidates fared well in various elections in the South and Midwest during the 1890s.

In 1892, farm leaders met in St.Louis to organize the People's or Populist party. At the national convention in Omaha, the Populists nominated General James B. Weaver of Iowa and drafted a platform calling for a graduated income tax, national ownership of railroads, telephone and telegraph, and a "subtreasury" plan to permit farmers to store nonperishable crops until market prices improved. The Populists were not revolutionaries but viewed themselves as a majority oppressed by the "establishment." Among colorful Populists were Congressman Tom Watson of Georgia, "Sockless Jerry" Simpson of Kansas, and Ignatius Donnelly of Minnesota, whose *Caesar's Column* pictured a future America where a few plutocrats tyrannized helpless workers and serfs. In the South, the Populists were unable to unite white and black farmers, as politicians played on racial fears to keep the region Democratic. Though defeated by Cleveland, Weaver polled 22 electoral votes.

### Showdown on Silver

Advocates of "free" silver wanted to inflate the currency to assist debtors in repaying long-term obligations in "cheaper" dollars. Bondholders naturally opposed such inflation because they benefited if the money supply remained restricted. Though the nation had previously adopted a policy of bimetallism, silver ceased to be used as a basis for currency in 1873. Mine owners demanded that the metal again be coined, and in 1878, the Bland-Allison Act authorized the purchase of $2 to $4 million of silver a month at the market price. In 1890, the Sherman Silver Purchase Act required the government to buy 4.5 million ounces of silver monthly, but as supplies increased, the price of silver plunged. President Cleveland believed that the silver issue, by shaking business confidence, had caused the Panic of 1893. He hence reverted to the gold standard by obtaining repeal of the Sherman Silver Purchase Act.

As the nation experienced a severe depression in 1894, several "armies" of the unemployed, one led by Jacob Coxey of Ohio, marched on Washington to demand relief. Coxey urged the government to authorize federal public works to the tune of $500 million. Coxey's "army" was dispersed by club-wielding policemen.

Meanwhile, the Supreme Court sided with business in several key cases. It refused to use the Sherman Antitrust Act to break up the Sugar Trust, invalidated a federal income tax, and denied the writ of *habeas corpus* to Eugene Debs for his role in the Pullman strike, which Cleveland broke through the sending in of federal troops.

Cleveland's presidency underwent a grave financial test, when the gold supply dropped to $41 million. Amidst a public outcry, the president permitted a group of bankers led by J. P. Morgan to underwrite a $62 million bond issue to revive the gold supply. Gold and silver met their final test in the 1896 election. Armed with an intense rhetorical weapon, "the Cross of Gold" speech, Bryan defeated the "goldbugs" at the Democratic convention and waged a spirited "free silver" campaign against the Republicans, who nominated Governor William McKinley. The Populists endorsed Bryan, a step that helped to undermine their credibility as a separate party.

### The Election of 1896

Few presidential campaign prior to 1896 raised such emotions. Republicans from the silver-mining states backed Democrat Bryan; Gold Democrats defected to Republican McKinley. Most newspapers, even those of Democratic inclination, endorsed McKinley. Viewed in the East as a dangerous radical, Bryan was declared "insane" by *The New York Times*. Bryan was the first presidential candidate to take to the stump, traveling 18,000 miles and making more than 600 speeches. McKinley's campaign was managed by Ohio businessman and "kingmaker" Marcus

Alonzo Hanna. Hanna raised $3.5 million from businessmen, often by intimidation. He sent speakers into doubtful districts and blanketed the nation with 250 million pieces of campaign literature. McKinley, who could not compete with Bryan's oratory, conducted a "frontporch" campaign in Canton, Ohio. That system conserved his energies and enabled him to avoid the appearance of seeking the presidency too openly, which was considered bad form at the time. Without leaving his doorstep, McKinley hence met thousands of people from throughout the nation. On election day, McKinley carried the East, the Midwest, and the Pacific Coast. Bryan won in the South, the Plains states, and the Rockies. Though the popular vote was close, McKinley took the electoral college 271-176.

**The Meaning of the Election**

Business interests voted heavily for McKinley, fearing a Bryan victory would bring economic chaos. Farmer in states bordering the Great Lakes, where the farm depression was less severe, also backed McKinley. Even a majority of the labor vote went to McKinley. Some industrialist coerced employees into voting Republican, but McKinley was highly regarded in labor circles. As governor, he had advocated arbitration of labor disputes, favored union organization, and had tried to persuade George Pullman to deal fairly with the strikers. Mark Hanna, too, had a reputation for treating his employees fairly. During the campaign some Republicans vowed to flee the country if Bryan were elected. With workers standing beside capitalist and with the farm vote split, the election did not divide the nation along class lines. As Mckinley emerged triumphant, the silver issue paled in significance. Moreover, gold discoveries in Alaska and South Africa and improved methods of extracting gold from low-grade ores led to a natural expansion of the money supply.

## People, Places, and Things

*Define the following concepts:*

political platform _____

_____

political boss _____

_____

"proletarian mob" _____

_____

civil service reform _____

_____

fiscal policy _____

_____

"subtreasury" plan _____

_____

spellbinders _____

_____

"free silver" _____

_____

"front-porch" campaign _____

_____

*Describe the following:*

Tammany Hall _____

_____

Stalwarts _____

_____

Half-Breeds _____

_____

Pendleton Act _____

_____

"Mulligan letters" _____

Mugwumps _____

Farmers Alliance _____

Populist party _____

*Caesar's Column* _____

"Crime of '73" _____

*Identify the following people:*

William Marcy Tweed _____

Rutherford B. Hayes _____

James A. Garfield _____

Chester A. Arthur _____

Charles Guiteau _____

_____

Grover Cleveland _____

_____

James G. Blaine _____

_____

Benjamin Harrison _____

_____

Roscoe Conkling _____

_____

Thomas Reed _____

_____

Mary E. Lease _____

_____

James B. Weaver _____

_____

William Jennings Bryan _____

_____

Mark Hanna _____

_____

## Map Exercise

Refer to the map below. Shade all the states carried by McKinley in the 1896 "watershed" election. Put dots on the states won by Bryan. Leave blank those states that had not yet been admitted to the Union by 1896.

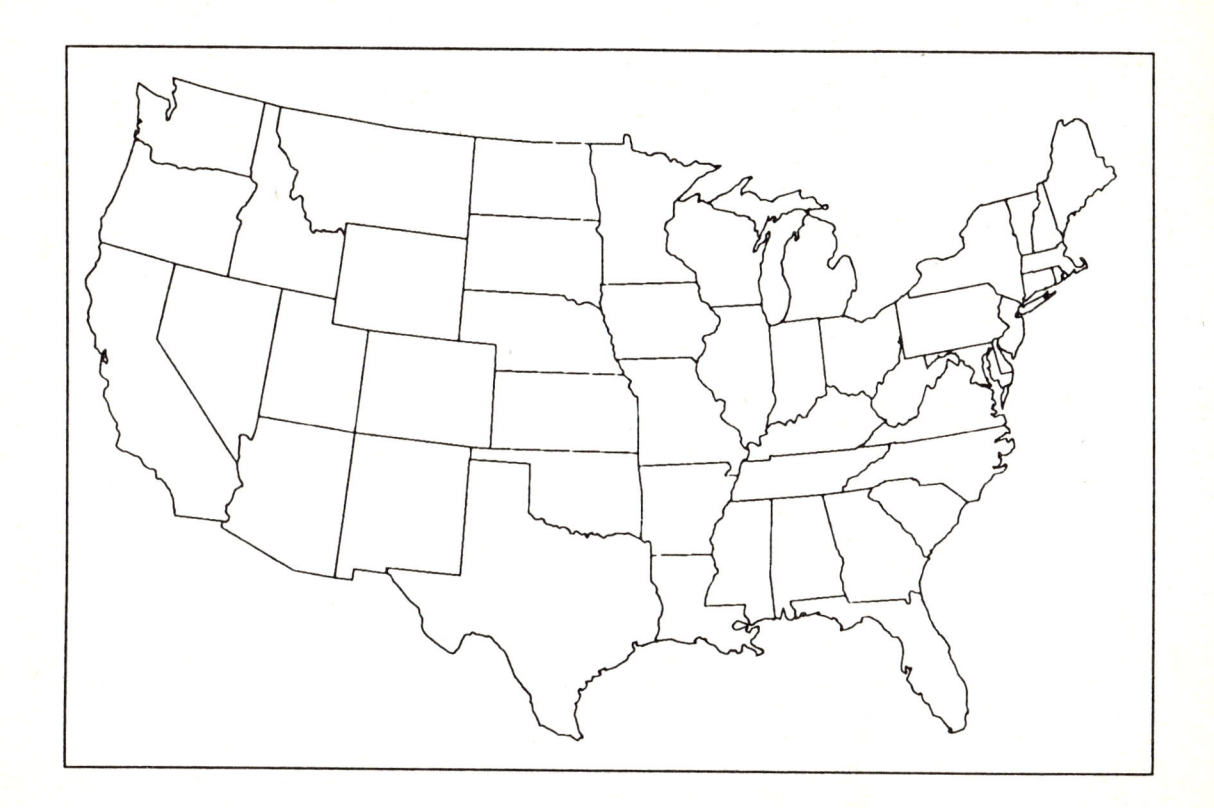

## Self-Test

### Multiple-Choice Questions

1. The Republicans won all of these presidential elections *except*:
   A. 1876
   B. 1880
   C. 1884
   D. 1888

2. What dismissed New York customs official later became president?
   A. Hayes
   B. Garfield
   C. Arthur
   D. Cleveland

3. The Mugwumps opposed the presidential candidacy of:
   A. James G. Blaine
   B. Roscoe Conkling
   C. Grover Cleveland
   D. Benjamin Harrison

4. The president who fathered a child out of wedlock was:
   A. Hayes
   B. Garfield
   C. Arthur
   D. Cleveland

5. The president who challenged the conventional wisdom of seeking reelection unless one stands for principle was:
   A. Hayes
   B. Arthur
   C. Cleveland
   D. Harrison

6. Thomas Reed was associated with:
   A. Organizational procedures in the U.S. House of Representatives
   B. Formation of the Populist party
   C. A plan to increase veterans' pensions
   D. Lowering the protective tariff

7. Congress first spent $1 billion in a single session in:
   A. 1870
   B. 1880
   C. 1890
   D. 1900

8. Which of these statements is FALSE regarding the 1892 election?
   A. For the third consecutive time, Grover Cleveland was the Democratic nominee.
   B. Benjamin Harrison was the unsuccessful incumbent.
   C. William Jennings Bryan secured endorsements of both Democratic and Populist parties.
   D. James Weaver garnered 22 electoral votes.

9. Populists called for all of the following *except*:
   A. Protective tariff
   B. Graduated income tax
   C. "Subtreasury" plan
   D. Increasing the money supply to aid debtors

10. Which of the following was *not* a Populist?
    A. "Sockless Jerry" Simpson
    B. Ignatius Donnelly
    C. Tom Watson
    D. Theodore Roosevelt

11. J. P. Morgan and Grover Cleveland worked to:
    A. Lower tariff barriers
    B. Keep the gold reserve above the $100 million level required by law
    C. Establish public works projects during the Panic of 1893
    D. Reform corrupt campaign practices of the 1890s

12. Jacob Coxey:
    A. Was the Populist presidential nominee in 1896
    B. Was McKinley's 1896 campaign manager
    C. Wrote *Caesar's Column*
    D. Led a march of the unemployed on Washington in 1894

13. "...You shall not press down upon the brow of labor this crown of thorns, you shall not crucify mankind upon a cross of gold," warned:
    A. Theodore Roosevelt
    B. William McKinley
    C. William Jennings Bryan
    D. Grover Cleveland

14. The "front-porch" campaign was waged by:
    A. Cleveland
    B. Arthur
    C. Harrison
    D. McKinley

15. Important gold discoveries occurred in the late 1890s in
    A. Peru and Venezuela
    B. South Africa and Alaska
    C. France and Russia
    D. Sweden and Egypt

16. The Farmers Alliance began in:
    A. Kansas
    B. Alabama
    C. South Carolina
    D. Texas

17. Richard Croker:
    A. Was a "boss" of Tammany Hall
    B. Managed Blaine's presidential campaign
    C. Helped secure Republican votes for Bryan in 1896
    D. Was William McKinley's campaign manager

18. Mark Hanna realized that campaign procedures had been irrevocably changed by the 1890s because of:
    A. The silver issue
    B. The impact of the Pendleton Act
    C. Bryan's taking to the stump in 1896
    D. The rise of the Populist party

19. Which of these politicians was *most* interested in foreign affairs?
    A. Hayes
    B. Arthur
    C. Cleveland
    D. Blaine

20. The Mulligan letters:
    A. Helped to defeat Cleveland in 1888
    B. Proved that Cleveland had fathered a child out of wedlock
    C. Undermined Blaine's reputation for personal integrity
    D. Secured support for Harrison among Irish-Americans in the 1888 campaign

**Essay Questions**

1. Explain why political leaders in the late nineteenth century avoided taking stands on public issues in light of sectional, partisan, ethnic, and economic differences among voters.

2. What conditions enabled political "bosses" and "machines" to organize voters? Identify some of the "bosses" and explain their reaction to reform movements.

3. Evaluate the administrations of Presidents Hayes, Garfield, Arthur, Cleveland, and Harrison in reference to their conceptions of the office and the use of executive power. Mention a few accomplishments of each president.

4. Show how farm discontent led to formation of the Populist party. List some of the goals of the Populists. Identify the leading Populist figures.

5. Discuss the election of 1896 in reference to candidates, parties, issues, political strategies and tactics, emotional climate, outcome, and lasting significance.


## Critical Thinking Exercise

Label each of the following statements concerning politics in the late nineteenth century as "T" for fact, "O" for opinion, or "F" for falsehood.

___ 1. William McKinley's victory in 1896 was possible because the Republicans were still the majority party, and McKinley obtained support from substantial Democratic defectors.

___ 2. The Bryan-McKinley race is considered a "watershed" election because it settled the question of the gold standard and ushered in a long era of Republican domination of the presidency.

___ 3. The American public held Congress in no higher esteem a century ago than it does today, according to opinion polls.

___ 4. Cleveland's handling of the gold reserve reflected his inability to deal with crises.

___ 5. Populists played a leading role in Benjamin Harrison's election as president.

___ 6. Abraham Lincoln erred in his original estimate of James Blaine as "one of the coming men of the country."

___ 7. Blaine's moderate views toward the South contributed to the support he received in the region in 1884.

___ 8. Bryan's defeat was fortunate because his program would have jeopardized the financial security of the nation.

____9. Thomas Reed's political courage would have been useful in the White House during an era when presidents tended to be cautious caretakers.

____10. McKinley's response, whether intentional or not, to Bryan's 1896 campaign strategy was nothing short of brilliant.

CHAPTER 22

# From Isolation to Empire

## Learning Objectives

*After reading Chapter 22, you should be able to:*

1. Explain American interest in Latin America and the Far East at the turn of the twentieth century.
2. List factors leading to the rise of imperialism in America.
3. Evaluate the Spanish-American War with reference to causes, key battles, outcome, and the peace treaty.
4. List reasons why Americans were divided over the question of annexing the Philippines in 1898.
5. Discuss the significance of the Open Door in China.
6. Review the timetable of events that led to construction of the Panama Canal.

## Overview

### America's Divided View of the World

Americans in the late nineteenth century showed little concern about events in Europe but indicated growing interest in Latin America and the Far East. The disdain toward Europe rested on a view of the United States as an "apart nation."

The United States pressed for compensation from Great Britain for Union merchandise sunk by Confederate cruisers that had been built in British naval yards during the Civil War. The British paid $15.5 million in settlement of the *Alabama* claims in the 1871 Treaty of Washington. There were also outbursts against Britain regarding her treatment of the Irish. Other squabbles developed with France and Germany over the banning of American pork.

### Origins of the Large Policy

During the Civil War, France had established a protectorate over Mexico, installing the Austrian Archduke Maximilian as emperor. Secretary of State William Seward demanded that the French withdraw, and the United States moved 50,000 troops to the Rio Grande. France pulled out, and nationalist rebels seized power and executed Maximilian.

In 1867, Seward arranged the Alaska purchase from Russia for $7.2 million, thereby ridding the continent of another foreign power. That same year Seward acquired the Midway

Islands (which had been discovered in 1859 by the American naval officer N. C. Brooks) and proposed annexing Hawaii, Cuba, and the Dominican Republic. American trade grew to the extent that by 1898 the nation was shipping abroad more manufactured goods than it imported.

Shifting intellectual currents encouraged interest in other nations. The Darwinist historian John Fiske claimed that American democracy was certain to spread peacefully over the entire world. The missionary Josiah Strong in *Our Country* claimed that God had ordained the Anglo-Saxon race to impress Christian institutions on all mankind.

Military and strategic needs dictated a colonial policy. Captain Alfred T. Mahan in *The Influence of Sea Power upon History* argued that a powerful navy and overseas bases would make the United States invulnerable in war and prosperous in peace. Therefore, he urged America to build a modern fleet, obtain coaling stations and bases in the Caribbean, annex Hawaii, and cut a canal across Central America. Leading followers of Mahan included President Harrison's secretary of the navy, Benjamin Tracy, and future President Theodore Roosevelt.

### The Course of Empire in the Pacific

American interest in the Far East can be traced to the first merchant ship dropping anchor in Canton harbor. Thereafter, merchants received major concessions in China through the Treaty of Wanghia in 1844.

Contacts were made with Hawaii as early as 1820. The Hawaiian monarchy was dominated by descendants of missionary families engaged in raising sugar and pineapples. In 1875, a reciprocity treaty admitted Hawaiian sugar to the United States free of duty in return for a promise to yield no territory to a foreign power. The McKinley Tariff of 1890 discontinued the duty on raw sugar and compensated American producers of cane and beet sugar through a bounty of two cents a pound. This policy destroyed the advantage Hawaiian sugar growers had gained in the reciprocity treaty.

In 1891, Queen Liliuokalani, an advocate of "Hawaii for Hawaiians," attempted to rule as an absolute monarch. She was overthrown in a coup supported by the United States minister, John L. Stevens. A treaty of annexation was drafted in the closing days of the Harrison administration, but President Cleveland withdrew the agreement because he believed that the Hawaiians opposed annexation, and he disapproved of the way the monarchy had been toppled. In 1898, Congress annexed the islands by joint resolution, a procedure requiring only a simple majority vote.

### The Course of Empire in Latin America

The Monroe Doctrine had conditioned Americans to the idea of protecting the national interest in the Western Hemisphere. As early as 1869, President Grant had supported construction of an interoceanic canal even though the Clayton-Bulwer Treaty made such a unilateral canal impossible at that time. In 1880, the French engineer Ferdinand de Lesseps formed a company to build a canal across the isthmus. President Hayes announced that the United States would not permit a European power to control such a waterway.

In 1889, the United States participated in its first Pan-American Conference, which met in Washington. There Secretary of State James Blaine tried to obtain a reciprocity agreement with the Latin American countries, but the major outcome of the meeting was the establishment of the Pan-American Union.

A minor disagreement with Chile brought the United States to the verge of war in 1891, when sailors from the U.S.S. *Baltimore* on shore leave in Valparaiso were set upon by a mob. Two crewmen were killed, and the United States threatened war until Chile agreed to pay reparations.

In 1895, President Cleveland became involved in a border dispute between Venezuela and British Guiana (later Guyana). He directed Secretary of State Richard Olney to dispatch a near-ultimatum to the British which declared that the "United States is practically sovereign on this continent." Britain finally agreed to Cleveland's call to arbitrate the dispute. The boundary tribunal ironically awarded most of the disputed land to Britain.


**The Cuban Revolution**

In 1896, General Valeriano Weyler arrived in Havana from Spain to assume duties as governor of Cuba. Determined to end the guerrilla warfare waged by Cuban nationalist rebels, Weyler herded the rural population into "reconcentration" camps. The American public, most newspapers, veterans' organizations, labor unions, and many Protestant clergymen sympathized with the Cubans, whom the press depicted as fighting for liberty and democracy against an autocratic Old World power.

When riots broke out in Havana in early 1898, McKinley sent the battleship *Maine* to protect American citizens. Thereafter Hearst's *New York Journal* printed a letter written to a friend in Cuba by the Spanish minister in Washington, Dupuy de Lome. The letter, stolen by a spy, denounced McKinley as a "bidder for the admiration of the crowd." On February 15, the *Maine* exploded and sank in Havana harbor; 260 crew members perished. A naval court of inquiry determined that the vessel had been sunk by a submarine mine, but it now seems more likely that an internal explosion destroyed the ship. Spain's culpability seems doubtful because such action would have guaranteed the entry of the United States.

After weeks of uncertainty, President McKinley drafted a message to Congress asking for authority to use the armed forces in Cuba. The Spanish government seemed to yield, but Cuban nationalists pressed for independence. War was at hand.


**The "Splendid Little" Spanish-American War**

On April 20, 1898, Congress by joint resolution recognized the independence of Cuba and authorized armed forces to drive out the Spanish. The Teller Amendment disclaimed any intention of annexing the island. Four days later Spain declared war on the United States. Though the war was fought to free Cuba, the early action took place in the Philippines, where Commodore George Dewey moved against the Spanish base at Manila Bay. Not one American life was lost.

Meanwhile, in the Cuban phase of the war, the United States won swift and total victory. Americans blockaded Santiago, where the Spanish admiral Pascual Cervera had docked his fleet. An expeditionary force commanded by General William Shafter landed at Daiquiri, and pressed toward Santiago. By July 1, American volunteers known as the "Rough Riders," trained in Tampa, Florida, stormed San Juan Hill. When Cervera tried to run the American blockade, he was stopped by five battleships and two cruisers. In four hours the Spanish force was destroyed; the American ships sustained little damage, and one seaman lost his life in the engagement.

After the surrender of Santiago, American troops occupied Puerto Rico. On August 12, a day before the fall of Manila, Spain agreed to vacate Cuba, to cede Puerto Rico and the island of Guam to the United States, and to permit the settlement of the Filipino issue at a peace conference beginning on October 1.

## Developing a Colonial Policy

The debate over taking the Philippines thrust the United States into the ranks of major world powers. In light of the Teller Amendment forsaking any claim over Cuba, logic would seem to have indicated that the United States would not annex the Philippines. Yet expansionists wanted to take the entire archipelago to expand the trade, wealth, and power of the United States. McKinley believed that the public wanted the islands, and business opinion shifted dramatically in support of annexation.

## The Anti-imperialists

An important minority of intellectuals argued that because Filipino statehood was not under consideration, it would be unconstitutional to annex the islands. Annexation would violate the spirit of the Declaration of Independence. Many who opposed annexation were partisan Democrats; others were governed by ethnic and racial prejudices. McKinley looked favorably on the commercial possibilities that would stem from acquisition of an empire. At the Treaty of Paris (1898) the United States acquired the Philippines but agreed to pay $20 million to soothe the feelings of the Spanish. The treaty was approved by the United States Senate when Bryan, as titular head of the Democratic party, did not openly oppose the treaty because to have done so would have left the nation technically at war with Spain. Moreover, Bryan hoped to use the issue in his planned 1900 presidential rematch with William McKinley.

## The Philippine Insurrection

In 1899, Filipino nationalists under Emilio Aguinaldo rose in guerrilla warfare against the United States, a three-year war that cost more in lives and money than the Spanish-American conflict. The rebellion, characterized by extreme brutality on both sides, continued even after McKinley sent a federal judge, William Howard Taft of Cincinnati, to become the first civilian governor of the islands. Though anti-imperialists continued to object to taking over territories without the consent of the local population, McKinley's reelection resolved the question of Philippine annexation.

## Cuba and the United States

McKinley quickly established military governments in Cuba, Puerto Rico, and the Philippines. In 1900, the Foraker Act established civil government in Puerto Rico. It did not give the Puerto Ricans American citizenship or self-government and placed tariffs on imports to the United States. The Supreme Court in *Downes v. Bidwell* upheld the tariff on Puerto Rican goods on the premise that the "Constitution does not follow the flag," a judgment stemming from the "insular cases." The court stipulated that Congress itself must develop colonial policy.

Americans found Cuba to be in a state of collapse and chaos after the war. Streets were littered with garbage and the corpses of horses and dogs. American soldiers had difficulty working with the Cubans, a factor attributed in part to racial prejudice. The United States helped to modernize sugar production, improve sanitation, establish schools, and restore order. McKinley appointed General Leonard Wood as military governor. The Platt Amendment granted independence to Cuba but held open the possibility that the United States would intervene if Cuban independence were threatened. In 1902, the United States vacated Cuba, but the economic ties continued.

## The United States in the Caribbean

The Caribbean countries were economically underdeveloped, socially backward, politically unstable, and desperately poor. A few families owned most of the land and dominated social and political life. Cynicism and fraud poisoned relations between the Caribbean nations and the great powers. In 1902, trouble broke out in Venezuela, when a dictator refused to honor debts owed to Europeans. Germany and Britain imposed a blockade of Venezuela to force payment. Under American pressure, the Europeans agreed to arbitrate the dispute.

In 1903, the Dominican Republic defaulted on $40 million worth of bonds. President Theodore Roosevelt arranged for the United States to take charge of Dominican customs service. This Roosevelt Corollary to the Monroe Doctrine declared that the United States would reluctantly "exercise . . . an international police power" in Latin America to maintain peace and stability. Roosevelt's policy brought order but engendered resentment in Latin America.

## The Open Door Policy

The United States tried to prevent the absorption of China by the great powers through the "Open Door" policy announced by McKinley's Secretary of State, John Hay. Hay asked that the trading rights of all countries be honored and that there be no discriminatory duties within the various spheres of influence. Tariffs were to be collected by the Chinese. When the great powers were noncommittal in their replies, Hay announced that the powers had "accepted" his recommendations.

Hay's policy was tested in the Boxer Rebellion of 1900. Chinese nationalists swarmed into Peking (Beijing) and drove foreigners within the walls of their legations, which were placed under siege. An international rescue expedition freed the foreigners. Fearing that the rebellion would lead to further expropriations, Hay sent off another round of Open Door notes.

Thereafter, the United States became involved in the settlement of the Russo-Japanese War, which began in 1904, when Japan attacked Russia in a quarrel over Manchuria. Theodore Roosevelt was asked to mediate the struggle in a conference at Portsmouth, New Hampshire. The Japanese were disgruntled over the treaty because they got no indemnity and only the southern half of Sakhalin Island.

Moreover, when the San Francisco school board instituted a policy of segregating Asian children in a special school, Japan protested. Roosevelt persuaded the San Franciscans to abandon segregation, and Japan through the "Gentlemen's Agreement" halted further Japanese immigration.

## The Isthmian Canal

In 1901, the United States and Britain signed the Hay-Pauncefote Treaty, which abrogated the 1850 Clayton-Bulwer Treaty. The United States agreed that any canal it might build would be "free and open to the vessels" of all nations. A route across Panama, then part of Colombia, was finally selected after consideration of a longer Nicaraguan link. In 1903, the United States signed the Hay-Herran Treaty to pay Colombia $10 million and annual rent of $250,000 for a canal route. The Colombian Senate rejected the treaty on grounds that the $10 million offer was insufficient.

Roosevelt therefore ordered the cruiser *Nashville* to Panama, where a revolution sparked by the French company erupted in November 1903. Roosevelt recognized the new Republic of Panama, and the United States acquired the Panama Canal Zone, a strip of land 10 miles wide across the new country. Historians have long criticized Roosevelt's aggressiveness in the canal incident, but he never wavered in his belief that he had acted in the national interest.

In 1921, the United States authorized $25 million to Colombia in return for recognition of the independence of Panama. The United States still dominated Panama by virtue of the canal zone, through which passed the first vessels in the summer of 1914.

President Taft's policy toward the outlying areas, termed "dollar diplomacy," assumed that economic penetration would stabilize underdeveloped areas and profit the United States without the need to commit troops or spend public funds. American investments reached $500 million in Cuba by 1920, and smaller investments were made in Haiti and the Dominican Republic. In Central America the United Fruit Company accumulated large holdings in banana plantations, railroads, and other ventures. Still other countries invested in Mexico's rich mineral resources.

"Non-colonial Imperial Expansion"

The United States acquired its colonies in the period between 1898 and 1903. Thereafter, a conviction that the costs of colonial administration outweighed the profits brought about a gradual retreat from imperialism. Critics of the policy claimed the United States exploited the underdeveloped countries and ignored the conflicting cultures and needs of colonial subjects. Yet, by 1914 the United States was a world power poised to guide the development of lesser developed countries with traditions far different from its own.

## People, Places, and Things

*Define the following concepts:*

- "large" policy _____

- joint resolution _____

- "reconcentration" camps _____

- archipelago _____

- anti-imperialists _____

- "insular cases" _____

- "spheres of influence" _____

- "yellow peril" _____

- isthmus _____

_____

- "dollar diplomacy" _____

_____

*Describe the following:*

Treaty of Washington _____

_____

Clayton-Bulwer Treaty _____

_____

- *Maine* _____

_____

- Rough Riders _____

_____

Teller Amendment _____

_____

- Platt Amendment _____

_____

- Roosevelt Corollary _____

_____

- Boxer Rebellion _____

_____

- Open Door policy _____

- Treaty of Portsmouth _____

- "Gentlemen's Agreement" _____

- Sakhalin Island _____

- Hay-Pauncefote Treaty _____

- *Nashville* _____

- United Fruit Company _____

- *Downes v. Bidwell* _____

*Identify the following people:*

- Maximilian _____

- William H. Seward _____

- N.C. Brooks _____

- Josiah Strong _____

- Alfred Mahan _____

- Liliuokalani _____

- John L. Stevens _____

- Valeriano Weyler _____

- Dupuy de Lome _____

- George Dewey _____

- Emilio Aguinaldo _____

- Theodore Roosevelt _____

- Leonard Wood _____

John Hay _____

_____

William Howard Taft _____

_____

## Map Exercise

Refer to the map on the following page. Place the letter in the blank that corresponds to the correct location.

_____ 1. Bahamas

_____ 2. Colombia

_____ 3. Costa Rica

_____ 4. Cuba

_____ 5. Dominican Republic

_____ 6. El Salvador

_____ 7. Florida

_____ 8. Guatemala

_____ 9. Haiti

_____ 10. Honduras

_____ 11. Jamaica

_____ 12. Mexico

_____ 13. Nicaragua

_____ 14. Panama

_____ 15. Puerto Rico

_____ 16. Venezuela

_____ 17. Virgin Islands

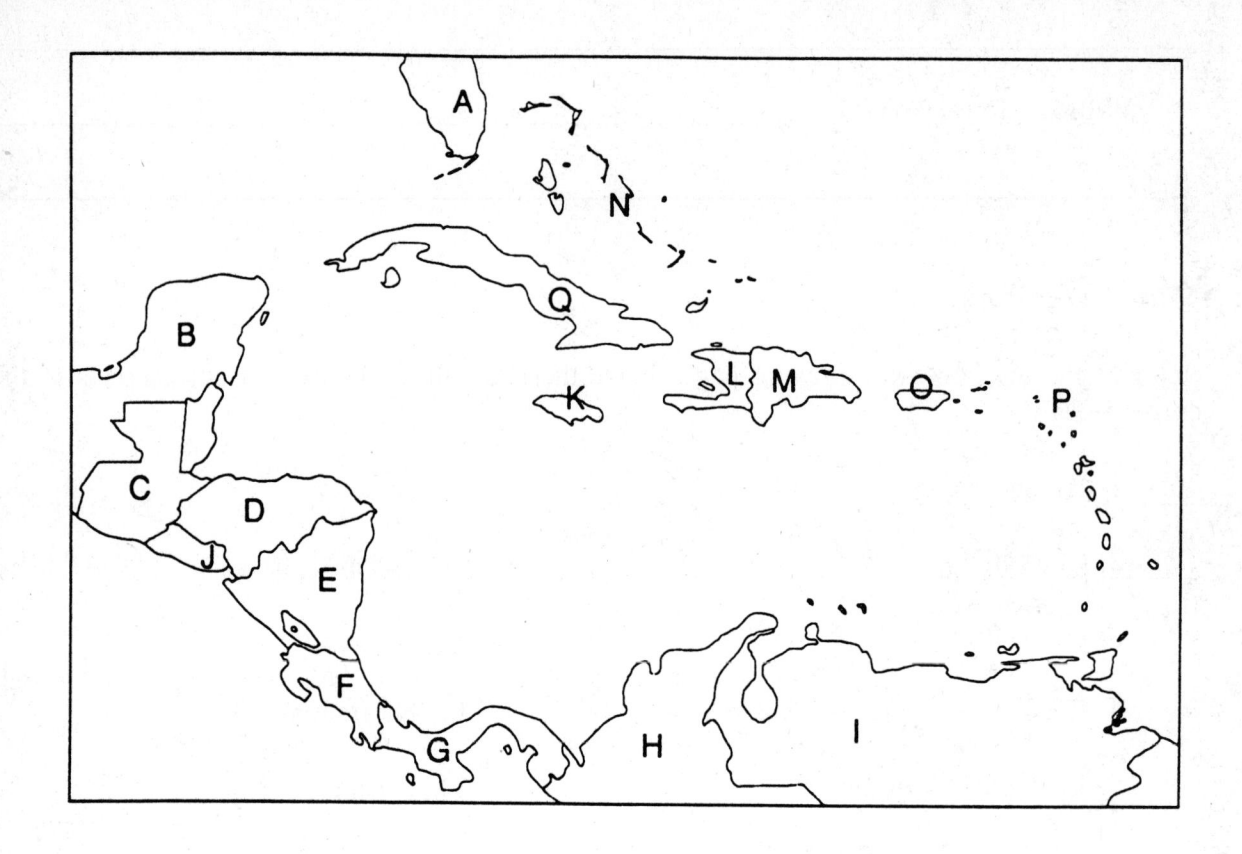

Refer to the map on the following page. Place the letter in the blank that corresponds to the correct location.

_____ 1. Australia

_____ 2. China

_____ 3. Guam

_____ 4. Japan

_____ 5. Korea

_____ 6. Manchuria

_____ 7. Midway

_____ 8. Philippines

_____ 9. Sakhalin Island

_____ 10. Wake Island

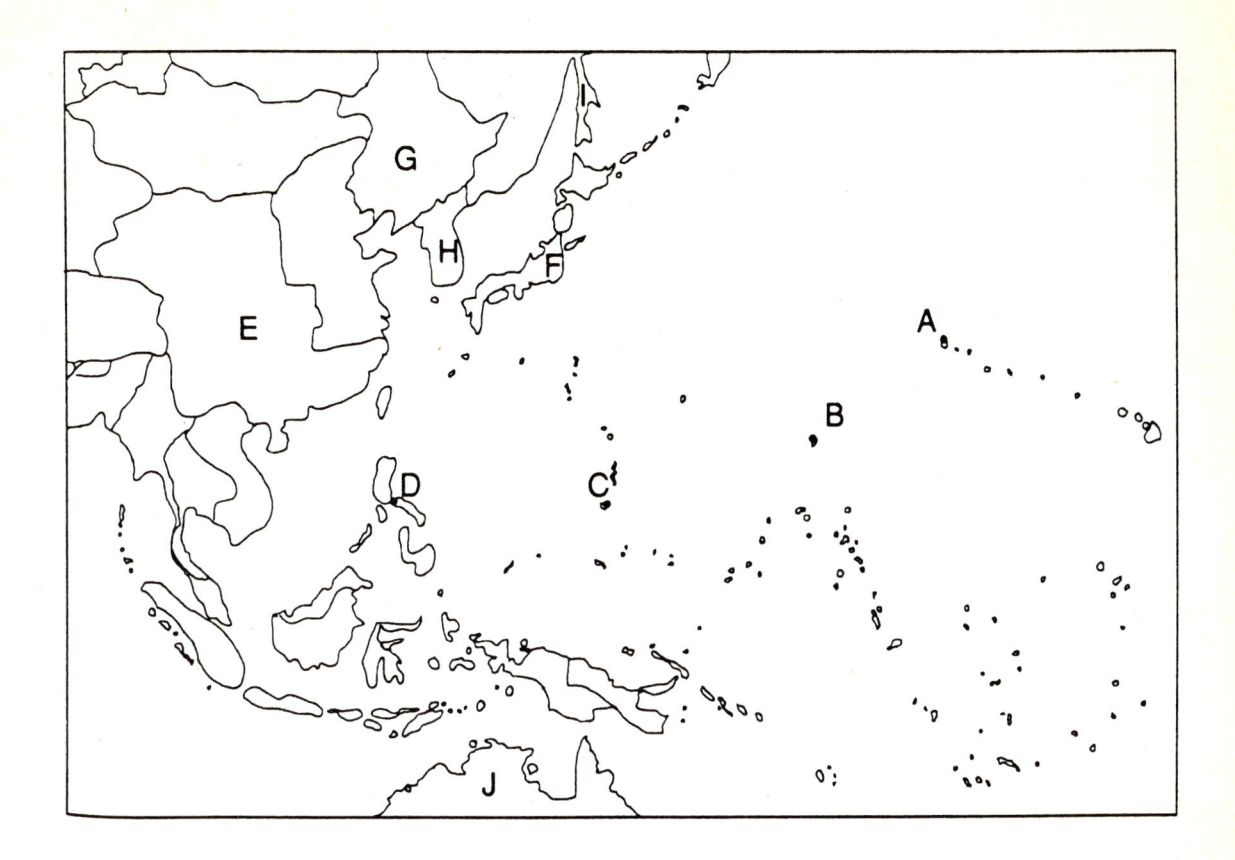

## Self-Test

**Multiple-Choice Questions**

1. ". . . the United States is practically sovereign on this continent," declared:
    A. Theodore Roosevelt
    B. James G. Blaine
    C. Richard Olney
    D. William McKinley

99

2. Josiah Strong:
   A. Advocated American intervention to collect customs in the Dominican Republic
   B. Said the United States was ordained by God to spread its Christian teachings worldwide
   C. Argued the anti-imperialist position regarding the Philippines
   D. Wrote *The Influence of Sea Power Upon History*

3. No nation can become a world power without a powerful navy represents the view of:
   A. Dupuy de Lome
   B. Emilio Aguinaldo
   C. Alfred T. Mahan
   D. Josiah Strong

4. Which of these statements regarding American interest in Hawaii is *false*?
   A. Hawaii became a territory during Cleveland's administration.
   B. In 1893, a revolt resulted in the overthrow of Queen Liliuokalani.
   C. The United States was instrumental in permitting a group of sugar growers to establish a Hawaiian republic.
   D. Hawaii did not become a state until 1959.

5. The explosion of the *Maine* precipitated United States participation in a war against:
   A. Spain
   B. Britain
   C. Germany
   D. Venezuela

6. San Juan Hill is located in:
   A. Sanitago, Chile
   B. Santiago, Cuba
   C. Manila
   D. San Juan, Puerto Rico

7. From the treaty ending the Spanish-American War, the United States acquired all of the following *except*:
   A. Guam
   B. Philippines
   C. Cuba
   D. Puerto Rico

8. Anti-imperialists objected to annexation of the Philippines for all of these reasons *except*:
   A. Inconsistency with the Teller Amendment
   B. The need for naval bases and coaling stations in the Far East
   C. To consider the Filipinos as colonists would violate the spirit of the Declaration of Independence
   D. The Aguinaldo revolt proved that the Filipinos did not desire American occupation

9. Pivotal "support" for the treaty ending the Spanish-American War is attributed to:
   A. William Jennings Bryan
   B. Theodore Roosevelt
   C. William McKinley
   D. John Hay

10. The military governor who supervised the rebuilding of Cuba after the Spanish-American War was:
    A. William Howard Taft
    B. Leonard Wood
    C. William Sampson
    D. George Dewey

11. The Foraker Act:
    A. Allowed America to build a future canal across Nicaragua
    B. Established a limited civil government in Puerto Rico
    C. Required American traders to respect "spheres of influence" in China
    D. Renounced American interests in occupying Cuba

12. Russia and Japan went to war in a desire to exploit the natural resources of:
    A. Sakhalin Island
    B. Korea
    C. Manchuria
    D. Philippines

13. The treaty ending the Russo-Japanese War was signed in:
    A. Russia
    B. Japan
    C. Britain
    D. The United States

14. "Dollar diplomacy" refers to:
    A. Construction of an interoceanic canal to assist world trade
    B. Encouragement of American trade and investments in such areas as Latin America and the Far East
    C. European investment in American finance
    D. Maintaining the right of transit across Panama

15. Why did Colombia reject the American canal offer?
    A. Germany submitted a better financial arrangement
    B. America decided instead to pursue the Nicaraguan route
    C. Colombia felt that the $10 million offer was too small in that the United States would pay $40 million to a French company that had been trying to build a canal
    D. Colombia rejected American policy regarding canal tolls

16. The Clayton-Bulwer Treaty was superseded by which agreement?
    A. Hay-Pauncefote
    B. "Gentlemen's Agreement"
    C. Hay-Herran
    D. Platt Amendment

17. Theodore Roosevelt's critics accused him of trying to annex what country when he took over its customs house in 1907?
    A. Cuba
    B. The Dominican Republic
    C. Venezuela
    D. Puerto Rico

18. The *Alabama* claims refer to United States policy with:
    A. France
    B. Spain
    C. Cuba
    D. Great Britain

19. John Fiske was a Darwinist who:
    A. Occupied the Midway Islands in 1867
    B. Insisted that the American system of government was so successful that it must be spread around the world
    C. Espoused religious justifications against American imperialism
    D. Negotiated the Peace of Paris, 1898

20. San Francisco became the subject of international attention in 1906 because of its policy of:
    A. Banning the importation of Hawaiian sugar
    B. Passing a resolution against the Open Door Policy
    C. Segregating Asian school children
    D. Recruiting Chinese laborers

**Essay Questions**

1. Explain how the Philippine annexation question divided Americans in 1898. Emphasize valid points held by both sides in the controversy. What was the ultimate outcome?

2. Evaluate the Spanish-American War, with emphasis on causes, principal battles, immediate results, the peace treaty, and long-term implications to American policy.

3. Explain how the Open Door policy and Boxer Rebellion worked to shift America from isolationism to interventionism.

4. Discuss principal events over a period of nearly 60 years that made possible construction of the Panama Canal.

5. Explain how the Roosevelt Corollary to the Monroe Doctrine affected American policy at the turn of the twentieth century.

## Critical Thinking Exercise

Label each of the following statements as "I" for isolationist attitudes toward foreign policy or "E" for expansionist or imperialist beliefs.

_____ 1. "The trade of the world must and shall be ours."

_____ 2. Colonial holdings promote the prosperity of a nation by providing markets for manufactured goods.

_____ 3. America has enough to be concerned with right here on the continent that it need not be excessively involved in world events.

_____ 4. Whenever America has become involved in distant wars of this century, she has emerged with as many problems as she faced before entering such wars.

_____ 5. It was inconsistent to annex the Philippines in view of the Teller Amendment.

_____ 6. Had the Platt Amendment not been revoked in 1934, Cuba might well be a free nation today.

_____ 7. Recent unrest in French-speaking Quebec, Canada, should give pause to those promoting Puerto Rican statehood.

_____ 8. No major power can shirk its foreign responsibilities for long and retain major-nation status.

____9. "We want peaceful commerce with all nations, and we want contact and communications, both cultural and diplomatic, with all the peoples of the planet."

____10. "We do not want to fight other peoples' wars or use the tax dollars of our citizens to pay other nations' debts."

CHAPTER 23

# The Age of Reform

## Learning Objectives

*After reading Chapter 23 you should be able to:*

1. Explain the origins of the Progressive movement.
2. Evaluate the motivation and state of mind of Progressives.
3. Discuss reforms at the city, state, and national levels in the early 20th century.
4. Evaluate the Roosevelt administration in regard to business and the Square Deal.
5. Evaluate the presidency of William Howard Taft and explain how Taft split the Republican party after 1909.
6. Analyze the election of 1912 regarding political parties, candidates, issues, results, and long-range implications.
7. Describe the reforms of the New Freedom.
8. Explain why nonwhites benefited little from progressivism.

## Overview

**Roots of Progressivism**

Historians categorize the period between the end of the Spanish-American War and American entry into World War I as the Progressive Era. "Progressive" in this sense refers to reform as a response to the burgeoning industrialism that followed the Civil War. The roots of Progressivism predated 1898, and remnants of the movement continued into the 1920s. Some Progressives demanded an end to corrupt political machines; others wished to regulate the industrial giants through stronger anti-trust laws; a third group proposed reforms on behalf of the urban poor, including an end to child labor, regulation of working hours and conditions, worker safety, and improved housing.

The historian Richard Hofstadter viewed Progressivism as a "status revolution" in which prosperous small businessmen and professional persons resented the power and prominence of industrial tycoons and were outraged over the activities of machine politicians. Progressive backing for reform harmonized with intellectual currents of the time -- the new social sciences, the Social Gospel, and pragmatism -- blended with their ideas of social improvement.

## The Muckrakers

A group of journalists encouraged Progressivism through their emphasis on the abuses of the political, social, and economic system. These "muckrakers," named after a character in John Bunyan's *Pilgrim's Progress*, flooded the press with articles on such topics as insurance, college athletics, prostitution, sweatshop labor, and political corruption. Henry Lloyd and Ida Tarbell tackled the Standard Oil monopoly in *Atlantic Monthly* and *McClure's*, respectively. Lincoln Steffens wrote hard-hitting articles which exposed the ties between big-city machines and business operators.

## The Progressive Mind

Progressives tried to arouse the conscience of the people to "purify" American life. They believed that human beings are by nature decent and well-intentioned and claimed that the evils of society lay in the structure of institutions, rather than weaknesses or sinfulness of individuals. Therefore, most Progressives believed that government should respond to the will of citizens who stood for traditional virtues. Despite its democratic rhetoric, Progressivism was paternalistic. Reformers frequently oversimplified issues and treated their values as absolute truth and morality. Though progressives stressed individual freedom, many backed prohibition. Nor did they challenge fundamental principles of capitalism or try to reorganize society. Many Progressives were anti-immigrant and anti-black.

## "Radical" Progressives: The Wave of the Future

Some Progressives espoused radical views. Eugene V. Debs ran for president on the Socialist ticket. William "Big Bill" Haywood, Mary "Mother" Jones, and Daniel De Leon organized a radical union, the Industrial Workers of the World, which proclaimed that the working class had nothing in common with its employers.

Progressive intellectual Sigmund Freud advanced the theory of psychoanalysis in *The Interpretation of Dreams*, which slowly revolutionized manners and morals. Among the "Bohemian" thinkers who flocked to New York's Greenwich Village were the dancer Isadora Duncan, the photographer Alfred Stieglitz, the "ashcan" artists, playwright Eugene O'Neill, birth-control advocate Margaret Sanger, and communist journalist John Reed, who wrote an eyewitness account of the Russian Revolution, *Ten Days That Shook the World*.

The creative writers of the era included the poets Ezra Pound, who yearned for an "American Renaissance," and the Chicagoan Carl Sandburg, who hailed his "City of Big Shoulders."

## Political Reform: Cities First

Progressivism began in the cities, where corruption and inefficiency had become rampant. Reformers worked to dismantle political machines from New York to San Francisco, where the legendary lawyer Abe Ruef made a fortune in illegal political activities. Progressive mayors included Samuel "Golden Rule" Jones in Toledo, Tom L. Johnson of Cleveland, Seth Low and John P. Mitchell of New York, and Hazen Pingree of Detroit. Some reformers created "home rule" charters and research bureaus, took over city utilities, and offered two new forms of municipal government.

The commission system, which began in Galveston in 1900, integrated legislative and executive functions in the hands of an elected commission. The city-manager system, epitomized by Dayton, Ohio, authorized a professional manager to administer city affairs on a nonpartisan basis.

**Political Reform: The States**

Progressives found they could not improve the cities unless legislatures were willing to cooperate, because municipalities are creations of states. A model for progressive policies was undertaken in Wisconsin by Republican Governor Robert M. La Follette, who claimed that the people would always do the right thing if properly informed. Despite the opposition of rail and lumbering interests, La Follette obtained a direct primary for nominating candidates, a corrupt practices act, and laws limiting campaign expenditures and lobbying. La Follette himself became a political "boss" through his use of patronage and demand for loyalty from subordinates. La Follette was prone to sense "conspiracies" when his programs attracted even mild opposition. His "Wisconsin Idea" spread across the nation from New Jersey to Oregon, where voters introduced the initiative, which allows voters to approve measures rejected by state lawmakers and to repeal legislation enacted by the legislatures.

**State Social Legislation**

The states gradually adopted social legislation to regulate employment. Utah restricted miners to an eight-hour day in 1896; New York's tenement law increased the area of open space on building lots and required toilets, ventilation, and fireproofing for each apartment. Judges sometimes used the Fourteenth Amendment restriction on depriving individuals of "life, liberty or property" as an excuse to overturn social legislation, but they also at times adopted a narrow interpretation of state police power to uphold such reforms as the Utah mining law.

In *Lochner v. New York*, the Supreme Court said the states could not limit bakers to a ten-hour day because individuals could work as many hours as they wished. In 1923, the Court in *Adkins v. Children's Hospital* overturned a minimum wage for women in the District of Columbia. After Congress passed laws to ban child labor, the Court overruled the legislation in *Hammer v. Dagenhart* in 1918. An attempt to amend the Constitution to prohibit child labor, submitted in 1924, failed to gain ratification.

By 1917, most states had limited the hours of women industrial workers, and some had set wage standards. In 1908, the Court had ruled in *Muller v. Oregon*, a landmark case argued by attorney Louis D. Brandeis, that the state could limit women laundry workers to a ten-hour day on grounds that long hours undermined the health of the women, the well-being of their families, and the good of the communities.

Many states improved worker safety, particularly after the 1911 Triangle Shirtwaist factory fire in New York City, which claimed the lives of nearly 150 women because the company had no fire escapes.

Reforms patterned on the La Follette formula were adopted under Governors Woodrow Wilson in New Jersey and Charles Evans Hughes in New York. Wilson obtained a public utility commission with authority to fix rates of rail, gas, electric, telephone, and express companies. Hughes crusaded for changes in insurance laws.

## Political Reform in Washington

On the national level Progressives pushed for adoption of the Nineteenth Amendment to grant women's suffrage, a goal promoted by feminists Susan B. Anthony, Elizabeth Cady Stanton, Carrie Chapman Catt, and Alice Paul. Feminists earlier had obtained voting rights in the West—Wyoming, Colorado, Utah, and Idaho—and demanded political, social, and economic equality with men.

The Progressive reform drive found further expression in the Sixteenth Amendment, authorizing federal income taxes, and the Seventeenth Amendment, which permits voters to choose directly their two United States senators. Meanwhile, Progressive congressmen, led by George Norris of Nebraska, reformed procedures in the House of Representatives in 1910 by stripping the Speaker of control over committee assignments and placing such selections in the hands of party caucuses.

## Theodore Roosevelt: Cowboy in the White House

At forty-two, Roosevelt succeeded to the presidency on the assassination of William McKinley in 1901. Earlier he had served in the New York assembly, on the national Civil Service Commission, and as New York City police commissioner, assistant secretary of the navy, governor of New York, and vice-president. He had even been a Dakota rancher, a soldier in the Spanish-American War, and a historian renowned for *The Winning of the West*.

His elevation to the presidency alarmed some conservatives, particularly after he adopted progressive policies. Yet Roosevelt's energy, enthusiasm, and sound thinking in a crisis served the nation well. He often got what he wanted by using his executive power rather than by persuading Congress to pass new laws.

Still, a number of Progressive measures passed Congress. The Newlands Act funneled proceeds from land sales in the West into irrigation projects. The Department of Commerce and Labor and Bureau of Corporations were established to discourage monopolies. The Elkins Act strengthened the Interstate Commerce Commission, made the receiving of rebates illegal, and required railroads to follow published rates.

## Roosevelt and Big Business

Roosevelt acquired the reputation of "trustbuster," but the designation was only partially accurate because he did not believe in breaking up corporations indiscriminately. He insisted that regulation was the best way to deal with large corporations. In 1902, he ordered the Justice Department to revive the Sherman Antitrust Act by filing suit against the Northern Securities Company, a creation of J. P. Morgan, James J. Hill and E. H. Harriman, who controlled the Great Northern, the Northern Pacific, and the Chicago, Burlington and Quincy railroads. The Supreme Court in turn directed the breakup of the company.

Roosevelt then ordered suits against Standard Oil and the American Tobacco Company. He assured corporate leaders that he was not opposed to size per se but to conditions that tended to create monopolies. The Bureau of Corporations worked with U. S. Steel and International Harvester to remedy deficiencies and avoid antitrust suits.

## Square Dealing — set up of his ideas

Roosevelt was the first president to use executive power to benefit organized labor. In 1902, anthracite miners struck for higher wages, an eight-hour day, and recognition of the United Mine Workers. The mine owners, who two years earlier had approved a 10 percent wage hike, refused concessions and prepared to starve the strikers into submission. Roosevelt, who sympathized with the miners and feared a coal shortage, called both sides to arbitration in Washington. When no settlement resulted, Roosevelt threatened to use federal troops to seize and operate the mines. This threat brought the owners, led by George Baer of Reading Railroad, to terms. The miners soon returned to work with a 10 percent wage increase and a nine-hour day. The owners obtained a 10 percent increase in the price of coal. Roosevelt was the main winner of the strike. Without calling on Congress for support, he expanded executive power. His action marked a step forward in the evolution of the modern presidency.

## T.R.: President in His Own Right

The popular Roosevelt was easily reelected in 1904 by defeating the conservative New York judge, Alton B. Parker. Encouraged by his landslide, Roosevelt pressed for further reforms. In 1906, the Hepburn Act gave the Interstate Commerce Commission the power to inspect the books of rail companies, to set maximum rates, and to control sleeping car and oil pipeline companies.

Congress passed meat inspection and pure food and drug legislation, which had been encouraged by the muckraker Upton Sinclair, whose *The Jungle* exposed filthy conditions in the Chicago slaughterhouses. Roosevelt agreed with the packers' demand that the government pay the costs of inspection. The Food and Drug Administration, through the government chemist Harvey Wiley, worked to enforce the ban on the manufacture and sale of adulterated and fraudulently labeled products.

## Tilting Left

Roosevelt never accepted the "lunatic fringe" of the progressive movement but steadily took more liberal positions. In 1908, he called a conference on conservation. He placed some 150 million acres of forest lands in federal reserves and enforced laws governing grazing, mining, and lumbering.

Meanwhile, the Panic of 1907 began with a run on several New York trust companies and spread to the Stock Exchange, where speculators found that they could not borrow to meet their obligations. In the emergency Roosevelt authorized the deposit of large amounts of government cash in New York banks.

Conservative or "Old Guard" Republicans blamed the panic on Roosevelt's "trust-busting," but the president denounced the "malefactors of great wealth" and endorsed federal income and inheritance taxes, regulation of interstate corporations, and reforms favored by industrial workers.

## William Howard Taft: The Listless Progressive

As his successor, Roosevelt chose Secretary of War Taft, who easily defeated Democrat William Jennings Bryan's third and final White House bid. Though Taft supported Progressive legislation, he never absorbed the progressive spirit of his times. He lacked the physical and mental stamina required of a modern president and preferred the judicial life. He was named chief justice in 1921 by President Warren G. Harding.

Taft followed Roosevelt's lead in enforcing the Sherman Act, expanding the national forest reserves, and promoting mine safety legislation. He approved enactment of an eight-hour day for workers under government contracts and even asked Congress to lower the tariff, something Roosevelt had avoided. While the House passed tariff legislation favored by Taft, protectionists in the Senate restored high rates on many items. Taft did little to assist Progressive senators who objected to the higher rates; instead he signed the Payne-Aldrich measure into law and proclaimed the measure the "best bill that the Republican party ever passed."

Taft also got into hot water with conservationists though he believed in stewardship of natural resources. Secretary of the Interior Richard Ballinger returned to the public domain certain waterpower sites that the Roosevelt administration had withdrawn. Chief Forester Gifford Pinchot objected when he learned that Ballinger was upholding claims of mining interests to Alaskan coal lands. When Pinchot persisted in criticizing Ballinger, Taft dismissed Pinchot.

## Breakup of the Republican Party

Pinchot's dismissal created a rift between Taft and Roosevelt that shattered the Republican party into Progressive and Old Guard factions and helped to ensure GOP defeats in elections from 1910 to 1916. Whereas Taft was tied to the Old Guard, Roosevelt in 1910 unveiled a comprehensive program of social legislation that he called the New Nationalism. Though earlier emphasis had been placed on breaking up trusts, Roosevelt proposed an expansion of federal power to regulate business. In 1911, Roosevelt and Taft began feuding over U.S. Steel's absorption of the Tennessee Coal and Iron Company.

The next year, Roosevelt declared his candidacy for the Republican presidential nomination and won most of the primaries, including the one in Taft's native Ohio. Since some Taft delegates had been chosen under questionable circumstances, Roosevelt challenged the right of 254 delegates to their seats. The Taft-dominated credentials committee awarded enough disputed seats to the president, who won the nomination on the first ballot.

Thereafter, Roosevelt ran as a third-party candidate under the Progressive or "Bull Moose" banner. He advocated a plethora of reforms, including strict regulation of corporations, a tariff commission, national presidential primaries, minimum wage and workers' compensation laws, and the elimination of child labor.

## The Election of 1912

On the 46th convention ballot, the Democrats nominated Woodrow Wilson, a political scientist and Princeton University president elected governor of New Jersey in 1910. Wilson's New Freedom claimed that the national government could best prevent unfair business practices by allowing competition, breaking up trusts, and establishing fair rules for conducting business. Roosevelt conversely believed that complexities of the modern world required regulation of the trusts, in effect the employing of Hamiltonian means to achieve Jeffersonian ends.

With a united Democratic party, Wilson received 435 electoral votes, to 88 for Roosevelt, and 8 for Taft. As representatives of the two segments of Progressivism, Wilson and Roosevelt together polled more than two-thirds of the popular votes.

## Wilson: The New Freedom

The Underwood Tariff reduced rates to their lowest level since before the Civil War. To compensate for lost revenue, Congress collected the first income taxes under the Sixteenth Amendment.

Wilson signed the Federal Reserve Act, which gave the nation a central banking system for the first time since the 1830s. The measure divided the nation into twelve banking districts, each under the supervision of a "banker's bank." All national banks (State banks had the option to join) had to invest 6 percent of their capital as a reserve requirement. The nerve center of the system was the Federal Reserve Board in Washington, which controled the amount of money in circulation through the manipulation of the reserve requirement and the rediscount rate, the commission charged the member banks by the reserve banks.

In 1914, Wilson replaced Roosevelt's Bureau of Corporations with the Federal Trade Commission, which issued cease and desist orders against "unfair" trade practices. The Clayton Antitrust Act outlawed both price discrimination that tends to foster monopoly and interlocking directorates, which act as a subterfuge for controlling competing companies. Wilson's aggressive use of presidential power was backed by the Democratic Congress, whose members were determined to make a good record. When lobbyists tried to block tariff reform, Wilson made a dramatic appeal to voters to contact their lawmakers.

## The Progressives and Minority Rights

Progressives were generally unconcerned about the conditions of immigrants. The Dillingham Commission proposed restrictions on the number of newcomers to be admitted to the United States, particularly those from southern and eastern Europe.

In the Dead Indian Land Act of 1902, Indians were given greater latitude to sell land allotments that they had inherited. Greater efforts were undertaken to improve the education of Indian children. Yet Indians, who did not gain citizenship until 1924, were relegated to a fundamentally inferior status in the Progressive era.

Segregation was rigidly enforced in the South. Few blacks attended high school; a common folk proverb held that "When you educate a Negro, you spoil a good field hand." Lynchings remained a persistent problem; indeed some 1,100 blacks were murdered by mobs between 1900 and 1914. Some southern progressives justified the disfranchisement of blacks on grounds that corrupt white politicians would therefore be unable to purchase black votes.

## Black Militancy

Breaking with the accommodationist leadership of Booker T. Washington, William E. B. Du Bois, a Massachusetts native who was the first black to earn a Ph.D. in the field of history from Harvard, wanted blacks to establish their own businesses, run their own newspapers and colleges, write their own literature, and preserve their identity, rather than amalgamate themselves into white society. Du Bois called for black education, the franchise, and civil rights. He believed that blacks could overcome the vices of immorality, crime, and laziness through the leadership of its "exceptional men," or "talented tenth."

In 1909, Du Bois joined a group of whites to form the National Association for the Advancement of Colored People, the flagship organization in the war against racial discrimination. Blacks also turned to the study of their past to stimulate pride in their heritage. Du Bois edited the NAACP journal, *The Crisis*; Carter G. Woodson founded the Association for the Study of Negro Life and History and edited the *Journal of Negro History*.

Such militancy produced few immediate gains for minorities. Though he had invited Booker T. Washington to dine at the White House, Theodore Roosevelt pursued a "lily-white" policy as the Bull Moose nominee in 1912. President Wilson was a segregationist who refused to appoint a privately-funded commission to study racial problems. Wilson's attitude alarmed Du Bois and another black militant, William Monroe Trotter, editor of the *Boston Guardian*, who lost his temper in an ugly confrontation with the president in 1914.

# People, Places, and Things

*Define the following concepts:*

Progressive _____

_____

"search for order" _____

_____

muckrakers _____

_____

"ashcan" artists _____

_____

psychoanalysis _____

_____

city manager _____

_____

commission government _____

_____

trustbuster _____

_____

bohemian _____

_____

rediscount _____

_____

interlocking directorate _____

_____

lobbyists _____

_____

"talented tenth" _____

_____

*Describe the following:*

*McClure's* _____

_____

*Pilgrim's Progress* _____

_____

Greenwich Village _____

_____

Wisconsin Idea _____

_____

*Muller v. Oregon* _____

_____

Triangle Shirtwaist Factory _____

_____

National Women's Suffrage Association _____

_____

Newlands Act _____

_____

*The Jungle* _____

_____

Payne-Aldrich Tariff _____

_____

New Nationalism _____

_____

New Freedom _____

_____

Federal Reserve Act _____

_____

Clayton Antitrust Act _____

_____

Federal Trade Commission _____

_____

*Identify the following people:*

Lincoln Steffens _____

_____

William "Big Bill" Haywood _____

_____

Samuel M. Jones _____

_____

Robert La Follette _____

_____

Susan B. Anthony _____

_____

George W. Norris _____

_____

Gifford Pinchot _____

_____

William E. B. Du Bois _____

_____

William Monroe Trotter _____

_____

Isadora Duncan _____

_____

Carl Sandburg _____

_____

# Self-Test

## Multiple-Choice Questions

1. Which of these was *not* a "muckraker"?
   A. John Bunyan
   B. Lincoln Steffens
   C. Upton Sinclair
   D. Ida Tarbell

2. The form of municipal government that took root in Galveston, Texas, in 1900 was:
   A. Commission type
   B. City manager
   C. Mayor council
   D. Interlocking directorate

3. The Progressive mayor who fought corruption in Ohio's largest city was:
   A. Tom Johnson
   B. Hazen Pingree
   C. Robert M. La Follette
   D. Samuel Jones

4. In *Muller v. Oregon*, the Supreme Court:
   A. Upheld a maximum ten-hour day for working women in Oregon
   B. Forbade Oregon from regulating the wages of working women
   C. Sanctioned freedom of contract in employment
   D. Held a series of state social welfare laws to be unconstitutional

5. Leon Czolgosz was the:
   A. Anarchist who assassinated President McKinley
   B. Reform mayor of New York City
   C. 1904 Democratic presidential nominee
   D. Mine owners representative in the 1902 coal strike

6. The Bureau of Corporations was superseded by the:
   A. Department of Commerce and Labor
   B. Federal Reserve Board
   C. Internal Revenue Service
   D. Federal Trade Commission

7. Most supportive of the Clayton Antitrust Act were:
   A. Farmers
   B. Labor unions
   C. Corporations
   D. Conservationists

8. The first president to assemble the White House Conservation Conference was:
   A. McKinley
   B. Theodore Roosevelt
   C. Taft
   D. Wilson

9. Funds for the Newlands Act came from:
   A. The income tax
   B. Corporation taxes
   C. User fees
   D. Revenues earmarked from the sale of public lands in the western states

10. Which of these is *mispaired*?
    A. Alfred Stieglitz—photography
    B. Sigmund Freud—psychology
    C. Margaret Sanger—feminism
    D. Seth Low—Tennessee Coal and Iron Company

11. Taft split the Republican party into "Old Guard" and "progressive" wings by his actions in all of these incidents *except*:
    A. The Ballinger-Pinchot dispute
    B. Credentials dispute at the 1912 Republican convention
    C. Payne-Aldrich Tariff
    D. Mine safety legislation

12. Which of these statements regarding the election of 1912 is *false*?
    A. Taft won the Republican nomination but lost the primaries
    B. The Democratic nominee was chosen on the 46th ballot
    C. The Progressive party candidate advocated breaking up the trusts
    D. The winner polled less than a majority of the popular vote

13. Which of these statements regarding the Federal Reserve Act is *false*?
    A. There are twelve Federal Reserve districts in cities such as New York, Chicago, Dallas, and San Francisco.
    B. National banks must participate in the system.
    C. The system is governed by a board appointed by the president.
    D. The Federal Reserve can reduce the rate of inflation by adding to the money supply.

14. Theodore Roosevelt is associated with all of the following *except*:
    A. Western ranching
    B. Big game hunts in Africa
    C. "New Nationalism"
    D. Formation of the NAACP

15. The black who took the leading role in challenging the leadership of Booker T. Washington was:
    A. Carter Woodson
    B. William E. B. Du Bois
    C. William Monroe Trotter
    D. Herbert Croly

16. The New Freedom did *not* include:
    A. Civil rights legislation
    B. Federal Reserve Act
    C. Underwood Tariff
    D. Clayton Act

17. Greenwich Village intellectuals included all of the following *except*:
    A. Isadora Duncan
    B. Abe Ruef
    C. Eugene O'Neill
    D. Alfred Stieglitz

18. The direct primary was first pushed by:
    A. Theodore Roosevelt
    B. Robert La Follette
    C. Woodrow Wilson
    D. Louis Brandeis

19. Which Supreme Court decision held that a ten-hour limit for bakers deprived those workers of the liberty of working as long as they desired?
    A. *Muller v. Oregon*
    B. *Hammer v. Dagenhart*
    C. *Holden v. Hardy*
    D. *Lochner v. New York*

20. Which of these was *not* a Republican?
    A. Richard Ballinger
    B. Gifford Pinchot
    C. Louis D. Brandeis
    D. Joseph Cannon

**Essay Questions**

1. Explain how the progressive movement developed as a response to the post-Civil War industrialism. Focus on the muckrakers and the Progressive mind.

2. Discuss political reforms at the municipal and state levels during the Progressive Era. Mention specific mayors and governors and their accomplishments.

3. Explain how Theodore Roosevelt helped to strengthen the executive function of the presidency, with reference to his policies toward business and the Square Deal.

4. Discuss the presidential election of 1912 in reference to parties, nominees, platforms, issues, campaign styles, results, and long-term significance.

5. Explain why the Progressive movement offered little hope to blacks and other minority groups desiring to improve their status. Refer to the new spirit of black militancy that appeared by the time of the Wilson administration.

## Critical Thinking Exercise

Circle the response in each listing that is *unrelated* to the other three.

1. Reform
   Improvement
   Status quo
   Change

2. Progressive
   "Old Guard"
   Liberal
   Trust-busting

3. New Nationalism
   Monopoly
   New Freedom
   Regulation

4. Accommodationist
   Segregation
   Equality
   "Lily-white"

5. John Mitchell
   "Mother" Jones
   Samuel Gompers
   Carter Woodson

6. Roosevelt
   Taft
   Wilson
   Bryan

7. Debs
   Sinclair
   Tarbell
   Steffens

8. New Freedom
   Anti-trust
   Centralized banking
   Laissez-faire

9. Isadora Duncan
   Eugene O'Neill
   Elbert Gary
   Alfred Stieglitz

10. Abe Ruef
    Tom Johnson
    Seth Low
    Rudolph Spreckels

CHAPTER 24

# Woodrow Wilson and the Great War

## Learning Objectives

*After reading Chapter 24, you should be able to:*

1. Explain the similarities and differences between the foreign policies of the Roosevelt/Taft and Wilson administrations.
2. Discuss the elections of 1916 and 1920 in reference to parties, nominees, issues, outcomes, and significance.
3. Outline the steps by which the United States became involved in World War I.
4. Explain how war mobilization affected the economy, the status of civil liberties, and the Progressive movement.
5. Understand the critical role American troops played in the world war.
6. Explain how the Paris Peace Conference revised the European map and established the League of Nations
7. Discuss Wilson's uncompromising stance in the final defeat of the treaty.
8. Evaluate the postwar "Red Scare."

## Overview

**Missionary Diplomacy**

A critic of "dollar diplomacy," President Wilson vowed to guide foreign affairs on an idealistic basis in a policy he termed "missionary diplomacy." Yet due to the strategic importance of the Panama Canal, Wilson wound up pursuing policies similar to those of Roosevelt and Taft. The Bryan-Chamorro Treaty of 1914 made Nicaragua a virtual American protectorate and gave the United States the option to construct a canal across that country.

Wilson refused diplomatic recognition to Mexico's "government of butchers" established by Victoriano Huerta following the earlier overthrow of Porfirio Diaz. Instead Wilson brought pressure against Huerta, and a tense situation exploded in 1914 when American sailors were humiliated and arrested in Tampico, Mexico. Wilson used the event to rationalize the sending of dispatch troops into Mexico to overthrow Huerta.

Argentina, Brazil, and Chile offered to mediate the dispute in a conference at Niagara Falls, Ontario. Though no settlement was reached, Huerta, hard pressed by Mexican opponents, abdicated. On August 20, 1914, General Venustiano Carranza entered Mexico City in triumph.

Thereafter one of Carranza's own generals, Francisco "Pancho" Villa, rose against him and seized control of Mexico City.

When Wilson realized the extent of Carranza's influence in Mexico, he recognized the Carranza government. In 1916, Villa, trying to undermine Carranza by forcing the United States to intervene, killed 16 Americans on a train in northern Mexico. He then crossed into Columbus, New Mexico, and murdered 19 others. Wilson responded by sending troops under General John Pershing to cross the border to pursue Villa, who drew Pershing deeper and deeper into Mexico. In early 1917, Wilson recalled Pershing's force, leaving the Mexicans to work out their own destiny.

## Outbreak of the Great War

World War I erupted when a young student, Gavrilo Princip, assassinated the Archduke Franz Ferdinand, heir to the Austro-Hungarian throne, on a summer day in 1914. This rash act precipitated general war because the major powers formed two great coalitions: the Central Powers (Germany, Austria-Hungary, and later Ottoman Turkey) and the Allied Powers (Great Britain, France, Russia, and later Italy, Japan, and the United States). Though the United States initially professed neutrality, most Americans sympathized with the Allies, who skillfully portrayed the Germans as ruthless barbarians. A minority of persons of German and Irish descent, the latter motivated by hatred of the British, sympathized with the Central Powers.

## Freedom of the Seas

The British forbade neutrals from trading with belligerent nations, and the United States did not try to force Britain's hand with a Jefferson-style embargo, which though it had failed in 1808, might have succeeded in 1914 because the Allies were so dependent on American supplies. Whereas commerce with the Central Powers was minuscule, that with the Allies soared from $825 million in 1914 to over $3.2 billion in 1916.

With the land war a bloody stalemate, the Germans challenged Allied control of the seas through the use of submarines. These vessels, which played a role in World War I not unlike that of American privateers in the Revolution and the War of 1812, depended on surprise attack. Therefore, the commanders of submarines could not give the crew and passengers of neutral ships time to get off in lifeboats before sinking the vessels.

Germany declared the waters surrounding Britain a war zone and announced that it would sink without warning all enemy merchant ships in the area. Neutral ships that entered the area did so at their own risk. Wilson warned the Germans he would hold them to "strict accountability" for any loss of American life or property resulting from such attacks.

On May 7, 1915, a submarine sank the British liner *Lusitania* off the Irish coast, causing the death of nearly 1,200 persons, including 128 Americans. The attack sorely tested American diplomacy, but Wilson kept open the lines of communication. When the French steamer *Sussex* was attacked in 1916, America issued another protest, and the Germans, in the *Sussex Pledge* agreed to stop sinking merchant ships without warning.

## The Election of 1916

Because Wilson's 1912 victory resulted from a split in the Republican ranks, his reelection was no foregone conclusion. To shore up his political base among Progressives, Wilson named Jewish attorney Louis D. Brandeis to the Supreme Court and approved a Farm Loan Act, the Keating-Owen Child Labor Act, and the Adamson Act, which established an eight-hour day for railroad workers and prevented a possible rail strike during the war.

The Republicans, including Theodore Roosevelt, nominated Associate Justice Charles Evans Hughes, a former New York governor. Wilson stressed preparedness, and Democratic speakers reminded voters that Wilson had "kept us out of war." Despite his ineffective personal style and campaigning, Hughes appeared to have won on election night. Late returns, however, gave Wilson California and a slim victory of twenty-three electoral votes.

## The Road to War

In 1915 and 1916, Wilson had sent his aide, Colonel Edward M. House on unsuccessful secret missions to London, Paris, and Berlin to try to mediate among the belligerents. Moreover, in early 1917, Wilson delivered a speech calling for "peace without victory," meaning that any settlement imposed by a victor would breed hatred and more war. Each nation should be treated equally, and nationality groups must exercise self-determination, Wilson said.

Thereafter, Germany renounced the *Sussex* pledge and announced the resumption of unrestricted submarine warfare against vessels headed for Allied ports. Germany hoped to starve the British into submission and to halt the flow of American supplies to Allied armies. Wilson responded by severing diplomatic relations with Germany. Within a month, Walter Hines Page, United States ambassador to Britain, released the infamous Zimmermann telegram, by which Germany had sought a secret alliance with Mexico. Congress then declared war by a vote of 82-6 in the Senate and 373-50 in the House. Wilson led his people into battle in the spirit of justice and humanity, not vengeance and victory.

## Mobilizing the Economy

Without the entry of the United States, World War I would have likely ended in 1918 on terms dictated by Germany. American men and supplies contained Germany's last offense and ensured its final defeat.

American industry was converted to war production in a haphazard fashion. Airplane, tank, and artillery construction proceeded too slowly to affect the war. America indeed was no "arsenal of democracy" in World War I; the typical doughboy in France was transported in a British ship, wore a British-style steel helmet, and fought with French ordnance.

Conversion of the economy to a wartime footing was directed by the War Industries Board, which allocated scarce materials, standardized production, fixed prices, and coordinated purchasing. In early 1918, Wilson appointed his son-in-law, Treasury Secretary William G. McAdoo, as director-general of the railroads. McAdoo's Railroad Administration ran the trains as a single system, pooled equipment, centralized purchasing, and raised wages and passenger rates.

Meanwhile, the mobilization of agricultural resources was directed by Herbert Hoover, a mining engineer who had headed the Belgian Relief Commission earlier in the war. To avoid rationing, Hoover successfully organized a campaign to persuade consumers to conserve food voluntarily.

## Workers in Wartime

With the army taking men from the labor force and with immigration reduced to a trickle, unemployment disappeared and wages rose. The cost of living soared, but the boom created unprecedented opportunities. Disadvantged groups, particularly southern blacks, were attracted to factory jobs in northern cities.

Wilson created the National War Labor Board, headed by former President Taft and Frank P. Walsh, a prominent lawyer, to settle labor disputes and prevent strikes. Union membership rose by 2.3 million during the war.

## Paying for the War

World War I cost the United States about $33.5 billion, excluding pensions and other postwar expenses. About $7 billion was lent to the Allies but spent in the United States, thereby contributing to national prosperity. Five Liberty and Victory Loan drives appealed to the patriotism of workers to support the war.

In addition to borrowing, the government collected about $10.5 billion in taxes, including the graduated income tax that took more than 75 percent of the income of the wealthiest citizens, a 65 percent excess-profits tax, and a 25 percent inheritance tax.

## Propaganda and Civil Liberties

Wilson tried to mobilize public opinion and to inspire Americans to work for a better world that he expected to emerge from the war. His Committee on Public Information headed by journalist George Creel depicted the war as a crusade for freedom and democracy. Most Americans supported the war without reservation, but a minority of those of German and Irish ancestry and those of pacifistic leanings were never reconciled to the war.

To control dissidents, the Espionage Act imposed fines of up to $10,000 and jail sentences of up to 20 years on persons convicted of aiding the enemy or obstructing recruiting. The Supreme Court upheld the Espionage Act in *Schenck v. United States*, a case involving a

Socialist who had mailed circulars to draftees urging them to refuse induction. The Court cited a "clear and present danger" as the premise for such restrictions on free speech.

The Sedition Act, reminiscent of laws passed by the Federalist Congress under President John Adams, made "saying anything" to discourage the purchase of war bonds a crime and made it illegal to "utter, print, write, or publish any disloyal, profane, scurrilous, or abusive language" about the government, the Constitution, or the military. Socialist Eugene Debs was sentenced to ten years for making an antiwar speech. The wartime hysteria in the United States exceeded anything that occurred in Britain or France.

## Wartime Reforms

The American war mobilization was an outgrowth of the Progressive Era, which aimed to eradicate social evils. Reformers worked on many issues largely unrelated to the war: women's suffrage, prohibition, health insurance, and the curtailment of prostitution and venereal disease.

## Women and Blacks in Wartime

Most feminists supported the war in the expectation that it would open new job opportunities for women. Moreover, opposition to the war would have lessened the chances of obtaining national women suffrage. Most unions were unsympathetic to enrolling women, and the government urged women to concentrate on such tasks as preparing bandages, knitting clothing, and food conservation. A report subsequently revealed that women who had gained employment were paid less than their male counterparts.

More than 500,000 southern blacks migrated to the North between 1914 and 1919. Many felt unwelcome in their new surroundings, but the newcomers fared better economically than those who remained in the South. All blacks drafted into the army had fought in segregated units, and only a handful were commissioned officers. W. E. B. Du Bois, in *The Crisis* backed the war and commended Wilson for denouncing lynchings. Most blacks seemed to view the war as a way to demonstrate their patriotism
and prove their worth.

## "Over There"

The ultimate aim of the war was the military defeat of the Central Powers. The navy reduced the threat of German submarines and provided convoys to escort merchant ships across the Atlantic. The American Expeditionary Force commanded by General Pershing reached Paris on July 4, 1917; soon the "doughboys" were playing a vital role in the war.

Germany launched a spring offensive in March 1918, aided by soldiers previously committed to the Russian front. By late May the Germans had reached the Marne River near Chateau-Thierry, 50 miles from Paris. In its first major engagement, the AEF drove the Germans from Chateau-Thierry and Belleau Wood.

In September, some 1.2 million doughboys fought in the Argonne Forest, one of the bloodiest battles ever waged. On November 11, the Allied armies forced Germany to sign an armistice.

American losses in the war amounted to 112,432 dead and 230,074 wounded. More than half the deaths resulted from disease. Germany lost 1.8 million; Russia, 1.7 million; France, 1.4 million; Austria-Hungary, 1.2 million, and Britain, 950,000.

**Preparing for Peace**

Wilson outlined his Fourteen Points for world peace in a speech to Congress in January 1918, calling for open diplomacy, freedom of the seas in war and peace, removal of the barriers to international trade, a reduction in armaments, and self-determination for the nationalities. Wilson further called for the return of Alsace-Lorraine to France, adjustment of Italian boundaries, establishment of an independent Polish state, and evacuation of Belgium.

Wilson hoped to maintain peace through a League of Nations, on which he felt that the fate of humanity rested. The epitome of self-confidence, Wilson decided to head the American delegation to the peace conference, becoming the first president to leave American territory while in office. As Wilson departed to Paris, he had been weakened by Republican victories in the 1918 elections and by dissatisfaction among western farmers who felt that they had been discriminated against during the war due to price controls on wheat. No partisan Republican was included on the peace commission, a strategic error in that the treaty would need Senate ratification.

**The Paris Peace Conference**

The "Big Four" at Paris included Wilson, British Prime Minister David Lloyd George, French Premier Georges Clemenceau, and Italian Prime Minister Vittorio Orlando. Clemenceau, whose concern lay with French security, had little interest in the Fourteen Points, noting that mankind had not kept God's Ten Commandments. Lloyd George agreed with many of Wilson's proposals but found them politically inoperable. He told a colleague, "If you want to succeed in politics, you must keep your conscience well under control." Orlando left the conference in a huff when his demands were unmet.

The victors forced Germany to admit responsibility for the war and to agree to pay $33 billion in reparations to the Allies. The new map of Europe left fewer people on "foreign" soil than in any earlier period of history though the Austrian Tyrol was put under the control of Italy. Former German colonies were placed under the mandate of the League of Nations. Except for the war guilt clause and heavy reparations, Wilson had achieved a moderate peace.

## The Senate and the League of Nations

A majority of senators favored the treaty and the League of Nations, but 37 Republicans signed a manifesto devised by Foreign Relations Chairman Henry Cabot Lodge of Massachusetts, opposing the League as part of the treaty with Germany. Wilson refused to compromise despite the Republican Senate majority, telling one Democratic senator, "Anyone who opposes me ... I'll crush!"

Led by Lodge, the reservationist senators agreed to ratify the treaty if fourteen modifications, a number matching Wilson's Fourteen Points, were met. Reservationists feared that Article 10 of the League Covenant, which committed signatories to protect the political independence and territorial integrity of all member nations, could lead to American troop commitments to resolve European disputes. Meanwhile, the irreconcilables, led by William Borah of Idaho refused to support an international organization under any circumstances.

Influenced by the attitude that he knew more about the issue than any of his opponents as well as his hatred of Lodge and his deteriorating health, Wilson rejected Lodge's reservations outright. Instead of making concessions to ensure passage, Wilson embarked on a national speaking tour by train. The mighty effort failed to sway the wavering senators; instead, it drained Wilson physically. In September, while speaking in Pueblo, Colorado, he collapsed. A few days later in Washington, he suffered a severe stroke that partially paralyzed his left side.

The Democrats joined the irreconcilables to defeat the treaty with Lodge's reservations. When Lodge allowed the original draft to come up for a vote, reservationists and irreconcilables joined to block the treaty. Wilson's refusal to accept compromise hence doomed the treaty along with American participation in the League.

## Demobilization

With the end of the war, the economy was quickly demobilized. Business boomed in 1919, though temporary shortages caused inflation, and the cost of living doubled between 1913 and 1920. Inflation in turn produced labor trouble, as over 4 million workers went on strike during 1919. Between July 1920 and March 1922, farm prices dropped sharply, and unemployment soared.

## The Red Scare

Radical labor activities caused millions of Americans to associate unions and strikes with the threat of communist world revolution. Though there were few communists in the United States, the Russian experience caused many to feel that a cadre of revolutionaries could seize power.

Organized labor in America had seldom been radical, but some labor leaders had been attracted to socialism. Americans failed to distinguish between the common ends sought by communists and socialists and the different methods by which they sought to achieve those ends.

- Niagara Falls Conference _____

_____

- Columbus, New Mexico _____

_____

- *Lusitania* _____

_____

- *Sussex Pledge* _____

_____

- Adamson Act _____

_____

- Zimmermann telegram _____

_____

- Committee on Public Information _____

_____

- American Expeditionary Force _____

_____

- National War Labor Board _____

_____

- Fourteen Points _____

_____

- Article 10 of League Covenant _____

_____

131

Palmer raids _____
_____

*Identify the following people:*

Victoriano Huerta _____
_____

Venustiano Carranza _____
_____

Pancho Villa _____
_____

Gavrilo Princip _____
_____

Franz Ferdinand _____
_____

Edward M. House _____
_____

Charles Evans Hughes _____
_____

Louis D. Brandeis _____
_____

Herbert Hoover _____
_____

John J. Pershing _____

_____

Georges Clemenceau _____

_____

Henry Cabot Lodge, Sr. _____

_____

William E. Borah _____

_____

Warren G. Harding _____

_____

James M. Cox _____

_____

J. Edgar Hoover _____

_____

## Map Exercise

Refer to the map on the following page. Place the correct letter beside each country that corresponds with its location.

_____ 1. Austria-Hungary      _____ 8. Norway

_____ 2. Belgium              _____ 9. Poland

_____ 3. Czechoslovakia       _____ 10. Portugal

_____ 4. France               _____ 11. Russia

_____ 5. Germany              _____ 12. Serbia

____6. Great Britain        ____13. Spain

____7. Italy                ____14. Turkey

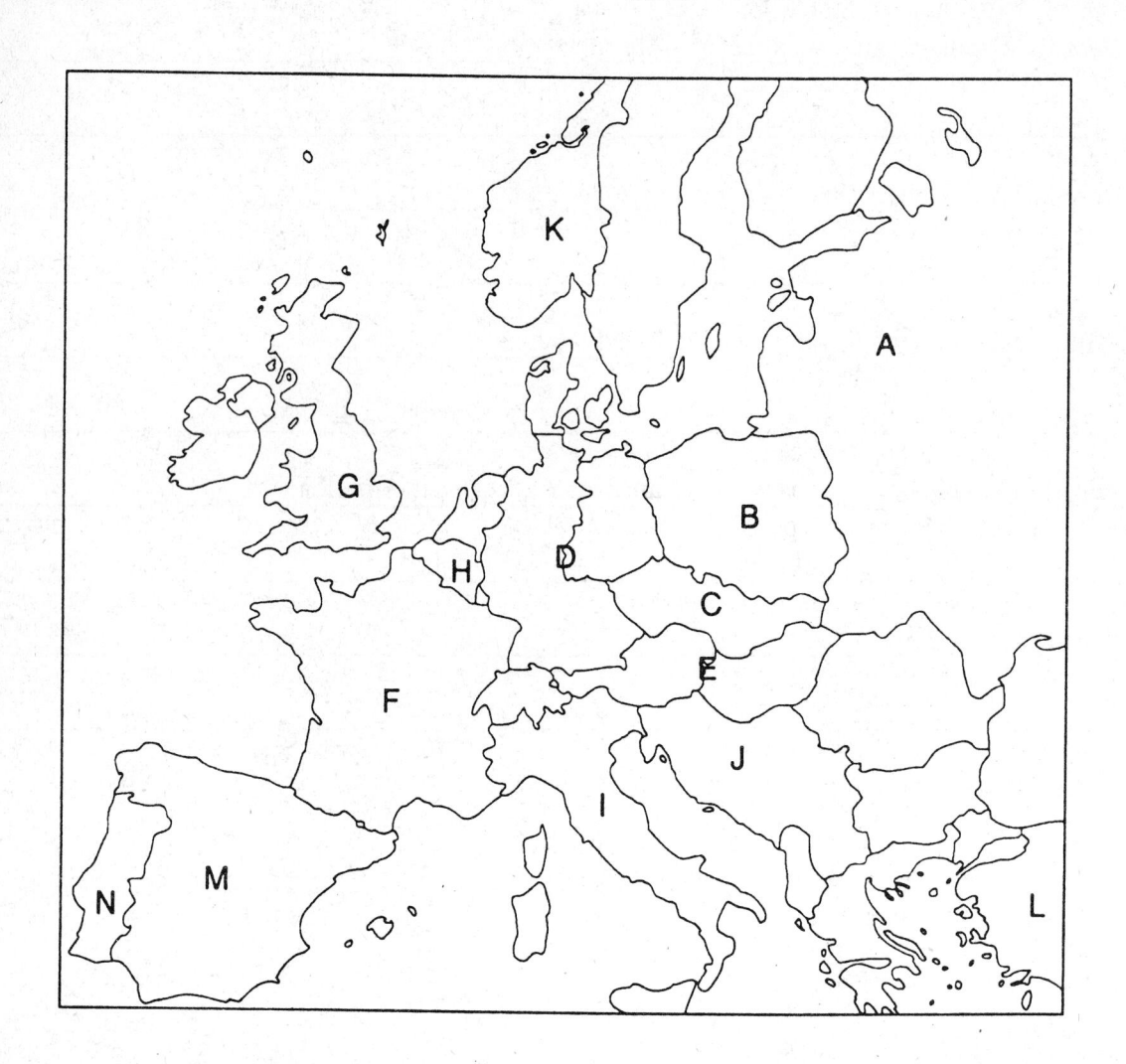

## Self-Test

**Multiple-Choice Questions**

1. After the sinking of the *Lusitania*, Woodrow Wilson did all of the following *except*:
   A. Demand that Germany pay indemnities for the victims
   B. Ask for the resignation of the hawkish Secretary of State William Jennings Bryan
   C. Insist that Germany stop attacking passenger vessels
   D. Continue the diplomatic dialogue with Germany

2. After the sinking of the *Sussex*, Germany:
   A. Warned that it would hold the Allies to "strict accountability" for interference with German shipping
   B. Launched an attack on Paris
   C. Invited Mexico to join the Central Powers
   D. Promised that merchant ships would not be sunk without warning ✓

3. Historians credit the Democrats with winning the 1916 election because
   A. The Republicans lost their status as majority party
   B. Wilson's supporters skillfully used the theme "He Kept Us Out of War" ✓
   C. Wilson's snub of Progressive Hiram Johnson helped the Democrats to win California
   D. The Republicans failed to take advantage of Wilson's Mexican policy

4. When he called for "peace without victory" in World War I, Wilson:
   A. Endorsed the concept of a "no-win" war
   B. Was seeking the backing of antiwar elements in America
   C. Felt that only a peace among equals, not a treaty between the victor and the vanquished, could endure ✓
   D. Was acknowledging the Allies' lack of preparedness to fight the Central Powers

5. To finance World War I, the United States relied on all of the following *except*:
   A. Higher income taxes
   B. Sale of war bonds
   C. Excess profits and inheritance taxes
   D. Temporary national sales taxes ✓

6. Which agency fixed prices for war materials and determined what manufacturers could use and to whom deliveries could be made?
   A. United States Peace Commission
   B. National War Labor Board ✓
   C. War Industries Board
   D. Office of Price Administration

7. The director of the Committee on Public Information was:
   A. Herbert Hoover
   B. J. Edgar Hoover
   C. W. E. B. Du Bois
   D. George Creel ✓

8. Eugene Debs was imprisoned for:
   A. Violating the Sedition Act
   B. Failure to pay income taxes
   C. His role in the Red Scare
   D. Making excess profits for his union during the war

9. Prior to assuming command of the American Expeditionary Force, General Pershing had:
   A. Directed the conscription of troops
   B. Handled relief efforts in France
   C. Sought to capture the Mexican bandit Pancho Villa
   D. Opposed the use of black troops in the military

10. Which of the following was *not* among the Fourteen Points?
    A. Open diplomacy
    B. Reducing armaments
    C. Ending tariff barriers
    D. Returning Alsace-Lorraine to Italy

11. Who of the following was *not* part of the American team at the Paris Peace Conference?
    A. Edward M. House
    B. Henry White
    C. Tasker Bliss
    D. Henry Cabot Lodge

12. Those demanding changes in the Paris peace treaty were known as:
    A. Reservationists
    B. Isolationists
    C. Irreconcilables
    D. Internationalists

13. To garner support for the treaty and the League, Wilson:
    A. Accepted changes needed to win Senate ratification
    B. Conducted an extensive speaking tour by train that ended in near disaster
    C. Mapped plans to run for a third term
    D. Asked Theodore Roosevelt to garner Republican support for the treaty

14. France and Britain intended to repay their war debts to the United States by:
    A. International trade
    B. Full payment in gold
    C. Tapping income from forthcoming German reparations
    D. Borrowing from European bankers

15. In the Zimmermann telegram, Germany:
    A. Apologized for the sinking of the *Lusitania*
    B. Declared war on France
    C. Proposed an alliance with Mexico against the United States
    D. Announced the resumption of unrestricted submarine warfare

16. The leader who likened the Fourteen Points to the unobeyed Ten Commandments was:
    A. Woodrow Wilson
    B. Theodore Roosevelt
    C. Georges Clemenceau
    D. David Lloyd George

17. David Lloyd George said political success rests with:
    A. Gaining public popularity
    B. Working diligently at the job
    C. Pragmatism to the exclusion of conscience
    D. Emphasizing binding principles

18. Wilson denounced the "government of butchers" that ruled in:
    A. Austria-Hungary
    B. Germany
    C. Mexico
    D. Haiti

19. Postwar strikes inadvertently helped to produce what future president?
    A. Harding
    B. Coolidge
    C. Hoover
    D. Franklin D. Roosevelt

20. Attorney General Mitchell Palmer:
    A. Believed that terrorists and revolutionaries were a serious threat to America in the postwar years
    B. Wrote the Covenant of the League of Nations
    C. Was the Democratic presidential nominee in 1920
    D. Fought the growing power of organized labor

**Essay Questions**

1. Explain how the idealism of Wilson's "missionary diplomacy" was often at odds with the reality the president faced in dealing with Mexico between 1913 and 1916.

2. Compare and contrast the elections of 1916, 1918, and 1920 in reference to parties, nominees, issues, outcome, and long-range significance.

3. Explain how the United States mobilized for war in Europe, with emphasis on preparedness, control over the economy, and the impact on the Progressive movement.

4. Discuss the American mission to Paris in 1919 in reference to goals, diplomatic achievement, and ultimate outcome.

5. Analyze the Red Scare of 1919 to 1921. Was it real or mostly imaginary? Explain your answer.

## Critical Thinking Exercise

The following statements refer to the Paris peace treaty and the League of Nations. List each statement as fact (F), opinion (O), or inference (I).

____1. Wilson was convinced his Fourteen Points would make the world "fit and safe to live in."

____2. Wilson's Fourteen Points, if fully implemented, would have made the world "fit and safe to live in."

____3. Wilson found that self-determination for European nationalities was difficult to achieve because there were too many regions of mixed population for every group to be satisfied.

____4. Self-determination for nationality groups after World War I would have prevented Adolf Hitler from later taking the Sudetenland section of Czechoslovakia.

____5. Wilson once told a colleague that there are two sides to every question—a right side and a wrong side.

____6. Wilson's decision to attend the Paris peace conference was a precedent-shattering step.

____7. Germany should not have been forced to sign the "war guilt" clause at the peace conference because Austria caused the war.

____8. The new European map drawn up in Paris in 1919 left fewer people on "foreign" soil than in any earlier period of history.

____9. The imposition of reparations on Germany was at odds with Wilson's "peace without victory" speech.

____10. Wilson's partisanship and personal stubborness played decisive roles in keeping the United States from joining the League of Nations.

CHAPTER 25

# Postwar Society and Culture: Change and Adjustment

## Learning Objectives

*After reading Chapter 25, you should be able to:*

1. Explain how and why America "closed the gates" to immigration in the 1920s.
2. Discuss changing social patterns as they affected families and young people in the 1920s.
3. Explain how women's issues assumed new interest in the 1920s.
4. Discuss the popularity of movies, radio, and sports in the 1920s.
5. Show how fundamentalism and prohibition contributed to urban-rural conflicts.
6. Understand the rise and fall of a renewed Ku Klux Klan.
7. Analyze the significance of the Sacco and Vanzetti case in reference to intellectual life in the 1920s.
8. Discuss literary trends of the 1920s.
9. Understand the roots of black nationalism that emerged in the 1920s.
10. Show how the automobile and airplane revolutionized American life.

## Overview

### Closing the Gates

Many European immigrants sought entry into the United States in the early decades of the twentieth century. In 1921, Congress enacted an emergency act establishing a quota system. Each year 3 percent of the number of foreign-born residents of the United States in 1910, about 350,000, could enter. The quota of each country was based on the number of its nationals here in 1910.

In 1924, the National Origins Act reduced the quota to 2 percent and the base year shifted to 1890, decreasing the proportion of southern and eastern Europeans admitted. The law reduced immigration to under 150,000 a year. Ultimately, the foreign-born percentage of the United States population fell from about 13 percent in 1920 to 4.7 percent in 1970. Western nations failed to meet their quotas, while southern and eastern Europeans awaited admission. Moreover, Jews, whether foreign-born or native, faced discrimination as they sought to enter colleges, medical schools, banks, and law firms.

## New Urban Social Patterns

The 1920 census revealed that for the first time a majority of Americans lived in urban rather than rural areas. Of 54 million urban residents, over 16 million lived in villages and towns and held the same ideas and values as rural citizens. Urbanization led to changes in family structure, as couples married more out of love and physical attraction than for social or economic advantage. In successive decades, people married later and had fewer children. Fewer than 10 percent of married women worked outside the home. Most male skilled workers earned enough to support a family in modest comfort. Working women tended to be either childless or highly paid professionals who could employ servants.

A debate brewed over the socialization and psychological development of children. One view stressed rigid training; the other, a permissive approach in which parents heeded their children's expressed needs. Psychologist and advertising magnate John B. Watson urged parents not to "hug and kiss" their children so as to foster independence. In *The Companionate Marriage* Benjamin Lindsey, a juvenile court judge, suggested "trial marriage" for young couples who practiced contraception.

## The Younger Generation

Young people of the 1920s were more unconventional than their forebears because they faced profound changes. Young men began to "pick up" their dates, rather than remain at the date's home and converse with her family. Young women wore makeup, shortened their hair and skirts, and even smoked in public. Some bemoaned the breakdown of moral standards, the fragmentation of the family, and the decline of parental authority. The rebelliousness was a youthful conformity shaped by peer pressure, particularly at the college level.

## The "New" Woman

Young people in the 1920s were more open about sex than their counterparts of earlier generations, but most did not engage in premarital relations. Birth control, largely a concern of married women in the 1920s, was promoted by Margaret Sanger, a former nurse who established the American Birth Control League in 1921.

Divorce laws were modified and women increasingly took jobs as clerks, typists, salespeople, receptionists, elementary teachers, domestics, and telephone operators. Most women's jobs were low-paying or unwanted by men. Another blow was dealt to working women in 1923, when the Supreme Court in *Adkins v. Children's Hospital* struck down a federal law that limited the hours of working women in the District of Columbia.

Feminists such as Alice Paul, founder of the Women's party and proponent of an equal rights amendment, were disappointed that suffrage did not bring equality with men. Meanwhile, the League of Women Voters worked for reforms, not all of which were directly related to women.

## Popular Culture: Movies and Radio

The first motion pictures, such as the eight-minute *The Great Train Robbery*, were brief, action-packed, and unpretentious. David Wark Griffith's *Birth of a Nation* in 1915 was a technical and artistic breakthrough best remembered for its sympathetic treatment of the Ku Klux Klan. As films moved to theaters, daily ticket sales soared. *The Jazz Singer* (1927) was the first major motion picture with sound. Color film soon followed.

Charlie Chaplin, who portrayed a sad-eyed little tramp, became the dominant star of the silent screen. Moreover, the animated cartoons of Walt Disney gave endless delight to millions of children.

Radio was developed before the Great War, and the first commercial station, KDKA, opened in Pittsburgh in 1920. Within two years over 500 stations were in operation. Congress limited the number of stations and parceled out wavelengths. The Federal Communications Commission was empowered to revoke the licenses of stations that failed to operate in the public interest but placed no controls on programming and advertising practices.

## The Golden Age of Sports

Greater leisure time and spending money of the 1920s allowed many people to attend athletic games. Perhaps the greatest all-around athlete of the century was the Indian Jim Thorpe, who had won the pentathalon and decathalon in the 1912 Olympics. Baseball was the single most popular sport, as Babe Ruth changed the nature of the game from one ruled by pitchers and low scores to one where hitting was the main thrust. In 1927, Ruth hit 60 home runs in a single season; he was so feared that more often than not he was given a base on balls.

Leading players in other sports included William Tilden (tennis), Bobby Jones (golf), Gertrude Ederle (swimming), Jack Dempsey (boxing), and Harold "Red" Grange (college football). Dempsey knocked out a succession of challengers only to be deposed by Gene Tunney in 1927. Ederle was not only the first woman to swim the English Channel but she did so faster than the four men who had previously made it across.

## Urban-Rural Conflicts: Fundamentalism

A resurgence of religious fundamentalism swept through rural areas in the 1920s. Concentrated among Baptists and Methodists, fundamentalists rejected Darwin's theory of evolution and stressed Divine Providence and a literal translation of the King James Bible. William Jennings Bryan, who devoted his later life to moral and religious causes, was perhaps the most prominent fundamentalist figure.

In 1925, Tennessee Governor Austin Peay signed into law a measure which forbade state school and college instructors from teaching "any theory that denies the story of Divine Creation of man as taught in the Bible." The American Civil Liberties Union financed a test case to challenge the statute. John T. Scopes, a biology teacher in Dayton, agreed to break the law by stating in class that man was descended from other primates. His arrest led to the sensational "monkey trial." Clarence Darrow of Chicago, Scopes's defense attorney, declared that civilization, not Scopes, was on trial. Such reporters as Henry L. Mencken of Baltimore flocked to Dayton to ridicule Bryan, who affirmed the biblical account that Eve was created from a rib of Adam and that a great fish had swallowed Jonah. Scopes, who was convicted and fined $100, subsequently left Dayton, the trial judge was defeated for reelection, and Bryan collapsed and died a few days after the trial ended.

### Urban-Rural Conflicts: Prohibition

The Eighteenth Amendment, ratified in 1919, forbade the manufacture, transportation, and sale of alcoholic beverages. Two years earlier the Lever Act, as a conservation endeavor, had outlawed the use of grain in the manufacture of alcoholic beverages. The lingering distrust of foreigners also played into the hands of prohibitionists because beer drinking was associated with the Germans. State and local laws had already made much of the country "dry" by 1917.

This "experiment noble in purpose" as Herbert Hoover called prohibition, drastically reduced the national consumption of alcohol. Arrests for drunkenness and deaths from alcoholism fell off sharply. Had the "drys" been willing to legalize wine and beer, the ban might have worked. Saloons were replaced by secret bars or clubs known as speakeasies, which operated with the sanction of the police.

Prohibition enhanced but did not originate the criminal empires of such gangsters as Al Capone of Chicago. Politicians denounced the evils of drinking but did not adequately fund the Prohibition Bureau to enforce the law. Prohibition also shook the Democratic party by creating a split between southern "drys" and northern "wets."

### The Ku Klux Klan

A new Ku Klux Klan was organized in 1915 by William J. Simmons, amid the distrust some felt toward foreigners, blacks, Catholics, and Jews. By 1923, two publicity agents had gained control of the Klan and claimed a total of 5 million members. The Klan vowed to return to an older, supposedly finer America and to stamp out nonconformity, but its membership declined when rival factions squabbled over money collected from dues. When the Indiana Klansman David C. Stephenson was convicted of assaulting and causing the death of a young woman, the rank and file began to desert the organization.

### Sacco and Vanzetti

In 1920, two men in South Braintree, Massachusetts, killed a paymaster and a guard in a daylight robbery of a shoe factory. Two Italian immigrants and anarchists, Nicola Sacco and Bartolomeo Vanzetti, were convicted of the murders. Their trial was a travesty of justice in which the judge called the defendants "those anarchist bastards." The pair was electrocuted, to the disillusionment of the intelligentsia. Some historians, impressed by ballistic studies of Sacco's gun, now suspect that he may have been guilty.

## Literary Trends

Most literature of the 1920s reflected the disillusionment of intellectuals, who became bitter critics of society due to the horrors of war and the activities of fundamentalists and "red-baiters." Young men and women crushed by the spirit of the age were dubbed the "lost generation." F. Scott Fitzgerald epitomized the new breed of authors in *This Side of Paradise*. *The Great Gatsby* dissected a millionaire whose love for another man's wife led to his own demise. Fitzgerald's own life descended into the despair of alcoholism. The expatriates left the United States to live in Paris. Ernest Hemingway graphically portrayed their world in *The Sun Also Rises*. In *A Farewell to Arms* he described the confusion and horror of war.

Iconoclastic H. L. Mencken founded the *American Mercury*, a magazine critical of middle-class interests and values. Mencken defined "Puritanism" as the "haunting fear that someone, somewhere, may be happy." Sinclair Lewis, in the novels *Main Street* and *Babbitt* assailed middle-class conformity and bigotry and portrayed businessmen as blindly orthodox in political and social opinions. Lewis went on to challenge the medical profession in *Arrowsmith*, organized religion in *Elmer Gantry*, and fascism in *It Can't Happen Here*. Lacking Mencken's ability to remain aloof, Lewis craved the good opinion and praise of his fellow authors.

## The "New Negro"

Southern blacks increasingly moved north after the war, populating urban ghettos amid de facto segregated conditions. Sociologists Robert and Helen Lynd in their classic analysis of "Middletown" (Muncie, Indiana) concluded that, despite school desegregation, blacks and whites in the North were segregated in churches, theaters, and other public accommodations.

The disappointments of the 1920s produced a new black militancy. W. E. B. Du Bois, who vacillated between support for integration and black separatism, tried but failed to create an international black movement. Marcus Garvey, founder of the Universal Negro Improvement Association, proposed that Negroes return to the African homeland of their ancestors. Garvey's *Black Star* steamship line went into bankruptcy, and he later was imprisoned for defrauding investors in various enterprises. Garvey's promotion of a "New Negro" sparked pride among blacks and made them willing to resist mistreatment.

Harlem, a white, middle-class residential section of New York City as late as 1910, became the largest black community in the world. The "Harlem Renaissance" of the 1920s gave new hope to black intellectuals such as the poet Langston Hughes.

## The "New Era"

The 1920s were exceptionally prosperous, as business boomed, real wages rose, and unemployment declined. Perhaps 40 percent of the total wealth of the world lay in American hands. Prosperity rested on the confidence of the business community, low interest rates, an increase in industrial output, and the efficiency of manufacturing.

The assembly line, perfected by Henry Ford, speeded production and reduced costs to make it possible for average citizens to own many products. The time-and-motion studies of Frederick W. Taylor, applied to hundreds of factories after the war, streamlined the manufacturing process.

### The Age of the Consumer

Advertising magnate Bruce Barton in *The Man Nobody Knows* described Jesus as the "founder of modern business," the man who "picked up twelve men from the bottom ranks . . . and forged them into an organization that conquered the world." Business worked to make goods more attractive and changed models frequently to entice buyers into the market.

The automobile had the single most important impact on the economy. By 1929, some 23 million private cars were on the highways, nearly one per family. The industry gave Americans a freedom not previously imagined and spurred the development of related businesses, triggered road-building, and fostered tourism.

### Henry Ford

Ford was the man most responsible for the growth of the automobile industry. His genius lay in reducing prices to match consumer buying power. By 1925 he had reduced the price of the Model T to under $300, while his Michigan factory turned out more than 9,000 cars per day. He also grasped the importance of high wages in stimulating output—in 1914 he established the $5 day, an increase of about $2 over prevailing wages. His assembly line increased the pace of work and made each worker more productive.

In time Ford became a billionaire who refused to deal with unions, spied on his employees, and fired any worker who drove any car but a Ford. When Ford failed to modernize, General Motors became a major competitor by offering better vehicles at slightly higher prices. Though uninformed on many topics, Ford spoke on controversial issues, denouncing alcohol and tobacco consumption. He once said that he would not give a nickel for all the art in the world, and he defined "history" as "more or less the bunk." Despite apparent anti-Semitism, his homespun style and intense individualism still caused many to regard him as a folk hero.

### The Airplane

The internal combustion engine with its high ratio of power to weight made the airplane possible; hence early experiments with planes occurred at about the same time that the prototypes of the modern automobile were being manufactured.

Wilbur and Orville Wright launched the first flight at Kitty Hawk, North Carolina, in 1903, five years before Ford produced the Model T. Another pair of brothers, Malcolm and Haimes

Lockheed built one of the first commercial planes. The war also accelerated advances in airplane technology.

In 1927, Charles Lindbergh flew his single-engine *Spirit of St. Louis* nonstop from New York to Paris in some 33 hours, a formidable achievement. "Lucky Lindy" became an international hero, one who shunned exploitation of his fame.

Another pioneer of aviation was William E. Boeing, who began flying passengers and mail between San Francisco and Chicago in 1927.

## People, Places, and Things

*Define the following concepts:*

quota system _____

_____

*e pluribus unum* _____

_____

eugenics _____

_____

bohemian _____

_____

nickelodeons _____

_____

decathalon _____

_____

fundamentalism _____

_____

cause célèbre _____

_____

Divine Creation _____

_____

speakeasy _____

_____

"lost generation" _____

_____

assembly line _____

_____

*Describe the following:*

American Birth Control League _____

_____

*The Great Train Robbery* _____

_____

*Birth of a Nation* _____

_____

*The Jazz Singer* _____

_____

Federal Communications Commission _____

_____

Scopes trial _____

_____

Comstock Act _____

_____

Prohibition Bureau _____

_____

Lever Act _____

_____

Ku Klux Klan _____

_____

Middletown study _____

_____

Universal Negro Improvement Association _____

_____

"Harlem Renaissance" _____

_____

*Identify the following people:*

John B. Watson _____

_____

Alice Paul _____

_____

Charlie Chaplin _____

_____

Robert "Bobby" Jones _____

_____

Jack Dempsey _____

_____

Gertrude Ederle _____

_____

Babe Ruth _____

_____

Clarence Darrow _____

_____

Al Capone _____

_____

Sacco and Vanzetti _____

_____

F. Scott Fitzgerald _____

_____

Ernest Hemingway _____

_____

Henry L. Mencken _____

_____

Sinclair Lewis _____

_____

Langston Hughes _____

_____

Henry Ford _____

_____

Charles Lindbergh _____

_____

Lockheed brothers _____

_____

William E. Boeing _____

_____

William J. Simmons _____

_____

## Self-Test

**Multiple-Choice Questions**

1. Which of these statements is *false*?
   A. New labor-saving machines enabled many women to escape the burdens of housework in the 1920s.
   B. The divorce rate increased during the decade.
   C. Family size increased as the standard of living rose.
   D. The changing role of women was reflected in new styles of dress and cosmetics.

2. Margaret Sanger was most closely associated with:
   A. The birth control movement
   B. Women's suffrage
   C. Equal pay for equal work
   D. The push for prohibition

3. Which of these is *mispaired*?
   A. Wright Brothers—Kitty Hawk
   B. Henry Ford—auto assembly line
   C. David Griffith—radio
   D. Charles Lindbergh—New York to Paris nonstop flight

4. Which of these statements regarding the motion picture industry is *false*?
   A. *The Jazz Singer* was the first motion picture to tell a complete story.
   B. *Birth of a Nation*, which depicted the Ku Klux Klan in a favorable light, marked a technological breakthrough in film.
   C. By 1920, all cities and most towns had at least one theater.
   D. The most popular star of the silent screen was Charlie Chaplin.

5. Leading sports figures of the 1920s included all of the following *except*:
   A. Jack Dempsey
   B. Robert Jones
   C. Gertrude Ederle
   D. Webster Thayer

6. *This Side of Paradise* and *The Great Gatsby* were written by:
   A. Ernest Hemingway
   B. F. Scott Fitzgerald
   C. Langston Hughes
   D. H. L. Mencken

7. All of the following were written by Sinclair Lewis *except*:
   A. *A Farewell to Arms*
   B. *It Can't Happen Here*
   C. *Arrowsmith*
   D. *Elmer Gantry*

8. Harold "Red" Grange was associated with:
   A. Radio
   B. The silent screen
   C. Baseball
   D. Football

9. Which of these statements does *not* apply to fundamentalism?
   A. Fundamentalists were mostly found among Protestants in the South.
   B. Urban sophisticates dismissed fundamentalists as boors and hayseeds.
   C. Fundamentalists were devoted to truths of the King James version of the Bible.
   D. Fundamentalists opposed laws to prohibit discussion of Darwin's theory of evolution in textbooks and classrooms.

10. The immigration law of 1924 worked to the advantage of:
    A. Anglo-Saxons
    B. Italians
    C. Jews
    D. Asians

11. In a "companionate" family:
    A. The mother attends to nearly all household duties
    B. The rearing of children is undertaken in a traditional, authoritarian manner
    C. Husbands and wives regard each other as equals regarding housework and occupations
    D. Divorce is not a viable alternative to marital difficulties

12. The juvenile court judge who proposed "trial marriages" as a potential way to reduce the divorce rate was:
    A. J. Walter Thompson
    B. John B. Watson
    C. Benjamin B. Lindsey
    D. Carrie Chapman Catt

13. The right of women to vote did *not* drastically alter politics because:
    A. Women failed to register to vote in large numbers
    B. Most women voted for candidates favored by their husbands
    C. The Nineteenth Amendment guaranteed sexual equality
    D. Most women began to concentrate on reforms regardless of partisanship

14. The animated cartoon is associated with:
    A. Walt Disney
    B. D. W. Griffith
    C. Charlie Chaplin
    D. William Tilden

15. The winner of the 1912 pentathalon and decathalon was:
    A. Babe Ruth
    B. Walter Camp
    C. Jack Dempsey
    D. Jim Thorpe

16. Prohibition might have been successful had:
    A. Its supporters been willing to legalize beer and wine
    B. The issue been left to the states
    C. Police more effectively enforced the ban on liquor sales
    D. Illegal liquor imports been halted

17. The Ku Klux Klan declined by the late 1920s because:
    A. Americans grew more tolerant of immigrants
    B. Factionalism sprang up, and rival leaders squabbled over the dues collected from the membership
    C. Church leaders denounced the Klan
    D. The Klan failed to influence state and local politics

18. The expatriates of the 1920s mostly lived in:
    A. France
    B. Russia
    C. England
    D. Canada

19. Marcus Garvey advanced the notion that:
    A. Blacks should concentrate in Harlem
    B. Blacks should push for integration into the full community
    C. God and Christ were black
    D. Blacks should elect only other blacks to state legislatures and Congress

20. Who called the study of history as "more or less the bunk"?
    A. William Boeing
    B. Langston Hughes
    C. Henry Ford
    D. Charles Lindbergh

**Essay Questions**

1. Discuss American immigration policy in the decade after World War I. Explain how and why Congress decided to "close the gates." Evaluate the wisdom of this policy.

2. Explain how the role of women changed in the 1920s in reference to family life, sexual matters, occupations, and attitudes.

3. Discuss the clash of rural and urban interests in the Scopes trial of 1925. Refer particularly to John T. Scopes, William Jennings Bryan, and Clarence Darrow.

4. Analyze prohibition as a "noble experiment" of the 1920s. List advantages and disadvantages to the drive to ban the sale, manufacture, and transportation of alcoholic beverages.

5. Discuss the pivotal role of Henry Ford in the revolution of transportation in the United States.

# Critical Thinking Exercise

Examine beyond the lines of the textbook to list the American literary or intellectual figures to whom the following analytical statements refer:

____1. Though he did not moralize against adultery, one of his greatest works depicted a tragedy resulting from an adulterous tryst.

____2. In an age of prohibition and traditional values, this literary genius fell prey to alcoholism and hedonism.

____3. This writer, who abhorred traditional values of his parents, particularly those of his mother, to embrace "individual expression," later followed the steps of his physician father in taking his own life.

____4. A diary that surfaced in 1990 disclosed that this late social critic himself exhibited many of the prejudices he had denounced during the twenties, particularly hostile attitudes toward blacks and Jews.

____5. His novel about one unscrupulous minister was critical of organized religion.

____6. Their scholarly analysis uncovered a phenomenon later called de facto segregation in the North.

____7. Before finally leaving the United States in disillusionment, he seemed at times to endorse black nationalism, integration into the white community, and an international black movement.

____8. This optimistic poet saw an unbounded future for the artistic and intellectual culture of blacks in the 1920s.

CHAPTER 26

# The New Era: 1921-1933

## Learning Objectives

*After reading Chapter 26, you should be able to:*

1. Evaluate the shortcomings of Harding's administration in reference to the personality and philosophy of the president.
2. Explain how the circumstances of the 1920s helped to make Calvin Coolidge a popular president.
3. Discuss the peace movement after World War I.
4. Explain how the "Good Neighbor" policy changed American relations with Latin America.
5. Show how Japan emerged as a militaristic Pacific power.
6. Understand how the issue of German reparations and Allied war debts undermined the European economy in the 1920s and 1930s.
7. Discuss the elections of 1928 and 1932 in reference to parties, nominees, issues, outcome, and long-term significance.
8. Explain how economic problems of the 1920s led to the stock market crash of 1929 and the depression of 1930.
9. Evaluate Herbert Hoover's policies to curb the Great Depression.
10. Show how the depression affected ordinary citizens.

## Overview

**"Normalcy"**

Party regular Warren Harding secured the 1920 Republican nomination as the result of a deadlock among GOP delegates. Harding's coining of the vulgarism *normalcy* as a substitute for *normality* exasperated those who insisted on proper erudition. Nevertheless, Henry Cabot Lodge declared Harding a vast improvement over Wilson, and voters agreed -- at least for a time. Though characterized as lazy and incompetent, Harding was hardworking and politically shrewd. He was also indecisive and unwilling to offend, two liabilities that doomed his administration. Though he named men of impeccable reputation to some departments, Harding was also committed to the "Ohio Gang" headed by Harry M. Daugherty, whom he made attorney general.

"Regulating" Business

Treasury Secretary Andrew Mellon, a multimillionaire banker and aluminum magnate, attempted to lower taxes on the wealthy, reverse the lower-tariff policies of Wilson, cut government expenses, and return to a form of laissez-faire. He proposed to eliminate inheritance taxes and reduce taxes on the wealthy by two-thirds but opposed lower rates on taxpayers earning less than $66,000 a year. Mellon claimed that freeing the rich from confiscatory taxation would foster investment in productive enterprises, the success of which would thereby create jobs.

Mellon's program was opposed by midwestern Republicans and southern Democrats loosely organized in the Farm Bloc. The revival of European agriculture after the war cut the demand for farm produce just as the increased use of fertilizers and machinery enlarged output. Therefore, farmers languished during the 1920s. Congress, though rejecting Mellon's more daring proposals, had by 1924 cut maximum taxes on income from 73 to 40 percent, reduced taxes on lower incomes, and raised inheritance levies.

The Fordney-McCumber Tariff granted protection to "infant industries" like rayon, china, chemicals, and toys but held to the Wilsonian principle of moderate protection for most products. Mellon balanced the budget and reduced the national debt by more than $500 million per year. Harding and Coolidge were so committed to Mellon's policies that they vetoed "bonus" bills in the name of economy to compensate veterans for their World War I service, a program pushed by the American Legion. Finally, in 1924, Congress established paid-up life insurance for veterans over Coolidge's veto.


The Harding Scandals

The Ohio Gang used its influence in corrupt ways. Jesse Smith, an influence peddler for Attorney General Daugherty, committed suicide when his dealings were exposed. Charles F. Cramer, assistant to Veteran Bureau Director Charles R. Forbes, also took his own life. Forbes, convicted of siphoning into his own pockets millions of dollars earmarked for the construction of veterans hospitals or medical supplies, was sentenced to two years. Daugherty himself was implicated in a fraud case but escaped imprisonment by taking the Fifth Amendment.

The worst scandal involved Interior Secretary Fall, who arranged for the transfer of naval oil reserves to his jurisdiction. Fall leased the properties to private oil companies without competitive bidding. Edward L. Doheny obtained a lease on the Elk Hills reserve in California, and Harry F. Sinclair of Mammoth Oil got access to Teapot Dome in Wyoming. A probe conducted by Senator Thomas J. Walsh of Montana disclosed that Doheny had "lent" Fall $100,000 in cash and Sinclair had given Fall over $300,000 in cash and securities. The three escaped conviction for defrauding the government, but Sinclair was later given nine months in jail for contempt of the Senate and tampering with a jury, and Fall was fined $100,000 and given a year in prison for accepting a bribe. In 1927, the Supreme Court revoked the leases.

The public learned of these scandals only after Harding's death of a heart attack in San Francisco. Harding was deeply mourned at the time of his death, but later revelations caused Americans to view him with scorn.

## Coolidge Prosperity

President Coolidge moved swiftly to clean up the Harding scandals in time to run for the office in his own right in 1924. He appointed Harlan Fiske Stone to replace Daugherty as attorney general, retained Mellon as treasury secretary, defended business interests, uttered folksy witticisms, and was highly admired among conservatives. The Democrats required 103 ballots to nominate John W. Davis, a conservative corporation lawyer and former Wilson solicitor general identified with Morgan banking interests, after the party deadlocked between the southern "dry" wing backing William G. McAdoo and the eastern "wet" element supporting New York Governor Alfred E. Smith.

Dismayed by the Coolidge/Davis choice, Robert M. La Follette entered the race as the nominee of a new Progressive party, which carried the support of the farm bloc, Socialists, American Federation of Labor, and a number of intellectuals. Coolidge handily defeated Davis, whose strength was confined to the South, and La Follette carried only his native Wisconsin.

## Peace Without a Sword

Harding permitted Secretary of State Charles Evans Hughes to exercise broad powers over foreign policy. Though many Americans were isolationist after the war, national leaders increasingly found international involvement unavoidable. In an attempt to maintain the "Open Door" in China and check Japanese expansionist tendencies in the Pacific, Hughes convened the Washington Naval Conference in 1921. The United States, Britain, France, Japan, and Italy agreed to stop building battleships for ten years and to reduce their fleet of capital ships to a fixed ratio. Japan later rebuffed the agreements and announced it would no longer limit capital tonnage. Moreover, the Japanese felt a sense of injury when they were given no quota under the National Origins Act of 1924. Japan apparently felt by the 1930s that the United States would not interfere with its domination of the western Pacific. Others in Japan seemed to view war with the United States as inevitable.

## The Peace Movement

Peace societies such as the Carnegie Endowment for International Peace flourished before and after World War I. In 1923, Edward W. Bok, retired editor of *Ladies' Home Journal*, was flooded with suggestions when he offered a $100,000 prize to the best plan for preserving peace.

Despite interest in the peace movement, the United States did not join the League's World Court out of apprehension that the organization might try to intervene in domestic matters. In 1928, the Kellogg-Briand Pact initially signed by 15 nations condemned war "as an instrument of national policy" amid optimism that another world war might be averted.

### The Good Neighbor Policy

Harding and Coolidge struggled with growing "Yankeephobia" south of the border. In the face of radicalism and instability in Mexico, which caused Americans with land and oil rights to suffer losses, Coolidge acted with restraint. He dispatched Dwight Morrow, father-in-law of Charles Lindbergh, to improve relations with Mexico.

Under President Herbert Hoover, the United States began to treat the Latin American nations as equals. Hoover reversed Wilson's policy of teaching the Latin Americans to "elect good men." The Clark Memorandum set aside the Roosevelt Corollary to the Monroe Doctrine, meaning the United States would no longer be so prone to intervention in the hemisphere. By 1934 the marines that had occupied Nicaragua, Haiti, and the Dominican Republic had been withdrawn, and the United States renounced the right to intervene in Cuba.

### The Totalitarian Challenge

In 1931, Japan conquered Chinese Manchuria and established the new state of Manchukuo, a violation of the Kellogg-Briand and Nine-Power pacts. Secretary of State Henry Stimson announced that the United States would not recognize the legality of seizures made in violation of American treaty rights. A few months later Japan attacked Shanghai and withdrew from the League of Nations, after the organization condemnd its agression. The lesson of Manchuria was not lost on Adolf Hitler, who assumed the German chancellorship in January 1933.

### War Debts and Reparations

Devastated from World War I, Germany could not pay the reparations she had been forced to accept at the peace conference in 1919. Therefore, the Allies could not repay the United States for loans made prior to American entry into the world war, some $10 billion, because they had expected to get that money from German reparations. The Europeans also claimed that they could not repay the loans in light of the high American tariff. The Allies explained that the money had been spent in the United States and had stimulated the American economy.

Two attempts were made to scale down the reparations—the Dawes Plan of 1924 and the Young Plan of 1929, but neither could remedy a defective international financial situation. Germany defaulted on the reparations, and the Allies abandoned all pretense of meeting their obligations to the United States, much to the consternation of President Coolidge.

### The Election of 1928

When Coolidge declined to seek reelection, the Republicans nominated Secretary of Commerce Herbert Hoover, the advocate of voluntary trade associations who urged capitalists to curb their selfish instincts. The Democrats nominated Governor Al Smith, who combined a cultural conservatism with humanitarian concern for the underprivileged. A product of New

York's Lower East Side slums, Smith became the first Roman Catholic nominated for president by a major party. Smith's religion, brashness and opposition to prohibition combined to hurt him in rural areas.

Hoover won a smashing victory and carried five southern states where Smith's Catholicism aroused resentment—the first real breakthrough in the South for a Republican presidential candidate since Reconstruction. The 1928 election also began a political realignment that was taking shape in the cities. Smith won the twelve largest cities, all of which had previously been Republican. In agricultural states Smith surpassed Davis's showing four years earlier. Moreover, a new coalition of urban workers and farmers would emerge by 1932.

## Economic Problems

Not all industries shared in the prosperity of the 1920s; coal and textiles faced competition from oil and new synthetics. Two hundred corporations controlled nearly half the nation's corporate assets. General Motors, Ford, and Chrysler turned out nearly all of the nation's vehicles. Four tobacco companies produced most of the nation's cigarettes. Retail merchandising was revolutionized by the growth of chain stores, epitomized by F. W. Woolworth and A&P, which took business from small shopkeepers.

Trade associations flourished in the 1920s, as producers formed voluntary organizations to exchange information, discuss policies toward government and the public, and regulate prices in their industries. Defenders argued that the associations made business more efficient, though they may well have been challenged under antitrust laws.

The weakest element in the economy remained agriculture. Farm prices slumped and farmers' costs mounted. George N. Peek, an Illinois plow manufacturer, proposed that the government buy the surplus farm production, sell it abroad on the world market, and assess an "equalization fee" on farmers to recover the inevitable losses. In 1927, and again in 1928, Congress passed the McNary-Haugen bill to stabilize farm prices, but Coolidge vetoed the measure both times, citing constitutional, philosophical, and practical objections.

## The Crash of 1929

Stock prices, already at a historic high, began to surge in the spring of 1928. Some conservative brokers warned that most stocks were overpriced, but the majority scoffed at pessimistic talk. The "bull market" continued through the first half of 1929, as many small investors put their savings into common stock. In September, the market wavered, and a month later, in a state of panic-selling, 16 million shares changed hands and prices plummeted.

## Hoover and the Depression

Despite popular misconception, the collapse of the stock market did not cause the Great Depression; stocks rallied late in the year, and business activity did not decline until the spring of 1930. The depression was a worldwide phenomenon caused by economic imbalances resulting from the world war.

The problem of underconsumption worked to speed the downward economic spiral. Manufacturers closed plants and laid off workers due to their mounting inventories. Automobile output dropped from 4.5 million units in 1929 to 1.1 million in 1931, costing many their jobs. In 1930 more than 1,300 banks closed; each failure deprived people of funds that they might have used to buy goods.

Hoover proposed a tax cut to increase consumers' spendable income, endorsed public works programs administered at the state level to create jobs for the unemployed, and urged lower interest rates to make it easier for businesses and farmers to borrow money. The program failed to check the economic slide. Hoover refused on constitutional grounds to allow federal funds to be used for the relief of individuals, placing the burden on states, cities, and private charities. By 1932, more than 40,000 Boston families were on relief, and in Chicago unemployment stood at 40 percent of the work force.

Hoover believed that federal loans to businesses were constitutional and approved the Reconstruction Finance Corporation to lend money to banks, railroads, and insurance companies. As time passed and the depression worsened, Hoover put more stress on balancing the federal budget, a factor that may have prolonged the depression.

In 1930 Hoover signed the Hawley-Smoot Tariff, which raised duties on most manufactured goods to prohibitive levels, and helped to bring about a financial collapse in Europe. He then proposed a one-year moratorium on all international obligations. Britain and other nations therefore devalued their currencies to encourage foreigners to buy their goods, an action that worsened the depression. As the economic situation deteriorated, Hoover lost the support of the people, who heaped contempt on him despite his devotion to duty and concern for the welfare of the country.


**Hitting Bottom**

In the spring of 1932 thousands faced starvation; only about a quarter of the unemployed received any public aid. Some who were evicted from their houses gathered in "Hoovervilles," or ramshackle communities made of packing boxes and rusty sheet metal. The prevailing despair prompted the socialist theologian Reinhold Niebuhr to remark that "Capitalism is dying, and ... it ought to die."

Some 20,000 veterans marched on Washington demanding immediate payment of their World War I "adjusted compensation." Hoover, fearing that the "Bonus Army" was composed of criminals and radicals, sent troops into Anacostia Flats to disperse the veterans. No one was killed, but the spectacle of tanks and tear gas being used against the veterans appalled many.

The severity of the depression caused some to demand radical economic and political changes. Some intellectuals even embraced communism because of its emphasis on economic planning and mobilization of the state to achieve social goals.

## The Depression and Its Victims

The depression had profound psychological effects on its victims as well as obvious economic ones. Those who lost jobs and could not find work fell into a state of apathy, often forfeiting their ambition and pride. Others declined to apply for public assistance out of shame. Despite difficulties, most workers did not become radical and held out hope for better times. The depression led to a sharp drop in the birth-rate and changes in family life that resulted when "breadwinners" came home with empty hands. Parental authority declined when there was less money available to supply children's needs.

## The Election of 1932

Certain of victory in 1932, the Democrats nominated Governor Franklin D. Roosevelt to challenge President Hoover. Under Roosevelt's tenure, New York had led the nation in providing relief for the needy, old-age pensions, unemployment insurance, and conservation and public power projects. Roosevelt's sunny, magnetic personality contrasted with that of the glum, colorless Hoover, who seemed more pessimistic with each passing day.

Born to wealth and social status, Roosevelt graduated from Harvard and embarked on a political career. Even an attack of polio in 1921 did not cause him to abandon his hopes for high office. Despite his physical handicap (he could walk only a few steps and only with the aid of steel braces), Roosevelt proved to be a powerful campaigner. He radiated confidence and humor when attacking the Republicans. He criticized Hoover for presiding over the "greatest spending administration in peace time in our history." In a contradictory stance, Roosevelt called for a balanced budget while also vowing to increase government spending to alleviate the dire need of the citizenry. Roosevelt promised to experiment with numerous possible solutions to the depression: "It is common sense to take a method and try it. If it fails, admit it frankly and try another. But above all, try something."

Roosevelt easily topped Hoover in the electoral college, 472 to 59. During the interval between the election and the inauguration, the depression worsened, as Roosevelt, Hoover, and the last "lame duck" session of Congress prior to the Twentieth Amendment could not agree on an interim economic policy.

## People, Places, and Things

*Define the following concepts:*

*normalcy* _____

_____

"infant industries" _____
_____

"adjusted compensation" _____
_____

jury tampering _____
_____

"Yankeephobia" _____
_____

totalitarian _____
_____

trade associations _____
_____

"equalization fee" _____
_____

"lame duck" _____
_____

*Describe the following:*

Fordney-McCumber Tariff _____
_____

Teapot Dome _____
_____

Washington Naval Conference _____

_____

Four-Power Treaty _____

_____

Nine-Power Treaty _____

_____

Kellogg-Briand Pact _____

_____

Good Neighbor policy _____

_____

Manchukuo _____

_____

Stimson Doctrine _____

_____

McNary-Haugen bill _____

_____

stock market crash _____

_____

Reconstruction Finance Corporation _____

_____

Hawley-Smoot Tariff _____

_____

"Hoovervilles" _____
_____

New Deal _____
_____

*Identify the following people:*

Andrew Mellon _____
_____

Charles Forbes _____
_____

Albert Fall _____
_____

Thomas J. Walsh _____
_____

"Ohio Gang" _____
_____

Harry Daugherty _____
_____

Harry Sinclair _____
_____

Calvin Coolidge _____
_____

John W. Davis _____

_____

Dwight Morrow _____

_____

Herbert Hoover _____

_____

Alfred E. Smith _____

_____

John J. Raskob _____

_____

George N. Peek _____

_____

Franklin D. Roosevelt _____

_____

John Nance "Cactus Jack" Garner _____

_____

Walter Lippmann _____

_____

Felix Frankfurter _____

_____

J. Reuben Clark _____

_____

# Self-Test

## Multiple-Choice Questions

1. The Dawes and Young plans:
   A. Were efforts to limit naval arms after World War I
   B. Provided financial assistance in rebuilding Europe after the war
   C. Sought to assist the Germans in making reparations
   D. Called for a moratorium on all war debts

2. The first Catholic nominated for president by a major party was:
   A. Franklin D. Roosevelt
   B. Alfred E. Smith
   C. Herbert Hoover
   D. John F. Kennedy

3. American and British capital ship tonnage was fixed at 525,000 tons by an international conference in:
   A. Paris
   B. London
   C. Shanghai
   D. Washington

4. Critics of the Reconstruction Finance Corporation claimed that it:
   A. Encouraged persons to remain jobless
   B. Subsidized farmers at the expense of industry
   C. Aided businessmen who were not directly affected by the depression
   D. Lent money without checks into the solvency of the firms

5. The Twentieth Amendment provided for:
   A. Repeal of prohibition
   B. Public works
   C. Federal support for farmers
   D. End to the "lame duck" session of Congress

6. Which of the following was *not* a member of Harding's Cabinet?
   A. William G. McAdoo
   B. Andrew Mellon
   C. Albert B. Fall
   D. Herbert Hoover

7. Andrew Mellon's philosophy would later be reflected in certain views of:
   A. Franklin D. Roosevelt
   B. Harry S. Truman
   C. Lyndon B. Johnson
   D. Ronald W. Reagan

8. Teapot Dome refers to a scandal involving:
   A. Indian reservations
   B. Liquor permits
   C. Oil leases
   D. Veterans hospitals

9. The nation that withdrew from the agreement limiting capital ship construction was:
   A. United States
   B. Japan
   C. Germany
   D. The Soviet Union

10. The "Colossus of the North" was:
    A. Nazi Germany
    B. The United States
    C. Canada
    D. Mexico

11. The Clark Memorandum:
    A. Reaffirmed the "Open Door" in China
    B. Encouraged "dollar diplomacy" in Latin America
    C. Abrogated the Platt Amendment
    D. Disavowed the tendency of the United States to intervene in routine Latin American matters

12. Instrumental in the nomination of Warren Harding was:
    A. Theodore Roosevelt
    B. Raymond Moley
    C. Robert La Follette
    D. Henry Cabot Lodge, Sr.

13. Harry Sinclair was jailed for:
    A. Fraud in the Teapot Dome leases
    B. Jury tampering and contempt of the Senate
    C. Income tax evasion
    D. Accepting a bribe

14. Robert La Follette carried which state in 1924?
    A. Michigan
    B. Wisconsin
    C. Minnesota
    D. Arkansas

15. In trade associations:
    A. Business operators discuss common problems of production and marketing and reach accommodations that decrease competition
    B. The courts found wholesale violations of antitrust laws
    C. The nation moved toward national economic planning
    D. "Adjusted compensation" was offered to bankrupt businesses

16. Why did President Hoover break up the veterans' bonus marchers of 1932?
    A. He had earlier vetoed "adjusted compensation."
    B. He believed that communists and radicals had infiltrated the ranks of the demonstrating veterans.
    C. Hoover opposed direct government aid to individuals.
    D. He believed that the right of free speech and assembly did not permit harassment of the national government.

17. Andrew Mellon favored which of these taxes?
    A. Inheritance taxes
    B. Tariffs
    C. Excess profits taxes
    D. Investment taxes

18. The Four-Power Treaty was *not* signed by:
    A. United States
    B. Germany
    C. Japan
    D. France

19. The Stimson Doctrine was specifically aimed at:
    A. Germany
    B. Britain
    C. Japan
    D. Soviet Russia

20. Prior to entering public service, Hoover had been:
    A. A medical doctor
    B. A missionary
    C. A mining engineer
    D. An economist

## Essay Questions

1. Show how corruptionists marred the Harding administration even though Harding himself was not involved in the scandals.

2. Explain how the Mellon financial program led to a balancing of the budget and a reduction in the national debt.

3. Explain how Charles Evans Hughes led the United States into an activist foreign policy during the 1920s despite the refusal to join the League of Nations.

4. Compare and contrast the Coolidge and Hoover administrations in reference to the economic conditions each president faced.

5. Why was the election of Franklin D. Roosevelt in 1932 one of the least surprising political events in history? Evaluate Roosevelt's campaign style and goals for the nation.

## Critical Thinking Exercise

Economics has been referred to as the "dismal science" because economists can examine identical sets of statistics and circumstances and reach diametrically opposite conclusions. Examine these statements regarding President Hoover and the Great Depression. Label the factual statements with "T", the opinion statements with "O", and the false statements with "F". In some cases you, like economists, may disagree as to whether the statement is truth, opinion, or falsehood.

\_\_\_\_1. Hoover rejected laissez-faire because he refused to follow Mellon's suggestion that the economic disaster be permitted to run its course, as the government had allowed the earlier panics of 1819, 1837, 1857, 1873, and 1893.

\_\_\_\_2. Because many factories could not sell their goods during the 1930s, they often closed plants and laid off workers and caused demand to decrease even more.

\_\_\_\_3. Had the depression been allowed to run its course, the American public would have worked harder and lived more moral, spiritual lives.

\_\_\_\_4. Hoover's program would likely have succeeded had he been reelected and not felt compelled to adjust to political realities.

\_\_\_\_5. In rejecting calls for a balanced budget during the depression, Hoover may have inadvertently prolonged and deepened the impact of the collapse.

____6. Only the national government possessed the power and the credit to deal adequately with the Great Depression.

____7. As the Hoover administration spent $500 million a year on public works, construction outlay rose sharply by 1932.

____8. Federal loans to businesses were constitutional because the money could be put to productive use and eventually repaid.

____9. Hoover's signing of the Hawley-Smoot Tariff is denounced today by supply-side economists.

____10. Prosperity cannot be restored by raids on the public treasury.

____11. Hoover was too rigidly wedded to a particular theory of government to cope with the depression.

____12. High American tariffs could have prevented the worldwide depression because they would have enabled Europeans to buy American goods more easily.

CHAPTER 27

# The New Deal, 1933-1941

## Learning Objectives

*After reading Chapter 27, you should be able to:*

1. Explain how Franklin Roosevelt sought to revive the economy amid the Great Depression.
2. Show how the New Deal tried to remedy social and economic problems.
3. Relate how the depression affected literature.
4. Explain how extremist critics tried to weaken Roosevelt.
5. Understand the reform measures of the "Second New Deal."
6. Evaluate Roosevelt's attempt to alter the Supreme Court.
7. Show the impact of the New Deal on women, blacks, and Indians.
8. Explain how the United States tried to steer clear of involvement as events moved toward another world war.

## Overview

### The Hundred Days

The special 1933 session of Congress known as the "Hundred Days" adopted dozens of "New Deal" measures without serious opposition. The day after his inauguration, President Roosevelt declared a nationwide bank holiday and forbade the exportation of gold. In the first of his "fireside chats" over radio, Roosevelt outlined a plan to reopen sound banks under Treasury licenses. A few weeks later, he took the country off the gold standard, hoping to cause prices to rise.

Congress established the Federal Deposit Insurance Corporation to guarantee bank deposits (initially $5,000) and separate investment and commercial banking. Lawmakers also created the Home Owners Loan Corporation to refinance mortgages and prevent foreclosures.

### The National Recovery Administration (NRA)

Congress addressed the problems of unemployment and industrial stagnation by creating the Civilian Conservation Corps, which provided jobs for young men in reforestation projects, and the National Industrial Recovery Act, which allowed manufacturers to draft codes of "fair business practices." The law enabled producers to raise prices and limit output without violating antitrust laws. NIRA allowed collective bargaining, established minimum wages and maximum hours, and abolished child labor, but it did not end the depression because producers raised prices and limited production instead of hiring more workers and increasing output.

Organized labor used the NIRA to persuade workers that Roosevelt wanted them to join unions. When the American Federation of Labor showed little enthusiasm in enrolling unskilled workers, John L. Lewis and garment trade unionists formed the Congress of Industrial Organizations, which in time rivaled the AFL in size and influence.

## The Agricultural Adjustment Administration (AAA)

The Agricultural Adjustment Act combined compulsory restrictions on production with subsidies to growers of wheat, cotton, tobacco, and pork. The money for these payments was raised by levying processing taxes on middlemen, such as flour millers, who passed the costs on to consumers. AAA sought to raise prices to a "parity" level with industry. Farmers could also qualify for rental payments by withdrawing acreage from cultivation.

To reduce 1933 output, Agriculture Secretary Henry A. Wallace ordered the destruction of crops in the field and the slaughter of millions of hogs at a time when some went hungry. Thereafter, acreage limits proved sufficient to raise some agricultural prices.

## The Tennessee Valley Authority (TVA)

During World War I, a government-owned hydroelectric plant at Muscle Shoals, Alabama, had provided power for factories making synthetic nitrate explosives. Roosevelt wanted to expand the plant into a broad experiment in social planning in the Tennessee Valley. Over the objection of private power companies, the TVA Act authorized a board to build dams, power plants, and transmission lines and to sell fertilizers and electricity to individuals and communities.

The TVA also promoted soil conservation, reforestation, flood control, navigation, and recreation. The authority provided a "yardstick" by which private power company rates could be tested.

## The New Deal Spirit

A majority of Americans in the 1930s considered the New Deal successful because some recovery had occurred amid the optimism of the Roosevelt administration. The New Deal borrowed ideas from the Populists on inflating currency, from Theodore Roosevelt's "New Nationalism" on the relaxation of antitrust laws, from the Progressive social workers on ways to help the downtrodden, and from Wilson's wartime agencies on ways to establish bureaucratic procedures. Rival officials within the administration and interest groups battled to implement their views.

## The Unemployed

At least 9 million remained jobless in 1934, but their loyalty to Roosevelt remained firm. Breaking with tradition, the Democrats increased their already large majorities in Congress in the off-year elections.

In May 1933, Congress had established the Federal Emergency Relief Administration, headed by Harry Hopkins. FERA dispensed $500 million through state relief organizations. Hopkins also persuaded Roosevelt to create the Civil Works Administration to provide work for the unemployed. When costs of the agency reached $1 billion in five months, the CWA was abolished. Despite charges that Hopkins's projects were wasteful, roads, bridges, schools, and other structures were built or refurbished.

In 1935, Hopkins was named to direct the Works Progress Administration, which spent $11 billion over eight years and employed 8.5 million. Besides public works, the WPA made numerous cultural contributions. The Federal Theater Project put actors, directors, and stagehands to work; the Federal Writers' Project turned out guidebooks; the Federal Art Project employed painters and sculptors; the National Youth Administration created part-time jobs for more than 2 million high school and college students.

Despite the public works programs, national unemployment during the New Deal never dropped below 10 percent, and in many places it was much higher.

## Literature in the Depression

Depression writers criticized many aspects of American life. John Dos Passos's trilogy, *U.S.A.*, portrays American society between 1900 and 1930 by interweaving five major characters from different walks of life. *U.S.A.* was a monument to the despair and anger of liberals in the 1930s, but after the depression Dos Passos abandoned his radical views.

John Steinbeck's *The Grapes of Wrath* describes the fate of the Joads, an Oklahoma farm family driven by drought and bad times to become migratory laborers in California. Steinbeck captured the bewilderment of the downtrodden and the brutality of their exploiters. In *Tortilla Flat* and *The Long Valley*, Steinbeck described the life of California cannery workers and ranchers.

Novelist William Faulkner depicted southern aristocrats and impoverished whites and blacks unable to escape from their surroundings. He burst into prominence with *The Sound and the Fury*, *As I Lay Dying*, and *Sanctuary*.

Thomas Wolfe of North Carolina wrote four autobiographical novels, *Look Homeward Angel*, *Of Time and the River*, *The Web and the Rock*, and *You Can't Go Home Again* which captured the despair of the depression and the divided nature of human beings.

## The Extremists

Roosevelt's moderation provoked several extremist critics, including Louisiana Senator Huey "Kingfish" Long, who professed an interest in the poor unaffected by recovery programs. Declaring "Every Man a King," Long's "Share the Wealth" movement attracted 4.6 million members. He proposed the confiscation of family fortunes of more than $5 million and a tax of 100 percent on all incomes exceeding $1 million a year. The money would be used to buy every family a "homestead" and provide an annual family income of $2,000 to $3,000 plus old-age and veterans' pensions and educational benefits.

Father Charles Coughlin, the Detroit-based "Radio Priest," claimed that inflating the currency would end the depression. Through his National Union for Social Justice, Coughlin attacked bankers, New Deal planners, and the farm program. He even alleged that Roosevelt was sympathetic toward communists and Jews.

Dr. Francis Townsend's "old-age revolving pensions" proposed paying every person 60 and over a pension of $200 a month, provided that the pensioners not hold jobs and would spend the checks within 30 days. Their purchases, he argued, would stimulate production and revitalize the economy. The scheme would have cost roughly half the national income at the time.

Prompted by the strength of the Long, Coughlin, and Townsend forces as well as a skeptical Supreme Court, Roosevelt shifted economic gears. He called for new taxes on corporations, and returned to enforcement of antitrust laws as a means to restore competition.

## The Second New Deal

In 1935, the New Deal Congress embarked on two landmark pieces of legislation still in place. The National Labor Relations (Wagner) Act restored labor guarantees wiped out by the Supreme Court in *Schechter v. United States*, the case which struck down the NRA. It gave workers the right to bargain collectively and prohibited employers from interfering with union activities. The National Labor Relations Board was established to supervise plant elections.

The Social Security Act authorized old-age insurance financed jointly by a tax on wages and payrolls. It created a federal-state unemployment insurance program. Social Security did not initially cover agricultural workers, domestics, and the self-employed. Over the years pension payments were increased and the classes of covered workers were enlarged. Within a few years the program became politically sacrosanct, the most protected of all New Deal laws.

The Public Utility Holding Company Act outlawed the pyramiding of electric and gas companies through the use of holding companies. The Rural Electrification Administration, created by executive order, lent money at low rates to utility companies and farm cooperatives in order to bring power to rural areas.

The Second New Deal imposed high taxes on large incomes and on estates and gifts. The imperatives of the depression forced Roosevelt to adopt deficit spending, a practice extolled by the British economist John Maynard Keynes. New Deal critics expressed alarm at the costs of government programs and the undermining of the foundations of American freedom and liberty.

## The Election of 1936

Governor Alfred M. Landon of Kansas, the 1936 Republican made little headway in his contention that he could administer the New Deal more efficiently than Franklin Roosevelt, the originator of the programs. A third candidate, Congressman William Lemke of North Dakota, polled few votes on a Union party banner. Huey Long had been assassinated in 1935, and his organization was taken over by the Reverend Gerald L. K. Smith, a rightist who branded the New Deal as "a slimy group of men culled from the pink campuses of America."

Roosevelt campaigned for the support of workers and the underprivileged, virtually writing off business as "economic royalists." Labor unions and blacks swung heavily to Roosevelt, who carried every state but Maine and Vermont. Republican Congressional ranks were decimated to 89 in the House and 16 in the Senate.

## Roosevelt and the "Nine Old Men"

Prior to 1937, the Supreme Court viewed the New Deal with apprehension. Four justices were anti-New Deal; two others, including Chief Justice Charles Evans Hughes, often sided with the conservatives. When major measures of the Second Hundred Days, including Social Security, were threatened by the Court, Roosevelt asked Congress to increase the number of justices to a maximum of 15 members, with a new appointee added for each sitting justice over the age of seventy. Roosevelt badly underestimated opposition to the plan from within his own party and was forced to back down. Yet in time, the persistent president was able to appoint a New Deal-majority to the Court, including Alabama Senator Hugo Black and William O. Douglas, the longest serving justice.

## The New Deal Winds Down

The Congress of Industrial Organizations recruited blacks and other minorities into the labor movement. CIO-sponsored "sit-down strikes" began at the General Motors plant in Flint, Michigan, in 1937. Fearful that efforts to clear the plant of striking workers would lead to sabotage, most employers capitulated to the union. The major steel companies recognized the CIO and granted higher wages and a 40-hour work week.

Though business conditions had improved since 1933, a "Roosevelt recession" developed in 1937. Roosevelt thereafter committed himself to heavy deficit spending. Another public works bill was passed, and a second AAA established marketing quotas and acreage limits for growers of staple crops. The Commodity Credit Corporation was empowered to lend money to farmers on their surplus crops. The Fair Labor Standards Act abolished child labor and established a national minimum wage of 40 cents an hour and a maximum work week of 40 hours, with time and a half for overtime.

When conservative Democrats raised objections to the New Deal, Roosevelt tried to "purge" them from the party. His intervention in various Democratic primary elections was flatly rebuffed by voters. Southerners in particular supported Roosevelt but resented his intervention

in their primaries. Anti-New Deal Democrats increasingly joined with Republicans, strengthened by the 1938 mid-term elections, into a "conservative coalition."
The conservatives failed to do away with accomplished reforms but succeeded in blocking additional legislation.

### Significance of the New Deal

The Great Depression finally ended when a massive war that broke out in Europe mobilized the world economy. At times Roosevelt favored deficit spending to check the depression; on other occasions, he proposed balanced budgets. The New Deal sometimes viewed the major economic problem as overproduction, and at other times suggested that the answer lay in more production. The New Deal in retrospect committed the nation to the idea that the federal government should accept responsibility for the national welfare and act to meet problems. New Deal programs, which vastly enlarged the federal bureaucracy, were increasingly accepted by both parties and may have prevented later declines from becoming catastrophes.

### Women as New Dealers: The Network

Women played an active role in the administration due to the influence of Molly Dewson, head of the Women's Division of the Democratic National Committee, and Secretary of Labor Frances Perkins, the first woman in the Cabinet.

First Lady Eleanor Roosevelt was a force in her own right through her newspaper column, "My Day," and as a speaker on public issues. She was particularly identified with efforts to obtain better treatment for blacks. In 1939, Mrs. Roosevelt resigned from the Daughters of the American Revolution after the group had refused to permit the use of its Washington auditorium for a concert by the black contralto, Marian Anderson. The President then arranged for Anderson to sing at the Lincoln Memorial.

### Blacks During the New Deal

Although blacks had supported Hoover's reelection, they voted overwhelmingly for Roosevelt in 1936. New Deal programs benefited many blacks though they were often paid at lower rates than whites under NRA codes. Blacks in the CCC were assigned to segregated units. Social Security excluded from coverage agricultural laborers and domestic servants, many of whom were minorities. In 1936, Roosevelt named Mary McLeod Bethune, founder of Bethune-Cookman College in Florida, to head the Division of Negro Affairs in the National Youth Administration, a position from which she developed educational and occupational programs for disadvantaged black youngsters.

## A New Deal for Indians

In 1924, Congress granted citizenship to all Indians, who continued to be treated as wards of the state. Indian Affairs Commissioner John Collier tried to preserve Indian culture, obtain jobs for Indians, and utilize modern medical advances and techniques of soil conservation. The Indian Reorganization Act of 1934 abolished the Dawes Act allotment system and encouraged Indians to return individually owned land to their tribes. Some Indians opposed the return of their lands to communal holdings, particularly those whose lands held oil and mineral rights. The New Deal provided relief to needy Indians living on reservations. Some critics charged Collier with segregating the Indians, whereas others accused him of promoting "pagan" practices and even trying to convert the Indians to "communism."

## The Role of Roosevelt

Brain Truster Rexford Tugwell found Roosevelt to be not "much at home with ideas" but always open to new facts and willing to take chances on potential solutions to problems. Roosevelt has been criticized for his lack of knowledge of economics, his vague political philosophy, and his administrative abilities. He encouraged rivalry among subordinates, assigned different agencies with overlapping responsibilities, failed to discharge incompetents, and delayed making important decisions.

Nevertheless, Roosevelt's fireside chats and bi-weekly press conferences convinced most that he had their welfare at heart. Roosevelt hence personified the government to the masses of citizens.

## The Triumph of Isolationism

While most Americans embraced isolationism, Roosevelt was already an internationalist. Isolationism seemed the dominant national view as a result of an investigation conducted by Senator Gerald P. Nye of North Dakota into the role played by munitions makers and bankers from 1914 to 1917. Some claimed that a "conspiracy" had dragged America into World War I.

Congress passed the Neutrality Act of 1935, which forbade the sale of munitions to all belligerents whenever the president should proclaim that a state of war existed. Thereafter, Italy invaded Ethiopia, and civil war broke out in Spain between the forces of General Francisco Franco, backed by Italy and Germany, and the leftist Spanish Republic, backed by communists. Congress therefore amended the Neutrality Act to cover civil wars.

## War Again in Europe

Roosevelt concluded that resisting aggression was more important than maintaining neutrality. In a 1937 speech, he had declared that the way to deal with "the epidemic of world lawlessness" was to "quarantine" it. Yet few seemed to follow the president's leadership away from isolationism.

The world moved closer to war when Japan again attacked China, and Nazi Germany demanded in 1938 that Czechoslovakia cede the German-speaking Sudetenland. Roosevelt was unable to obtain repeal of the Neutrality Act so that the United States could sell arms to Britain and France in the event of war. In August 1939, Germany and Russia signed a nonaggression pact, a prelude to their joint assault on Poland.

Hitler's troops invaded Poland on September 1, at last provoking Britain and France into a declaration of war. Congress then permitted the sale of arms on a cash-and-carry basis, but American vessels were forbidden to trade with the belligerents. Poland quickly fell to Hitler's army, and after a winter lull that cynics called the "phony war," the *Blitzkrieg* swept through the Low Countries, Scandinavia, and France. The British army retreated from Dunkirk, and Hitler proceeded to bombard and starve the British into submission. Epic air battles over England during the summer of 1940 ended in Nazi defeat, but the Royal Navy could not halt German submarine attacks.

Roosevelt transferred 50 overage destroyers to the British in exchange for naval bases. To strengthen national unity, he brought two Republicans, Henry Stimson and Frank Knox, into his Cabinet as secretary of war and navy, respectively. By September 1940, the first peacetime draft in American history was affecting 1.2 million men.


**A Third Term for FDR**

Roosevelt cast aside the two-term precedent set by George Washington to seek a third term. Vice-President Garner, disenchanted with Roosevelt and the New Deal, refused to run again. Roosevelt therefore dictated the selection of Agriculture Secretary Henry Wallace as Garner's successor.

The Republicans rejected both major announced candidates, Robert Taft of Ohio and Thomas E. Dewey of New York, and nominated a "dark horse" and former Democrat, Wendell Willkie, the Indiana-born utilities executive who had opposed the TVA. Roosevelt won rather handily despite Willkie's claim that the nation was headed to war.

Two competing groups quarreled over the proper U.S. policy. The Committee to Defend America by Aiding the Allies favored all-out aid to Britain, and the America First Committee, which included aviator Charles Lindbergh, took an isolationist stance.


**The Undeclared War**

When Winston Churchill informed Roosevelt that the "cash-and-carry" system was insufficient for British security needs, Roosevelt persuaded Congress to enact the Lend-Lease Act. The measure called for spending $7 billion for war materials that the president could sell, lend, lease, exchange, or transfer to any country whose defense he deemed vital to that of the United States.

Most of the aid went to Britain, but by November 1941, $1 billion was put at the disposal of the Soviets, who had been invaded by the Nazis in spite of the Hitler-Stalin nonaggression pact. After attacks on two American ships, the *Greer* and the *Reuben James*, Congress allowed the arming of merchant ships and permitted them to carry cargoes to Allied ports. For all practical purposes, the United States was already at war.

## People, Places and Things

*Identify the following concepts:*

- bank holiday _____
  _____

- Hundred Days _____
  _____

- fireside chats _____
  _____

- parity _____
  _____

- TVA "yardstick" _____
  _____

- interest-group democracy _____
  _____

- old-age revolving pensions _____
  _____

- payroll tax _____
  _____

- "economic royalists" _____
  _____

court-packing scheme _____

_____

• sit-down strikes _____

_____

destroyers-for-bases deal _____

_____

dark horse _____

_____

*Describe the following*:

FDIC _____

_____

CCC _____

_____

NRA _____

_____

AAA _____

_____

TVA _____

_____

WPA _____

_____

U.S.A. _____

_____

"Share the Wealth" movement _____

_____

Social Security Act _____

_____

*Schechter v. United States* _____

_____

NLRB _____

_____

REA _____

_____

CIO _____

_____

Fair Labor Standards Act _____

_____

"Quarantine" speech _____

_____

Sudetenland _____

_____

Lend-Lease Act _____

_____

*Greer* _____

_____

*Identify the following people:*

Henry A. Wallace _____

_____

Wendell L. Willkie _____

_____

Harry L. Hopkins _____

_____

Huey P. Long _____

_____

Charles Coughlin _____

_____

Alfred M. Landon _____

_____

Hugo L. Black _____

_____

Eleanor Roosevelt _____

_____

Frances Perkins _____

_____

Gerald P. Nye _____

_____

Francisco Franco _____

_____

John L. Lewis _____

_____

Winston Churchill _____

_____

William Faulkner _____

_____

## Map Exercise

Refer to the map on the following page. Match the country or region with its location as designated on the map.

____1. Austria      ____7. Italy
____2. Belgium      ____8. Norway
____3. Denmark      ____9. Poland
____4. France      ____10. Spain
____5. Great Britain      ____11. Sudetenland
____6. Holland

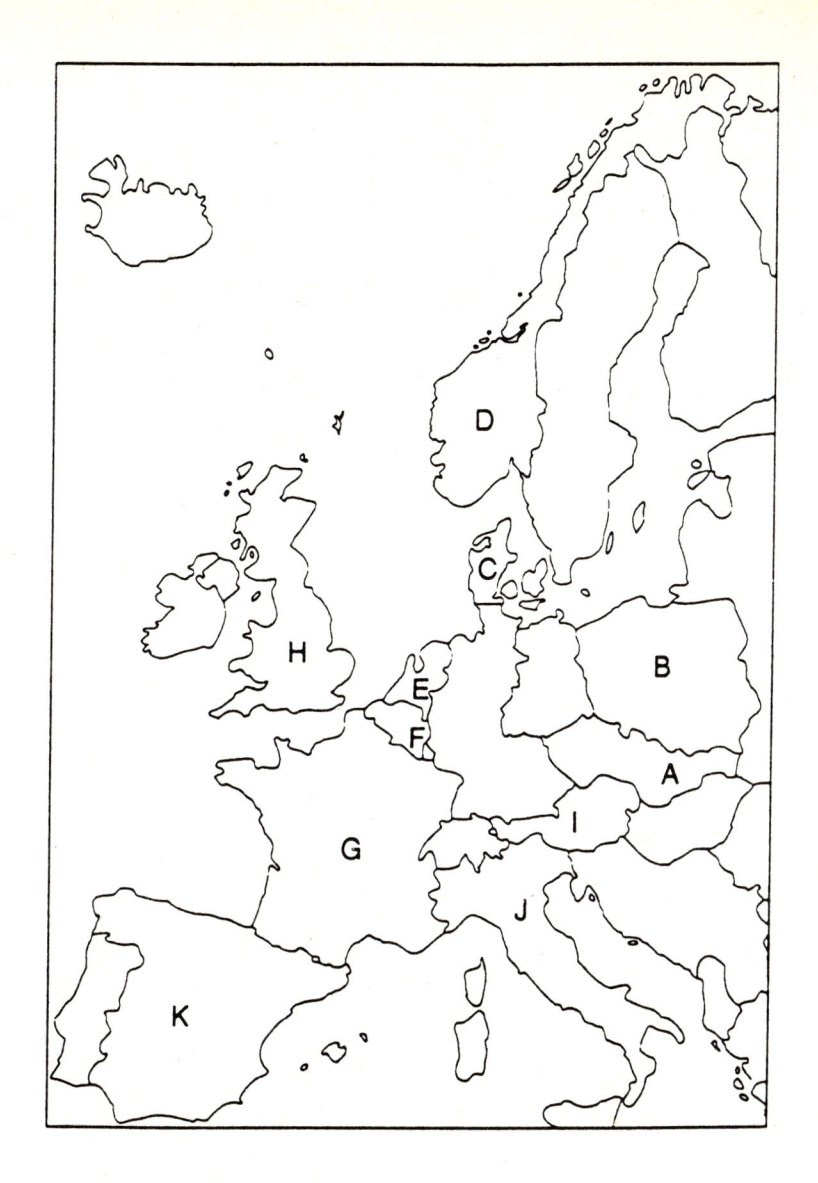

## Self-Test

### Multiple-Choice Questions

1.  Which of the following was *not* part of the Roosevelt administration?
    - A. John Nance Garner
    - B. Henry A. Wallace
    - C. Frances Perkins
    - D. Charles Lindbergh

183

2. FDIC is involved in what field?
   A. Banking
   B. Stock market
   C. Agriculture
   D. Manufacturing

3. The AAA of 1933 included all of the following *except*:
   A. Restrictions on production with subsides to growers of wheat, cotton, tobacco, and pork
   B. Rental payments to farmers for removing land from production
   C. A tax on farm processors
   D. A guarantee of parity

4. The NRA approved business codes if all of the following conditions were met *except*:
   A. Marketing quotas
   B. Maximum hours and minimum wage limits
   C. Elimination of child labor
   D. Guarantees of collective bargaining to unions

5. The NRA was declared unconstitutional because it:
   A. Accented production quotas
   B. Gave legislative authority to an executive agency
   C. Levied a questionable tax on farm producers
   D. Was an executive order, not congressional law

6. The TVA was initially involved in all of these activities *except*:
   A. Oil drilling
   B. Navigation
   C. Recreation
   D. Sale of electricity

7. The Wagner Act:
   A. Gave organized labor the right to bargain collectively
   B. Authorized "sit-down" strikes
   C. Forbade the United States from transferring arms to Britain
   D. Sought to curb the role of bankers and munitions makers who had profited from World War I

8. Unemployment insurance is part of which program?
   A. Fair Labor Standards Act
   B. Wagner Act
   C. National Labor Relations Act
   D. Social Security Act

9. Which of these was *not* an "extremist" critic of Roosevelt?
   A. Rexford Tugwell
   B. Charles Coughlin
   C. Francis Townsend
   D. William Lemke

10. Roosevelt could ultimately claim credit in the dispute over the Supreme Court because:
    A. Congress impeached two justices who had thwarted New Deal programs
    B. Congress enlarged the Court three years after the "court-packing" dispute
    C. The Court gradually shifted to the political left with the appointments of Justices Hugo L. Black and William O. Douglas
    D. The Court struck down the "conservative coalition"

11. The first permanent federal minimum wage was fixed at:
    A. 10 cents an hour
    B. 25 cents an hour
    C. 40 cents an hour
    D. $1 an hour

12. John Collier:
    A. Attempted to improve life for American Indians
    B. Headed the National Youth Administration
    C. Advised Roosevelt on economic policies
    D. Organized the Committee to Defend America by Aiding the Allies

13. John Steinbeck's most acclaimed novel is:
    A. *The Grapes of Wrath*
    B. *The Web and the Rock*
    C. *Sanctuary*
    D. *Tortilla Flat*

14. William Faulkner wrote all of the following *except*:
    A. *The Sound and the Fury*
    B. *Sanctuary*
    C. *U.S.A.*
    D. *As I Lay Dying*

15. Roosevelt's "Hundred Days" did *not* include the:
    A. Social Security Act
    B. Federal Deposit Insurance Corporation
    C. Home Owners Loan Corporation
    D. Federal Securities Act

16. The economist who advocated deficit spending was:
    A. Henry Morgenthau, Jr.
    B. John Maynard Keynes
    C. Raymond Moley
    D. Adam Smith

17. Social Security is financed by:
    A. A joint tax on wages and payrolls
    B. A tax on food processors
    C. Direct levies on business
    D. Income taxes

18. The Nazi invasion of Poland:
    A. Voided the nonaggression pact with the Soviets
    B. Started World War II
    C. Led the United States to revise its neutrality laws
    D. Led to the Munich Conference

19. Most Lend-Lease aid went to:
    A. Spain and Italy
    B. Britain and the Soviet Union
    C. France and Sweden
    D. Japan and Canada

20. During the 1930s, the lowest level of unemployment was:
    A. 5 percent
    B. 10 percent
    C. 15 percent
    D. 20 percent

## Essay Questions

1. Explain how the NRA, AAA, and TVA sought to revive the economy during the Great Depression. Evaluate each program.

2. Show how the "Second New Deal" promoted reforms that still affect workers and consumers.

3. Explain why many regard the New Deal as a success even though it did not end the depression.

4. Using specific examples, evaluate the impact of the New Deal on women, blacks, and Indians.

5. Discuss the elections of 1936 and 1940 regarding parties nominees, issues, outcomes, and significance. Why had Franklin Roosevelt become unbeatable in national elections?

## Critical Thinking Exercise

Label each of the following statements that refer to the New Deal as "T" for true, "F" for false, or "O" for opinion.

____1. Roosevelt reversed the thrust of NRA because he had increasing troubles both with business interests and the Supreme Court.

____2. Roosevelt's attempt to purge his party of reactionaries in the 1938 campaign strengthened the hand of liberals.

____3. Roosevelt's fireside chats convinced many that he had each citizen's welfare in mind.

____4. Had he attempted to do so, Roosevelt was the one president who could have convinced Americans to abandon free enterprise in favor of socialism.

____5. "Roosevelt was not really very much at home with ideas."

____6. The national government should work diligently to remedy specific social problems.

____7. Roosevelt's practice of dividing authority among competing administrators gave the national government remarkable flexibility.

____8. Roosevelt's handling of the depression and World War II clearly make him the singlemost outstanding president, eclipsing even Washington and Lincoln.

____9. New Deal programs succeeded in reducing national unemployment to historic low levels.

____10. One legacy of the New Deal was to strengthen the hold of interest groups over the government.

____11. New Deal programs probably kept many intellectuals from falling into even deeper despair during the turbulent 1930s.

____12. Roosevelt repudiated the Keynesian doctrine that deficit spending could stimulate a lagging economy.

CHAPTER 28

# War and Peace

## Learning Objectives

*After reading Chapter 28, you should be able to:*

1. Explain how and why the attack on Pearl Harbor led to United States entry in World War II.
2. Show how World War II changed the American home front.
3. Explain how the war affected blacks, Hispanics, and Indians.
4. Describe the treatment of Japanese-Americans in the war.
5. Evaluate the contribution of women to the war effort.
6. Outline the European and Pacific war strategy and tactics.
7. Show how the atomic bomb helped to end the war.
8. Offer contrasting views over how the Cold War developed.
9. Explain the significance of Yalta and Potsdam to the postwar international order.

## Overview

**The Road to Pearl Harbor**

Secretary of State Cordell Hull demanded that Japan withdraw from China and not attack the French and Dutch colonies in Southeast Asia. Japan might have accepted limited annexations in return for the removal of American trade restrictions. However, Hitler's invasion of the Soviet Union in mid-1941 removed the threat of Russian intervention in the Far East. Therefore, Japan occupied Indochina despite the risk of war with the United States.

Roosevelt retaliated by freezing Japanese assets and placing an embargo on oil. Japan agreed to refrain from renewed expansion in Indochina if the United States and Britain would lift their economic blockade and halt aid to China. When America rejected such demands, Japan prepared to attack the Dutch East Indies, British Malaya, and the Philippines.

Attempting to immobilize the United States Pacific fleet, Japan launched a surprise aerial raid on the naval base at Pearl Harbor, Hawaii. The American commanders, Admiral Husband Kimmel and General Walter Short, had taken precautions against sabotage but were unprepared for an aerial attack. On the morning of December 7, 1941, Japanese planes reduced the Pacific fleet to a smoking ruin: 2,300 servicemen were killed, 1,100 were wounded, and 150 planes were destroyed. The next day Congress declared war on Japan. The Axis powers honored their obligations to Japan and declared war on the United States on December 11.

## Mobilizing the Home Front

About 15 million men and women who entered the armed services had to be fed, clothed, housed, and supplied with equipment ranging from typewriters to airplanes. Congress granted President Roosevelt wide emergency powers and did not meddle in military strategy or administrative problems, which abounded due to confusion, inefficiency, and bickering within the bureaucracy. Roosevelt attempted to pay a large part of the costs of the war by collecting taxes, rather than by borrowing. He moved to base taxation on the ability to pay, to ration scarce raw materials and consumer goods, and to regulate wages and prices. The war stimulated the gross national product, which increased from $91.3 billion in 1939 to $166.6 billion by 1945. Though 8 million were unemployed in June 1940, unemployment disappeared after Pearl Harbor.

## The War Economy

Supreme Court Justice James F. Byrnes assumed the role of an "economic czar" through management of the Office of War Mobilization, which set priorities and prices. Rents, food prices, and wages were strictly regulated; items in short supply were rationed. Wages and prices soared during 1942 but stabilized in 1943, scarcely changing until controls were lifted after the war.

Increased factory output and conscription caused a labor shortage, which augmented the bargaining power of organized labor. The National War Labor Board arbitrated disputes and stabilized wages.

The standard of living for most workers improved during the war though gasoline rationing made pleasure driving nearly impossible. Plastics replaced metals in many items. Rationed items were given in amounts adequate for the needs of most, and America had both guns and butter. Heavy borrowing was undertaken because government spending doubled between 1941 and 1945.

To ensure collection of taxes, Congress adopted the payroll-deduction system under which employers withheld the taxes owed by workers from their paychecks and turned the money over to the government.

## War and Social Change

The war vastly increased the mobility of the American people. Not only were service personnel transported around the world, but new defense plants drew workers to such places as Oak Ridge, Tennessee, where an atomic energy plant opened. Although the population had risen by only 3 million in the 1930s; it increased by 6.5 million from 1940 to 1945, augmented by rising marriage and birth rates.

## Minorities in Time of War: Blacks, Hispanics, and Indians

Black leaders stressed the inconsistency of fighting for democracy abroad while minorities were denied civil rights at home. The treatment of blacks in the military improved compared to the situation in World War I, and the first black general was commissioned. Segregation was maintained in the armed forces, and black soldiers were often given inferior facilities in army camps, especially in the South.

More than 5 million blacks moved from rural areas to cities between 1940 and 1945 in search of work. A. Philip Randolph, president of the Brotherhood of Sleeping Car Porters, organized a march on Washington in 1941 to demand equality for blacks. Roosevelt responded with the Fair Employment Practices Committee, which prohibited discrimination in plants operating under defense contracts.

Blacks often found the welcome mat withdrawn as they moved to the North. In 1943, a bloody race riot broke out in Detroit; by the time federal troops restored order, 25 blacks and 9 whites lay dead. In Los Angeles attacks occurred on Hispanic "zoot suiters," gangs who wore broad-brimmed fedoras, long coats, and pegged trousers.

Black attitudes toward the war hardened. Some conservatives demanded that black editors critical of Roosevelt be indicted for sedition. Roosevelt misjudged the depth of black anger and urged black leaders to hold their demands in abeyance until after the war.

The war encouraged assimilation of the Indians, more than 24,000 of whom served in the armed forces. Thousands left the reservations to work in defense plants.

## The Treatment of German-, Italian-, and Japanese-Americans

Americans of German and Italian ancestry opposed the Hitler and Mussolini governments and were sufficiently assimilated into the population to protect themselves against abuse during the war.

Intolerance flared in the relocation of the West Coast Japanese in internment camps in Wyoming, Arizona, and other interior states. About 110,000 Americans of Japanese ancestry were sent into such camps against their will and despite the fact that they had committed no crime nor expressed disloyalty to the United States. The internment camps were established in a climate of fear stemming from the attack on Pearl Harbor. The Supreme Court upheld the relocation order in *Korematsu v. United States*, but near the end of the war, in *Ex Parte Endo* it forbade the internment of loyal Japanese-American citizens. Those interned were finally compensated by Congress in 1990.

## Women's Contribution to the War Effort

The need for women workers mushroomed when servicemen went to war. By 1945, more than 19 million women were employed. Additional thousands served in the Women's Auxiliary Air Corps and in naval, marine, and air corps auxiliaries. Although some men objected to their wives taking jobs, labor needs and the employer's willingness to hire women prevailed. Women worked as riveters, cab drivers, welders, machine tool operators and in other occupations formerly the domain of men. "War brides" faced the problems of limited housing and loneliness created by their husbands being away. Women had to deal with shortages, ration books, and other inconveniences.

## Allied Strategy: Europe First

Hitler's armies, which had reached Leningrad and Moscow, prepared for an assault on Stalingrad on the Volga River in 1942. German divisions under General Erwin Rommel began a drive across North Africa to the Suez Canal. U-boats were taking a toll in the North Atlantic, and Japan was overrunning the Far East. Military strategists concentrated first on Europe because Japan's conquests were in remote regions. If Russia surrendered, Hitler might be able to invade Britain.

In late 1942, an Allied army commanded by General Dwight D. Eisenhower struck at French North Africa. The French Vichy commandant, a Nazi collaborationist named Admiral Jean Darlan, switched sides when Eisenhower landed. The Allies defeated Rommel's Afrika Korps by early 1943. Air attacks on Germany continued, and the Russians pushed the Germans back from Stalingrad.

Meanwhile, the Allies invaded Sicily from Africa and proceeded to the Italian mainland. Despite Mussolini's fall from power, the campaign in Italy required months of fighting across the rugged Italian peninsula. Monte Cassino, halfway between Naples and Rome did not fall until May 1944. The capital itself was taken a month later. The Italian campaign was discouraging to the Allies though it weakened the enemy.

## Germany Overwhelmed

The Allies landed along the coast of Normandy, France, on June 6, 1944, thereby launching the second European front of the war. This liberation of France was a striking success. The American Third Army under General George S. Patton moved from Brittany and then veered eastward toward Paris. By September the Allies were fighting on the edge of Germany.

On December 16, the Nazis launched a counterattack, hoping to break through to Antwerp, Belgium, and split the Allied armies in two. The Germans drove about 50 miles into Belgium, but once the element of surprise had been overcome, their advance collapsed. This "Battle of the Bulge" delayed Eisenhower's offensive and cost the United States 77,000 casualties, but it exhausted Germany's last reserves.

The Allies pressed to the Rhine, and German cities fell almost daily. Americans then overran Nazi concentration camps where some 6 million Jews had been slaughtered. Roosevelt did not order the removal of refugees and refused to bomb the death camps, such as Auschwitz in Poland, on grounds that the destruction of German soldiers and military equipment took priority over any other objective.

With Russian shells reducing Germany to ruins, Hitler took his own life in his Berlin air raid shelter. On May 8, 1945 (V-E Day), Germany surrendered.

**The Naval War in the Pacific**

The Navy's aircraft carriers had escaped destruction at Pearl Harbor. Commanders discovered that carrier-based planes were more effective against warships than the heaviest naval artillery because of their greater range and concentrated firepower. In the Battle of the Coral Sea in May 1942, Japan tried to cut off Australia from American aid. Though Japan damaged the American carrier *Lexington* and sank two other ships, her troop transports were forced to turn back.

Japan then proceeded to Midway Island, where Americans destroyed four Japanese carriers and some 300 planes. The United States lost only the carrier *Yorktown* and a destroyer. The tide had turned, but victory came slowly.

General Douglas MacArthur, American commander in the Philippines, fought the Japanese at Manila until Roosevelt had him evacuated by PT boat to escape capture. Thereafter, MacArthur led an American army back to the Philippines. A second drive under Admiral Chester Nimitz was undertaken across the Central Pacific toward Tokyo.

**Island Hopping**

America proceeded to eject the Japanese from the Solomon Islands to protect Australia from attack. In August 1942, a series of land, sea, and air battles raged around Guadalcanal Island. Once again American air power was decisive. Meanwhile, Nimitz led the campaign to liberate the Gilbert and Marshall islands, where enemy soldiers fought like the Spartans at Thermopylae for every foot of ground. Resisting surrender, the Japanese had to be blasted and burned from tunnels, but in every case Nimitz's forces prevailed. MacArthur leapfrogged along the New Guinea coast toward the Philippines and landed on Leyte. There his forces destroyed Japan's seapower and reduced its air force to a band of kamikazes. MacArthur liberated Manila in February 1945. Iwo Jima and Okinawa subsequently fell to the Americans, but Japan still showed no willingness to surrender.

**"The Shatterer of Worlds"**

In 1944, Roosevelt was elected to a fourth term, easily defeating New York Republican Governor Thomas E. Dewey. The Democrats nominated Missouri Senator Harry S. Truman for vice-president, rejecting the controversial incumbent, Henry Wallace. With Roosevelt's sudden death of a cerebral hemorrhage in April 1945, Truman was hence thrust into the presidency.

Government-sponsored atomic research had been underway since 1939. Some $2 billion was spent before a successful bomb was exploded at Alamogordo, New Mexico, on July 16, 1945, under the direction of J. Robert Oppenheimer. Truman, who believed that use of the bomb would bring the war to an end and in the long run save American lives, warned Japan of the consequences of carrying on the struggle.

When Japan ignored the admonition, the Superfortress *Enola Gay* on August 6 dropped an atomic bomb on Hiroshima. The weapon took 78,000 lives and injured another 100,000. When Japan still hesitated to surrender, a second bomb blasted Nagasaki three days later. Thus ended the greatest war of history. As many as 20 million persons had been killed, including nearly 300,000 Americans.

Despite the destruction, the postwar years seemed promising because fascism had been annihilated, the communists promised cooperation in rebuilding Europe, and isolationism had vanished in America. The great powers moreover signed the United Nations charter, drafted at San Francisco in June 1945.


## Wartime Diplomacy

Americans naively failed to understand that Joseph Stalin, *Time* magazine's 1943 "Man of the Year," was as brutal as Hitler and Mussolini. The media had downplayed differences between the United States and its Soviet allies during the war. Former Ambassador Joseph E. Davies claimed that Stalin was committed to Jesus's teachings on the "brotherhood of man." Wendell Willkie's *One World* hailed the Russian people and their "effective society."

At the conference in Yalta, Ukraine, the Americans, British, and Soviets called for drafting a charter for the United Nations. The locus of authority in the new organization lay in the 11-member Security Council, over which any of the great powers could block UN action through the power of veto. The UN which America joined ironically incorporated most of the same limitations that Henry Cabot Lodge had proposed in his 1919 reservations to Article X of the League of Nations Covenant.


## Mounting Suspicions

The term "Cold War" refers to the four decades of postwar tensions between the United States and the Soviet Union. Americans felt compelled to halt the spread of communism out of fear that the Soviets were intent on world domination. An alternative view maintains that the Soviets, who endured assault by the Nazis and suffered the greatest numerical losses of the war, sought to protect themselves against another possible invasion.

Roosevelt admitted privately during the war that the Soviet Union would annex territory and possess preponderant power in eastern Europe, but publicly he held out hope that the Soviets would permit the promised free elections. Such elections were not held until 1990.

### Yalta and Potsdam

At the Yalta Conference, Roosevelt and Churchill agreed to Soviet annexation of large sections of eastern Poland in exchange for the unfulfilled promise of free Polish elections. Roosevelt feared that Polish-Americans would be irate if the Soviets took over their homeland. Shortly before his death, Roosevelt conceded that he could not "do business" with Stalin, who continued to hold eastern Europe in check.

In July 1945, President Truman met at Potsdam (near Berlin) with Stalin and Clement Attlee, the incoming British prime minister who had succeeded Churchill. The Allies agreed to try the Nazi leaders as war criminals and approved the division of Germany into four occupation zones held by the Americans, the French, the British, and the Soviets.

The war thrust Britain and France to the status of second-class powers, while the Americans and Soviets, the "superpowers," were destined to compete in the coming decades for power and influence.

## People, Places, and Things

*Identify the following concepts:*

cryptanalyst _____

_____

economic czar _____

_____

payroll-deduction system _____

_____

"guns and butter" _____

_____

zoot suit _____

_____

internment camp _____

_____

collaborationist _____

_____

*kamikazes* _____

_____

island hopping _____

_____

Cold War _____

_____

cerebral hemorrhage _____

_____

*Describe the following*:

Oak Ridge _____

_____

FEPC _____

_____

*Korematsu v. United States* _____

_____

Atlantic Charter _____

_____

Stalingrad _____

_____

Kasserine Pass _____

Afrika Korps _____

D-Day _____

"Battle of the Bulge" _____

Leyte _____

Iwo Jima _____

*Enola Gay* _____

Hiroshima _____

*One World* _____

Yalta Conference _____

Potsdam _____

*Identify the following people:*

Walter C. Short _____

_____

James F. Byrnes _____

_____

A. Philip Randolph _____

_____

Charles Drew _____

_____

Erwin Rommel _____

_____

Dwight David Eisenhower _____

_____

Douglas MacArthur _____

_____

Thomas E. Dewey _____

_____

Joseph Stalin _____

_____

Harry Truman _____

_____

Clement Attlee _____

_____

Albert Einstein _____

_____

## Map Exercise

Refer to the Pacific map on the following page. Place the correct letter beside the choice that represents the location of the following:

____1. Dutch East Indies

____2. Gilbert Islands

____3. Guadalcanal

____4. Hawaii

____5. Indochina

____6. Iwo Jima

____7. Luzon

____8. Malaya

____9. Marshall Islands

____10. Midway Island

____11. Mindanao

____12. Okinawa

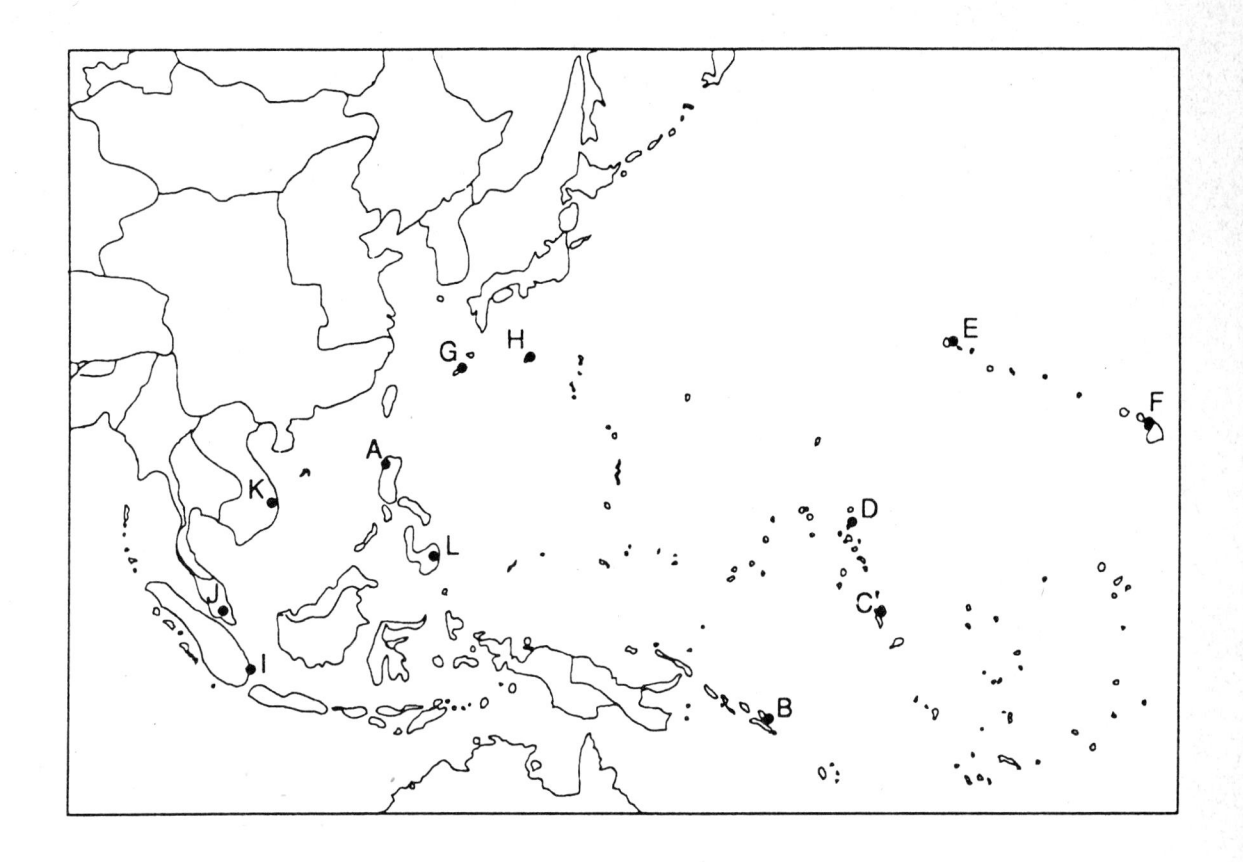

Refer to the European map on the following page. Place the correct letter beside the choice that corresponds with the location of the following:

____ 1. Belgium

____ 2. Berlin

____ 3. El Alamein

____ 4. Naples

____ 5. Netherlands

____ 6. Normandy

____ 7. Poland

____ 8. Rome

____ 9. Sicily

____ 10. Stalingrad

____ 11. Switzerland

____ 12. Vichy

199

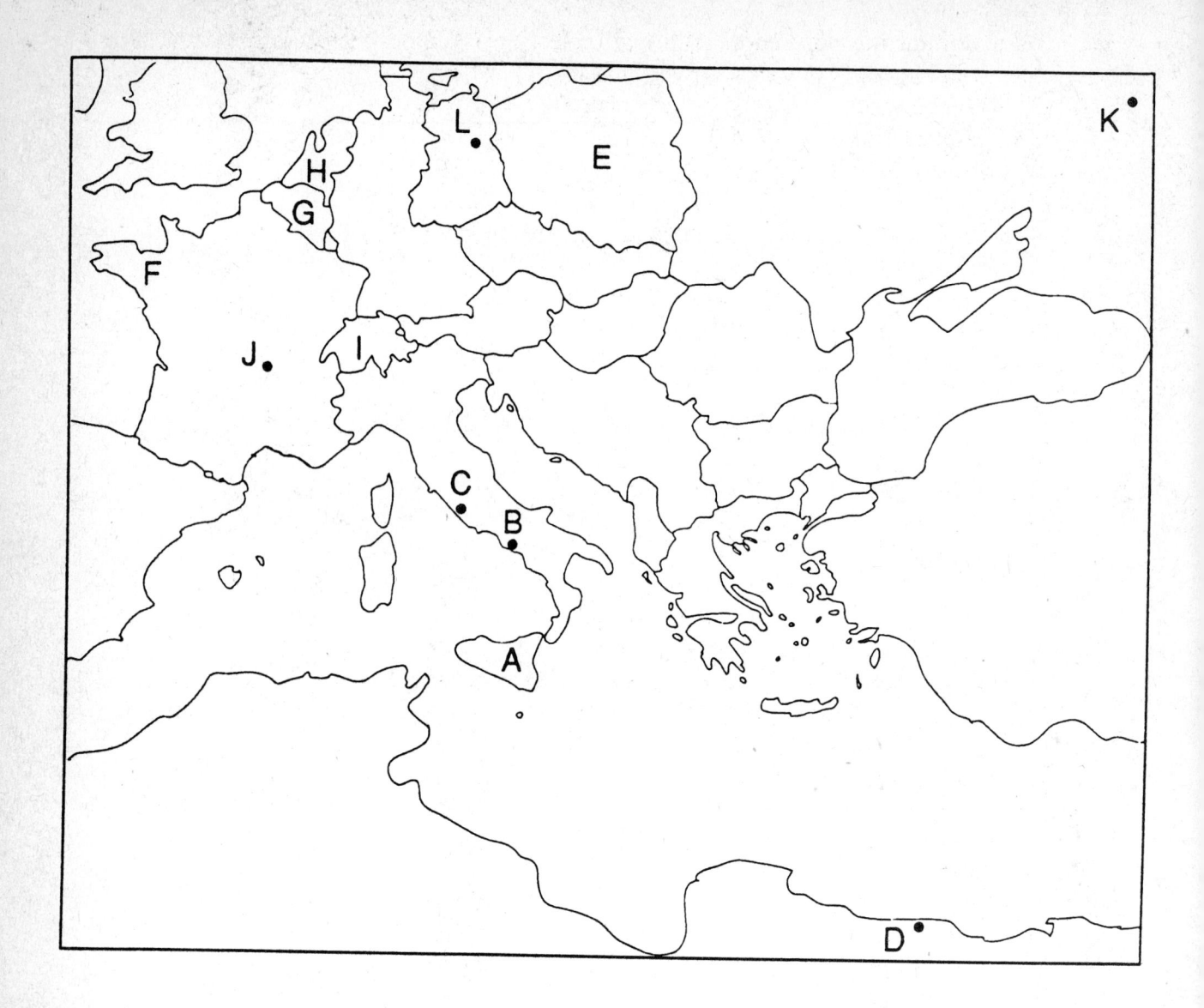

## Self-Test

**Multiple-Choice Questions**

1. At the height of its power, Japan controlled all of the following *except*:
   A. Philippines
   B. Guam
   C. Indochina
   D. Australia

2. What admiral was accused of failing to protect Pearl Harbor from Japanese attack?
   A. Jean Darlan
   B. Walter Short
   C. William Halsey
   D. Husband Kimmel

3. Winston Churchill, in fighting the war, insisted upon:
   A. Using the atomic bomb on Nazi Germany
   B. Opening a second front through Sicily and Italy
   C. Voiding the U.S.-Soviet alliance
   D. Support for the anti-Nazi French

4. Joseph Stalin obtained control over eastern Europe through the conference at:
   A. Washington
   B. Yalta
   C. Potsdam
   D. Teheran

5. The Cold War refers to:
   A. Fighting in northern Siberia during World War II
   B. Rivalry between France and Britain in the postwar era
   C. Ongoing tensions between the Soviets and the West, particularly the United States, after World War II
   D. American "island hopping" in the Pacific

6. All of the following were agreed upon at Potsdam *except*:
   A. Four occupation zones in Germany
   B. Plans for collecting German reparations
   C. Free elections in Poland
   D. Trying certain Nazi leaders as war criminals

7. Roosevelt won his *fourth* term by defeating:
   A. Henry Wallace
   B. Thomas Dewey
   C. Wendell Willkie
   D. Alfred Landon

8. American leaders had presumed an attack such as the one on Pearl Harbor would probably have occurred in:
   A. China
   B. The Philippines
   C. California
   D. Midway

9. In 1943 one of the worst racial riots in United States history swept through:
   A. New Orleans
   B. Philadelphia
   C. Detroit
   D. Los Angeles

10. For the Russians, the *most* important battle of World War II was waged in:
    A. Tokyo
    B. Moscow
    C. Leningrad
    D. Stalingrad

11. How did Dwight Eisenhower justify his 1942 arrangement with Admiral Jean Darlan?
    A. The Germans had already overrun Italy and were pressing toward Sicily.
    B. Eisenhower was able to press quickly across North Africa against the Germans because he did not first have to fight Vichy forces.
    C. Eisenhower knew the Allies were no match for the Afrika Korps.
    D. The arrangement would postpone the need for an Allied invasion of France.

12. Commanders in World War II found which of the following to be the *most* effective in fighting the war?
    A. Hand grenades
    B. Carrier-based planes
    C. Battleships
    D. Armored tanks

13. Douglas MacArthur was obsessed with leading American forces to regain control of:
    A. Japan
    B. Guadalcanal
    C. Midway
    D. The Philippines

14. The most glaring case of suppression of civil liberties during World War II dealt with:
    A. The internment of Japanese-Americans
    B. Imprisonment of communist leaders
    C. Jailing opponents to conscription
    D. Deporting Italian-Americans to Italy

15. The United States supported:
    A. The exiled Free French forces led by Charles de Gaulle
    B. Victory in Europe as the first priority
    C. A negotiated settlement with Japan after 1944
    D. Rommel's forces in North Africa

**Essay Questions**

1. Show how the breakdown of diplomacy between the United States and Japan culminated in the bombing of Pearl Harbor. Why was the United States unprepared for this disaster?

2. Explain how World War II finally pulled America out of the depths of the Great Depression. Exactly how was the home front mobilized?

3. Give specific examples of how minority groups, including blacks, Hispanics, and Japanese-Americans, fared during the war.

4. Explain how the Allies in Europe brought about the ultimate Nazi defeat.

5. Discuss "island hopping" in the Pacific theater and evaluate the strategic role of the atomic bomb in the conclusion of the war.

## Critical Thinking Exercise

Students sometimes confuse the two world wars. Place a Roman numeral "I" beside each statement that refers to World War I and a "II" beside each statement that refers to World War II. Place the letter "B" beside each statement that refers to both wars. Place the letter "N" beside each statement which refers to neither war.

_____ 1. American battle losses were more severe numerically than those of the European allies.

_____ 2. Germany wound up on the losing side of the war.

_____ 3. Poison gas was used in the war, one of the few times in history.

_____ 4. An international organization was proposed to establish permanent world peace after the war.

_____ 5. The American president spoke of "peace without victory."

_____ 6. America declared war only after an attack on her territory.

_____ 7. Italy switched sides during the war.

_____ 8. Mexico maintained neutrality in the war.

_____ 9. Switzerland maintained neutrality in the war.

_____10. Japan switched sides during the war.

_____11. Spain remained neutral during the war.

_____12. The French government at Vichy failed to obtain American and British recognition.

_____13. America began deducting income taxes from worker paychecks for the first time.

_____14. Japan was an enemy of China in the war.

_____15. Sweden was overrun by enemy armies in the war.

CHAPTER 29

# The American Century

## Learning Objectives

*After reading Chapter 29, you should be able to:*

1. Discuss changes in American life-styles that surfaced after World War II.
2. Understand the tenets of the containment policy.
3. Explain how America conducted foreign policy in the postwar years toward Japan, China, the Soviet Union, Britain, France, Germany, the Middle East, and Cuba.
4. Discuss ramifications of the Korean War to American policy.
5. Evaluate the anticommunist crusade of Senator Joseph McCarthy and its impact on civil liberties.
6. Compare and contrast the styles and philosophies of Presidents Truman and Eisenhower.
7. Explain how civil rights emerged as a political force in the 1950s and 1960s.
8. Analyze the elections of 1948 and 1960 as to nominees, issues, outcomes, and significance.

## Overview

### The Postwar Economy

President Truman slowly demobilized the armed forces in an attempt to prevent sudden economic dislocation. Most returning veterans hence found jobs because the demand for automobiles, homes, clothing, and appliances kept factories operating at capacity. The GI Bill of Rights offered subsidies to those wishing to continue their education, start businesses, or purchase homes.

Cutting taxes and the removal of rationing and price controls caused a period of rapid inflation. The economic turmoil enabled the Republicans to gain control of Congress in 1946 for the first time in sixteen years.

Overriding Truman's veto, Congress passed the Taft-Hartley Act, which forbade a national closed shop, the requirement that new workers join the union as a condition of employment. States could enact closed shop legislation or allow the open shop, under which workers have a choice of whether to join a union. Taft-Hartley outlawed secondary boycotts and strikes called due to disputes between unions over the right to represent workers. Most importantly, the law authorized the president to seek injunctions for up to 80 days (a "cooling-off" period) to halt strikes that endangered the national interest. Taft-Hartley made it more difficult to organize industries but did not weaken labor because it permitted union shop contracts, which forced workers into the union after accepting employment.

**Postwar Society: The Baby Boomers**

With the marriage rate soaring, the family again became the focus of a wholesome personal life in the postwar years. Income tax deductions encouraged taxpayers to have children and to borrow money to purchase houses and furniture.

The material progress of the new generation encouraged people to be conformists for the sakes of their families and employers. Many college-educated women sacrificed plans for a professional career to concentrate on home management and child development. The need to subordinate one's personal interests to the requirements of employers is described in William Whyte's *Organization Man* and in novels like Sloan Wilson's *The Man in the Grey Flannel Suit*.

**The Containment Policy**

The Soviet Union dominated eastern Europe, controlled Outer Mongolia, parts of Manchuria and northern Korea, and had annexed the Kurile Islands and regained the southern half of Sakhalin Island from Japan. It was further fomenting trouble in oil-rich Iran.

American and Soviet attitudes contrasted on the question of nuclear weapons. Atomic Energy Commissioner Bernard Baruch proposed outlawing such weapons under United Nations supervision, but the Soviets refused to permit the UN to inspect their stockpiles. When the West offered gestures of goodwill toward the Soviets, Stalin rebuffed them.

Because postwar cooperation failed, George F. Kennan, a Foreign Service officer, proposed a policy of "containment" by which the United States would prevent communism from spreading beyond its 1947 boundaries. Containment, which Kennan said could be a "duel of infinite duration," was tested when communists tried to overthrow the Greek monarchy. Because mounting financial pressures had forced the British to end aid to Greece, Congress appropriated $400 million under the Truman Doctrine to support "free peoples who are resisting attempted subjugation by armed minorities or by outside pressures." The result was the establishment of a military-dominated government in Greece. The Truman Doctrine also helped Turkey to overcome a similar communist threat.

**The Marshall Plan**

Kennan, moreover, proposed a broad program to finance European economic recovery. Secretary of State George C. Marshall outlined this "Marshall Plan" in the 1947 Harvard commencement address. After communists staged a coup in Czechoslovakia in 1948, drawing another country behind the "Iron Curtain," Congress appropriated over $13 billion through a 16-nation Committee for European Economic Cooperation. The results exceeded expectations; by 1951, western Europe was booming.

Meanwhile, a crisis over Berlin threatened the fragile peace. When the communists shut off access to West Berlin in a bid to starve the divided city into surrender, Truman ordered the airlifting of food, fuel, and other goods to maintain more than 2 million West Berliners. After a year the Soviets lifted their blockade.

## Dealing with Japan and China

President Truman decided not to allow the Soviet Union any significant role in the occupation of Japan, which was governed after the war by American troops commanded by General MacArthur. The Japanese, who showed remarkable adaptability amid military defeat, accepted political and social changes that involved universal suffrage, parliamentary government, and the deemphasis of the importance of the emperor. Though Japan lost its empire, the nation emerged economically strong, politically stable, and firmly allied with the United States.

China, however, was the scene of a prolonged conflict between communist forces loyal to Mao Tse-tung and the anticommunist nationals led by Chiang Kai-shek. Truman sent General Marshall to China to seek a settlment, but neither Mao nor Chiang would make concessions. After Marshall became secretary of state, civil war resumed in China.

## The Election of 1948

The Republican congressional victory in 1946, coupled with defections within the Democratic party, gave the GOP considerable hope of unseating Truman in 1948. South Carolina Governor (later Republican Senator) Strom Thurmond led a walkout of southern conservatives and ran as a States' Rights party nominee. Former Vice-President Henry Wallace, who claimed the containment policy was a threat to world peace, ran to Truman's left under a new Progressive banner. The Republicans again nominated the over-
confident New York Governor Thomas Dewey.

Truman's "give 'em hell" campaign stirred millions of voters, who supported the New Deal and who admired the President's fight against the odds. The success of the ongoing Berlin airlift moreover aided Truman in the election. Dewey's lackluster campaign failed to attract independents, and he actually polled fewer popular votes in 1948 than he had in 1944. To the surprise of the pollsters and nearly everyone except himself, Truman prevailed by 2.3 million popular votes and 114 electoral votes.

As Truman took office in his own right, he proposed the "Fair Deal," an extension of New Deal programs. Congress extended Social Security, increased the minimum wage, and funded housing programs.

## Containing Communism Abroad

In order to strengthen ties with the European democracies and to guarantee mutual security, the North Atlantic Treaty Organization was organized in 1949. Disturbed by news that the

Soviets had produced an atomic bomb, Congress appropriated $1.5 billion to arm NATO. General Eisenhower became the first NATO commander.

In Asia, communist armies of Mao Tse-tung drove the remnants of Chiang Kai-shek's forces to the island of Taiwan (formerly Formosa), amid cries by conservatives that Truman had not backed the nationalists with enough vigor and had underestimated Mao's commitment to world revolution.

## Hot War in Korea

In early 1950, Secretary of State Dean Acheson deliberately excluded Korea from what he described as the "defensive perimeter" of the United States in Asia. The perimeter included Japan, Taiwan, and the Philippines. In June the communist North Korean army crossed the 38th Parallel and overran South Korea.

With United Nations support but without a congressional declaration of war, Truman dispatched American troops to defend Korea. Sixteen nations nominally supported the UN mission under the command of General MacArthur, but more than 90 percent of the troops were American. MacArthur's forces fought successfully on two fronts about Pusan, at the southern tip of Korea, and Inchon, some 50 miles south of the 38th parallel. By October, MacArthur's forces had driven the communists out of South Korea. The general then gained permission to drive the communists off the entire Korean peninsula beyond the Yalu River, thereby risking Chinese intervention.

On November 26, 1950, 33 Chinese divisions smashed through MacArthur's line, and the once triumphant advance became a disorganized retreat. The UN army rallied south of the 38th Parallel, and by the spring of 1951 the front had been stabilized. MacArthur therefore asked that he be allowed to (1) bomb Chinese installations north of the Yalu, (2) blockade the coast of China, and (3) employ Chinese Nationalist troops in the war. When Truman rejected these proposals for fear that they might lead to a third world war, MacArthur appealed to the public and Congress over the commander-in-chief's head. Truman hence dismissed MacArthur for insubordination. In closing out his long military career, MacArthur delivered his "Old Soldiers Never Die" address before a joint session of Congress.

General Omar N. Bradley, chairman of the Joint Chiefs of Staff, however, explained that the showdown MacArthur proposed "would involve us in the wrong war, at the wrong place, at the wrong time, and with the wrong enemy." Armistice talks began in 1951 and dragged on for two years as thousands more died along the battlefront.

## The Communist Issue at Home

The Korean War highlighted the paradox that at the pinnacle of its power, the influence of the United States in world affairs was declining. Despite billions spent on armaments and foreign aid, national security seemed far from assured.

Furthermore, recurring communist espionage convinced many that conspirators were undermining American security. In 1947, Truman established the Loyalty Review Board, which discharged 2,700 government workers over a ten-year period for association with "totalitarian" or "subversive" organizations.

In 1948, former *Time* magazine editor Whittaker Chambers, a convert from communism, charged that Alger Hiss, president of the Carnegie Endowment for International Peace and a former State Department official, had been a communist in the 1930s. Hiss denied the charge and sued Chambers for libel. Chambers produced microfilm which revealed that Hiss had copied classified documents for dispatch to Moscow. Hiss could not be indicted for espionage due to the statute of limitations; instead he was indicted for perjury. His first trial ended in a hung jury, but his second trial, ending in January 1950, resulted in a five-year jail term.

Moreover, it was disclosed that three scientists, Klaus Fuchs of Britain and Julius and Ethel Rosenberg of the United States, had betrayed atomic secrets to the Soviets. The Rosenbergs were subsequently executed for treason in the summer of 1953.

## McCarthyism

In 1950, Wisconsin Senator Joseph R. McCarthy pressed the communists-in-government issue in a speech before the Women's Republican Club in Wheeling, West Virginia. McCarthy charged that the State Department was "infested" with at least 57 communists. The accusations, which were never proved, fed the worries of Americans fearful over Soviet power, the Korean War, the loss of the nuclear monopoly, and stories about spies. A Senate committee headed by Maryland Democrat Millard Tydings concluded that McCarthy had no evidence for his allegations.

McCarthy in turn lashed out at international expert Owen Lattimore of Johns Hopkins and such diplomats as John S. Service and John Carter Vincent, both already under attack for their criticisms of Chiang Kai-shek's Nationalist regime in China.

For a time, McCarthy exercised considerable political might. His intervention in senatorial elections played a role in the defeat of Senator Tydings in 1950.

## Dwight D. Eisenhower

After five straight presidential losses, the Republicans were looking for a sure winner in 1952. In nominating Eisenhower, the GOP rebuffed Ohio Senator Robert A. Taft, son of a former president and favorite of the party's midwestern, mostly isolationist, wing. Eisenhower's war record, his genial tolerance, and desire to avoid controversy proved appealing to voters. His promise to "go to Korea" was a political masterstroke.

The Democrats nominated the urbane Governor Adlai Stevenson of Illinois, whose grandfather had been Cleveland's second vice-president. Disillusionment over Korea coupled with the belief that the Democrats had occupied the White House for too long were handicaps Stevenson could not overcome. Eisenhower scored an electoral landslide, 442-89, even winning four southern states.

As president, Eisenhower scorned "creeping socialism," called for more local control of government affairs, and promised to cut federal spending to balance the budget and reduce taxes.

He gave his Cabinet considerable authority and used a military-type staff system. But he was unwilling to repeal existing social and economic legislation or to reduce military expenditures. He embraced a Keynesian approach to economic problems by trying to halt downturns in the business cycle through stimulation of the economy. He approved extension of social security, creation of the Department of Health, Education and Welfare (later Health and Human Services), and construction of interstate highways.

**The Eisenhower-Dulles Foreign Policy**

Eisenhower kept his promise to go to Korea. By July 1953 the communists agreed to an armistice, perhaps influenced by a hint that the United States might use "tactical" atomic bombs. Korea remained divided, and the war had cost 33,000 American dead and more than 100,000 wounded.

Meanwhile, Eisenhower and Secretary of State John Foster Dulles (whose grandfather and uncle had held the top-ranking Cabinet position in the Harrison and Wilson administrations, respectively) embraced a "New Look" in foreign affairs designed to steer clear of involvment in such "local" conflicts as the Korean War. Instead of waiting for communist powers to make a move and then contain them, the United States should put more emphasis on atomic bombs and less on conventional power. Potential enemies would face "massive retaliation" if they became aggressors. When in 1953, the Soviets followed the United States in perfecting a hydrogen bomb, the limits of massive retaliation became apparent. Years later, President Ronald Reagan proposed the "Strategic Defense Initiative" to replace the policy of massive retaliation.

**McCarthy Self-destructs**

After the death of Stalin, Nikita Khrushchev emerged as the new master of the Soviet Union. Khrushchev appealed to the antiwestern prejudices of "third world" countries emerging from colonialism by offering them economic aid and pointing to Soviet achievements in science and technology. He claimed that the launching of *Sputnik* was proof that communism would "bury" the capitalist system. Later Khrushchev spoke of "peaceful coexistence" between communism and capitalism.

McCarthy, meanwhile, continued to investigate communist infiltration by sending his young aide, Roy M. Cohn, to Europe to uncover subversives in the United States Information Service. In 1954, McCarthy accused the army of trying to blackmail his committee and announced a broad investigation. The televised Army-McCarthy hearings disclosed no subversion, and public opinion quickly turned against McCarthy. With President Eisenhower applying pressure behind the scenes, the Senate censured McCarthy in December 1954; his influence waned, and he died of cirrhosis of the liver in 1957.

## Asian Policy After Korea

In 1954, forces of the Vietnamese communist Ho Chi Minh besieged a French army at Dien Bien Phu. Facing heavy losses, France asked the United States to commit air power to the battle, but Eisenhower refused on grounds that a limited air strike would fail. France surrendered and joined Britain, Russia, and China in signing an agreement at Geneva dividing Vietnam along the 17th Parallel.

The northern sector became communist North Vietnam; the southern zone remained in the hands of the emperor, Bao Dai. Thereafter, the anticommunist Ngo Dinh Diem overthrew the emperor and became president of South Vietnam. An election to settle the future of Vietnam scheduled for 1956 never materialized, and Vietnam remained divided. Dulles responded to the situation in Vietnam with creation of the now-defunct Southeast Asia Treaty Organization, whose members included the Philippines, Thailand, and Pakistan.


## The Middle East Cauldron

Troubled by the establishment of Israel, neighboring Arab countries vowed to destroy the new Jewish state. Yet the outnumbered Israelis easily drove out their foes, including one million Palestinian Arabs, and thereby created a refugee problem in nearby countries and renewed calls for a Palestinian state.

Eisenhower tried to ease Arab resentment against the United States by supporting the new Egyptian government of Colonel Gamal Abdel Nasser. America planned to lend Nasser money to build the Aswan High Dam on the Nile but would not sell him arms. When Khrushchev agreed to an arms sale, Nasser allied with the Soviets, and Eisenhower withdrew the offer to finance the dam.

In retaliation, Nasser nationalized the Suez Canal, an action that outraged the British and French, who tried to reclaim the canal by force. Israel also attacked Egypt. Khrushchev threatened to launch atomic missiles against France and Britain if they did not withdraw. Eisenhower called upon Britain and France to pull out of Egypt, a position that created friction in the western alliance.

Prime Minister Anthony Eden announced a ceasefire, Israel withdrew her troops, and the crisis subsided with Egypt keeping control of the canal.

The Soviets used the Suez crisis to recover the prestige they had lost as a result of their brutal suppression of the Hungarian revolt, which broke out a week before the Suez crisis. Though America failed to come to the aid of the Hungarians, the "Eisenhower Doctrine" issued in 1957 declared that the United States was "prepared to use force" anywhere in the Middle East against "aggression from any country controlled by international communism."


## Eisenhower and the Soviet Union

Eisenhower met with Nikita Khrushchev in Geneva in July 1955 in the first of numerous postwar "summit" conferences. The "spirit of Geneva" softened rhetorical tensions between the two nations though there was no specific agreement to halt the Cold War. The next year Eisenhower was reelected, defeating Adlai Stevenson even more decisively than he had in 1952.

Attempting to match Soviet gains in space, the United States launched a small earth satellite, Explorer I, in January 1958. Dulles resigned in April 1959, a month before he died of cancer. Eisenhower then assumed much of the conducting of diplomacy.

Meanwhile, Vice-President Richard M. Nixon visited the Soviet Union, where he defended the merits of capitalism and freedom in the "kitchen debate" with Khrushchev. Thereafter, the Soviet premier toured the United States, and another summit was set for May 1960 in Paris.

Days before the scheduled conclave, the pilot of an American U-2 reconnaissance plane, Francis Gary Powers, was shot down by antiaircraft fire over the Soviet Union. Eisenhower assumed responsibility for the espionage mission, Khrushchev accused the United States of "cowardly" aggression, and the summit was abruptly cancelled.

## Latin America Aroused

The United States tended to neglect Latin America during the Cold War years and supported military regimes in the region. Resentment grew against the United States. In the spring of 1958 Vice-President and Mrs. Nixon made what was supposed to be a goodwill tour of Latin America. In Lima, Peru, Nixon was mobbed; in Caracas, Venezuela, radical students pelted his limousine with eggs and stones. The Nixons had to abandon the remainder of their trip.

A year later, a revolutionary movement headed by Fidel Castro overthrew the Cuban president, Fulgencio Batista, and Eisenhower recognized the new government. Castro soon proved to be a communist, confiscated American property without providing compensation, suppressed civil liberties, and allied with the Soviet Union. His trade treaty with the Soviets allowed the Russians to obtain sugar at a bargain, an action which prompted the United States to stop the importation of Cuban sugar. Khrushchev vowed to defend the Castro regime with atomic weapons should the United States intervene. Shortly before he left office, Eisenhower broke diplomatic relations with Cuba.

## The Politics of Civil Rights

Fears of subversion led to a repression of civil liberties—passage of the Smith Act of 1940, the McCarran Internal Security Act of 1950, and the Supreme Court decision *Dennis v. United States*, all of which limited free speech and association in the name of anticommunism. Meanwhile, J. Robert Oppenheimer, one of the fathers of the atom bomb, was denied a security clearance on the grounds that he had associated with communists and communist sympathizers.

Meanwhile, American blacks, resentful of their continuing status as second-class citizens, grew more militant. Eisenhower completed integration of the armed forces, but it was the Supreme Court that moved against school segregation. *Brown v. the Board of Education* decreed "separate-but-equal" to be "inherently unequal" in the District of Columbia and the seventeen states with compulsory segregation laws. The next year the Court ordered the states to proceed with school desegregation "with all deliberate speed."

White citizens' councils opposed to integration sprang up throughout the South. In 1956, segregationists blew up a high school in Clinton, Tennessee. The following year Eisenhower dispatched paratroopers and summoned National Guardsmen to federal duty in Little Rock, Arkansas, to enforce the desegregation of Central High School. Nine black students thereafter began to attend class, and soldiers were stationed at the school to protect them.

In 1957, Congress passed the first Civil Rights Act since 1875; the law established a Civil Rights Commission with investigatory powers and a Civil Rights Division in the Department of Justice.

The Court that compelled desegregation also defended constitutional rights of criminal suspects, including the right of counsel for indigents (*Gideon v. Wainwright*) and the right to remain silent when being interrogated by police (*Miranda v. Arizona*).

In *Baker v. Carr* the court halted unequal representation in state and local legislative bodies, establishing the principle of "one man, one vote." In another landmark case, *Griswold v. Connecticut*, the Court invalidated a state law banning the use of contraceptives on grounds that it violated one's "right of privacy."

**The Election of 1960**

Vice-President Nixon, the Republican nominee, had skyrocketed to prominence as a critic of communist subversion in government. His defense of American values had won him much national praise, as he sought the presidency on the strengths of the Eisenhower record. The Democrats nominated Senator John F. Kennedy of Massachusetts, with his convention rival, Senator Lyndon B. Johnson of Texas, as his running mate. The son of a wealthy businessman, Kennedy was only the second Catholic to gain a major party nomination. Kennedy stressed youth and vigor and promised to open a "New Frontier."

Four televised debates between the candidates, observed by some 70 million viewers, which focused on style and perception, helped turn the tide for Kennedy. His Catholicism strengthened Kennedy in eastern cities but weakened him in farm districts and in the West. Though his electoral margin was 303-219, Kennedy barely topped Nixon in popular votes. Kennedy's victory thrilled minority groups (Jews, blacks, blue-collar "ethnics," and Catholics) at the expense of the traditional white Protestant majority, which heavily preferred Nixon.

People, Places, and Things

*Identify the following concepts*

closed shop _____

_____

union shop _____

_____

"cooling-off period" _____

_____

baby boomers _____

_____

Iron Curtain _____

_____

defensive perimeter _____

_____

privileged sanctuaries _____

_____

statute of limitations _____

_____

"big lie" _____

_____

"creeping socialism" _____

_____

"massive retaliation" _____

_____

"peaceful coexistence" _____

_____

George Kennan _____

_____

Chiang Kai-shek _____

_____

Mao Tse-tung _____

_____

Strom Thurmond _____

_____

Omar Bradley _____

_____

Whittaker Chambers _____

_____

Julius and Ethel Rosenberg _____

_____

Joseph McCarthy _____

_____

Adlai Stevenson _____

_____

John Foster Dulles _____

_____

Roy M. Cohn _____

_____

Gamal Abdel Nasser _____

_____

Fidel Castro _____

_____

## Map Exercise

Refer to the Middle Eastern map on the following page. Place the correct letter that corresponds with the location of the following:

____1. Arabian Sea

____2. Egypt

____3. Gulf of Aden

____4. Gulf of Oman

____5. Iran

____6. Iraq

____7. Israel

____8. Jordan

____9. Kuwait

____10. Persian Gulf

____11. Red Sea

____12. Saudi Arabia

____13. Syria

____14. United Arab Emirates

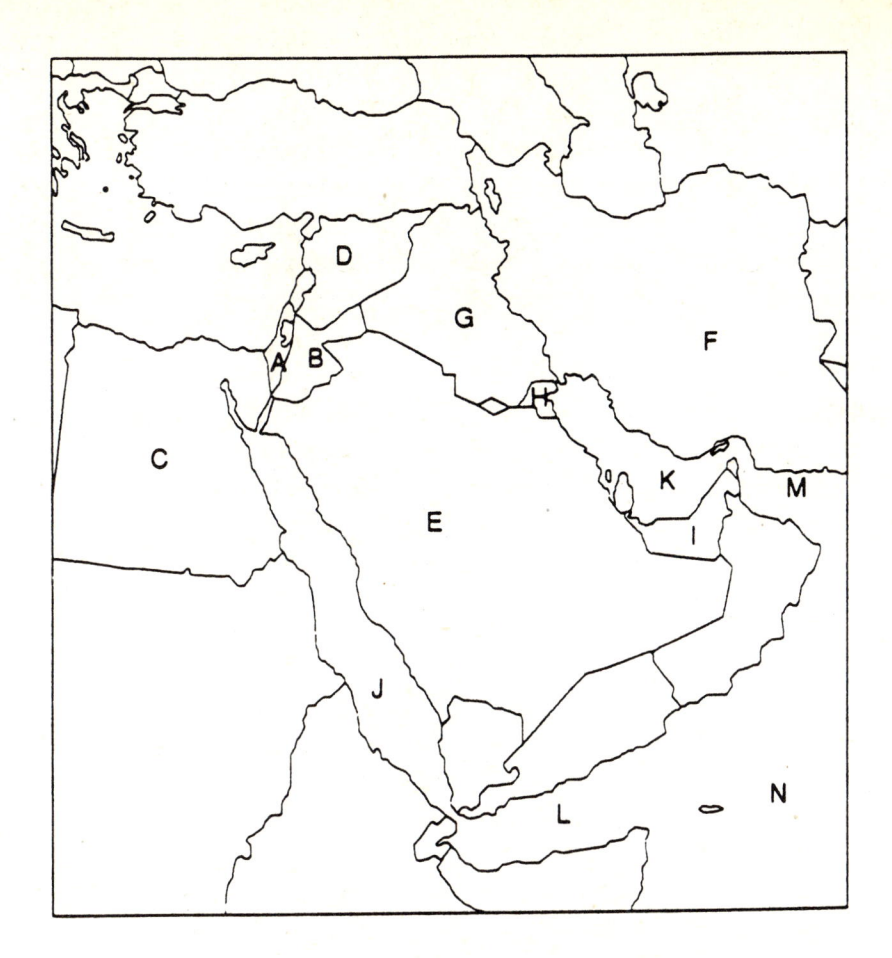

## Self-Test

**Multiple-Choice Questions**

1. "Containment" refers to:
    A. Preventing integration in southern public schools
    B. Keeping communism within its existing boundaries
    C. Support for the United Nations to prevent war
    D. Preventing the spread of nuclear weapons to smaller countries bent on aggression

2. "Privileged sanctuaries" were held by the:
   A. South Koreans
   B. Communist Chinese
   C. North Vietnamese
   D. Taiwanese

3. For John F. Kennedy, the key presidential primaries were in:
   A. Oregon and California
   B. New Hampshire and Florida
   C. Wisconsin and West Virginia
   D. New York and Texas

4. The Truman Doctrine opposed communist movements in:
   A. France and Italy
   B. Jordan and Syria
   C. Greece and Turkey
   D. Guatemala and Honduras

5. When the communists placed a blockade of highway, river, and rail traffic into Berlin in 1948, the United States:
   A. Ceded Berlin to the Soviet sphere of influence
   B. Threatened to use atomic weapons in the dispute
   C. Airlifted supplies into West Berlin
   D. Permitted the communists to annex Hungary in exchange for acknowledging American interest in West Berlin

6. Problems in the Middle East since 1948 stem from all of the following factors *except*:
   A. The absence of a Palestinian national homeland
   B. Soviet activities in the oil-rich area
   C. The refusal of most Arab states to recognize the right of Israel to exist
   D. American reluctance to assist Israel

7. The first NATO commander was:
   A. George Marshall
   B. Dean Acheson
   C. Dwight Eisenhower
   D. Omar Bradley

8. General MacArthur attempted to unite Korea under western control as far north as:
   A. Pusan
   B. Inchon
   C. Seoul
   D. The Yalu River

9. How many Americans died in the Korean War?
   A. 2,500
   B. 33,000
   C. 58,000
   D. 113,000

10. MacArthur proposed to win the Korean War by all of the following measures *except*:
    A. Using Nationalist Chinese troops in the struggle
    B. Employing atomic weapons against China and the Soviet Union
    C. Blockading the Chinese coast
    D. Bombing communist supply bases within northeastern China

11. The principal advocate of "massive retaliation" as a deterrence against communist aggression was:
    A. John Foster Dulles
    B. George F. Kennan
    C. George C. Marshall
    D. John F. Kennedy

12. France withdrew from Indochina after a military defeat at:
    A. Pusan
    B. Dien Bien Phu
    C. Bao Dai
    D. The Mekong River

13. Gamal Abdel Nasser was associated with all of the following *except*:
    A. Nationalization of the Suez Canal
    B. Recognition of Israel's right to exist
    C. Construction of the Aswan High Dam
    D. Close Egyptian-Soviet ties

14. Which of the following is *mispaired*?
    A. Roy Cohn—communist investigations
    B. Klaus Fuch—espionage
    C. Robert F. Kennedy—Justice Department
    D. Whittaker Chambers—Loyalty Review Board

15. The Taft-Hartley Act did *not* include:
    A. The outlawing of union shop contracts
    B. A ban on secondary boycotts
    C. A federal prohibition against the closed shop
    D. An 80-day cooling-off period to avoid strikes

16. The Fair Deal did *not* include:
    A. The interstate highway system
    B. A 75-cent per hour minimum wage
    C. Proposed health insurance through Social Security
    D. More federal housing programs

17. Alger Hiss went to prison for:
    A. Espionage
    B. Perjury
    C. Tax evasion
    D. Conspiracy

18. Targets of Senator Joseph McCarthy did *not* include:
    A. Owen Lattimore
    B. John S. Service
    C. Whittaker Chambers
    D. John Carter Vincent

19. The Civil Rights Act of 1957 provided for all of the following *except*:
    A. Establishment of the investigatory Civil Rights Commission
    B. Creation of the Civil Rights Division within the Justice Department
    C. The obtaining of injunctions to stop election officials from interfering with blacks seeking to register and vote
    D. School desegregation "with all deliberate speed"

20. Which of the following is *false* regarding the election of 1960?
    A. Kennedy's Catholicism helped him to win big eastern states.
    B. Nixon lost the entire South over the school desegregation issue.
    C. The shift of a few thousand votes in a few critical states would have altered the outcome.
    D. Nixon ran on the essence of the Eisenhower record.

**Essay Questions**

1. Outline specific ways that the Truman administration tried to halt the spread of communism in the early years of the Cold War.

2. Evaluate the rise and fall of Senator Joseph McCarthy as a factor in domestic politics of the Cold War.

3. Analyze the successes and shortcomings in the foreign and domestic policies of the Eisenhower administration.

4. Explain how and why civil rights for minorities became a domestic political issue by the middle 1950s.

5. Evaluate the election of 1960 in reference to parties, nominees, issues, political traditions, and long-range significance.

## Critical Thinking Exercise

Though instructors rarely require students to recite dates of key events, time and sequence are important concepts in the effective learning of history. Consult an outside reference work if needed to arrange these events in chronological order.

_____ 1. Election of Kennedy

_____ 2. Election of Truman

_____ 3. Eisenhower's reelection

_____ 4. U-2 spy incident

_____ 5. "Kitchen Debate"

_____ 6. *Griswold v. Connecticut*

_____ 7. Truman fires MacArthur

_____ 8. Censure of Senator Joseph McCarthy

_____ 9. Hiss conviction

_____ 10. Overthrow of Fulgencio Batista

_____ 11. Little Rock desegregation crisis begins

_____ 12. Final settlement in Korean War

_____ 13. Launching of *Sputnik*

_____ 14. Hungarian crisis

_____ 15. Nixon's goodwill tour of Latin America

CHAPTER 30

# The Best of Times, The Worst of Times

## Learning Objectives

*After reading Chapter 30, you should be able to:*

1. Evaluate the controversial administrations of Presidents Johnson and Nixon.
2. Show how the civil rights movement and the Great Society changed America.
3. Discuss the American role in the Vietnam War and show how the war contributed to domestic divisions.
4. Outline the significance of the election of 1968 in reference to parties, primaries, nominees, issues, strategies, outcome, and long-range implications.
5. Explain how Nixon tried to wind down American involvement in the Vietnam War.
6. Interpret the impact of detente on American foreign policy.
7. Explain how a "third-rate burglary" led to the forced resignation of a president.
8. Evaluate the impact of the Yom Kippur War, the Arab oil embargo, and OPEC price manipulation in the 1970s.

## Overview

### John Fitzgerald Kennedy

President Kennedy projected an image of originality and imaginativeness combined with moderation and good sense. He sought to teach the country to respect its most talented minds. On one occasion, he invited Nobel Prize winners to the White House and called the group "the most extraordinary collection of talent. . .that has ever been gathered {here} with the possible exception of when Thomas Jefferson dined alone."

Kennedy flouted convention by appointing his younger brother, Robert F. Kennedy, as attorney general. His inaugural address called upon Americans to "Ask not what your country can do for you. Ask what you can do for your country."

### The Cuban Crises

In an effort to tie economic aid to internal reforms in Latin America, Kennedy proposed the Alliance for Progress. When pro-Soviet activity erupted in the region, however, Kennedy attempted to strike back. In April 1961, he approved the Bay of Pigs invasion, an attempt by Cuban exiles to overthrow Fidel Castro. The Cuban public did not rally behind the exiles, who quickly surrendered. The affair exposed the United States to anti-imperialist criticism without toppling Castro. Kennedy imposed an economic blockade on Cuba and authorized a CIA attempt to assassinate Castro.

Kennedy met with Khrushchev in Vienna in June 1961. During the meeting he failed to convince the Soviet leader that he would resist pressure with determination. Khrushchev then closed the border between East and West Berlin and erected a wall of concrete blocks and barbed wire across the city to prevent East Germans from fleeing to the West.

Kennedy committed the United States to a bold space program, which sparked patriotic fervor in 1962, when John Glenn {later United States senator from Ohio}, became the first American to orbit the earth. Still the Soviet cosmonaut Yuri Gagarin had orbited the earth nearly a full year earlier.

Meanwhile, U-2 flights revealed that the Soviets were sending planes, conventional weapons, and guided missiles to Cuba and erecting launching pads. Kennedy declared that the Soviet's "deliberately provocative" buildup was unacceptable. For days, an impasse developed. Then Khrushchev agreed to withdraw the missiles in return for Kennedy's lifting of the blockade and his pledge not to try again to topple Castro. To many, Kennedy's handling of the crisis seemed to repair the damage done to his reputation by the Bay of Pigs fiasco.

As the arms race continued, most nations, but not France and China, signed the Nuclear Test Ban Treaty in 1963 to halt the atmospheric testing of atomic weapons.

**Kennedy's Domestic Program**

Having promised "to get the country moving again," Kennedy proposed to cut personal and corporate income taxes so that consumers would have more money to spend and corporations would invest in new facilities for producing desired goods. A coalition of Republicans and conservative southern Democrats resisted the tax-reduction scheme and further blocked Kennedy's plans for urban renewal, higher minimum wage, federal aid to education, and medical care for the aged.

**Tragedy in Dallas**

On November 22, 1963, while motorcading through Dallas, Kennedy was shot in the head by the assassin Lee Harvey Oswald and died almost instantly. Before he could be tried, Oswald was himself murdered, in full view of television cameras, by nightclub owner Jack Ruby while being transferred from one place of detention to another. The fact that Oswald had defected to Russia in 1959 and then returned to the United States convinced some that a conspiracy lay at the root of the tragedy. An investigation headed by Chief Justice Earl Warren concluded that Oswald acted alone, but doubts persisted in many minds.

Kennedy's election had initially seemed to mark the beginning of a new era in American history, but the assassination actually marked the end of the old one.

## Lyndon Baines Johnson

Plunging into the presidency, Lyndon Johnson benefited from the outrage Americans felt toward the Kennedy assassination. Johnson was often depicted as heavy-handed, subtle, devious, domineering, persistent, or obliging, whatever might advance his political interest. He once noted that while some politicians desired "power so they can strut around to 'Hail to the Chief' ...I wanted it to use it."

Johnson sought to enact Kennedy's unfinished agenda. Early in 1964 Kennedy's tax cut was passed, and the resulting economic stimulus caused a boom. Thereafter, an expanded version of another Kennedy measure, the Civil Rights Act of 1964, became law.

## "We Shall Overcome"

The origin of the civil rights movement is usually traced to the Alabama capital city of Montgomery, where in 1955, seamstress Rosa Parks refused to give her seat to a white passenger. Parks, secretary of the local NAACP, was arrested, and blacks boycotted the city bus lines. During the year-long boycott, some 350 persons carried more than 10,000 people back and forth to their jobs every day.

Plunging to the forefront of the movement was black minister Martin Luther King, Jr., an Atlanta native whose oratorical skills helped raise public attention and funds for the cause. In 1956, the Supreme Court struck down the bus segregation law, and Montgomery desegregated its transportation system. King's success in Montgomery led to the formation in 1960 of his Southern Christian Leadership Conference. Other groups in the civil rights struggle were the NAACP and CORE.

Thereafter, in 1960, four black students in Greensboro, North Carolina, refused to leave the lunch counter of a chain store until they were served, staging the first "sit-ins" across the South. In May 1961, civil rights forces organized a "freedom ride" across the South to test federal regulations prohibiting discrimination in interstate transportation.

Meanwhile, Elijah Muhammad and Malcolm X broke with the integrationist King and stressed "black nationalism," and called upon blacks to be thrifty and industrious but to view whites with suspicion and even hatred.

Jailed for leading demonstrations in Birmingham, Alabama, King outlined his policy of non-violent protest in "Letter from Birmingham Jail," which explained why civil rights advocates could wait no longer for their freedom.

At first, a cautious President Kennedy urged state officials to take the lead in enforcing desegregation, but the Birmingham demonstrations prompted the President to support a comprehensive new civil rights bill that made racial discrimination in hotels, restaurants, and other public accommodations illegal. When the bill ran into congressional opposition, civil rights forces organized a march on Washington attended by some 200,000 in August 1963. There King delivered his "I Have a Dream" speech, expressing the hope that his children would be judged according to the "content of their character" rather than the "color of their skin."

**The Great Society**

The Civil Rights Act of 1964 prohibited discrimination by employers against blacks and women, broke down remaining legal barriers to blacks voting in the South, and outlawed most forms of segregation. Johnson's success in steering the measure through Congress convinced him that he could be a reformer in the tradition of Franklin Roosevelt. Noting the number of poor in an otherwise affluent society, Johnson proposed direct economic assistance to the needy. Singled out for attention was the impoverished Appalachia region of the Southeast.

The Economic Opportunity Act of 1964, better known as "the war on poverty," created the Job Corps, community action agencies, college work-study, and training programs for the unskilled.

In 1964, Johnson easily defeated the conservative Republican Senator Barry M. Goldwater of Arizona after pledging to create a "Great Society" that would more evenly distribute the wealth of America. Goldwater opposed expanding social programs and advocated a tough stance in foreign affairs.

Soon voluminous Great Society measures were enacted on a scale reminiscent of the New Deal:

Medicare
Medicaid for the indigent
The Elementary and Secondary Education Act
Preschool Head Start program
Revised immigration act abandoning the quota system
Crime control
Slum clearance
Clean air
Model cities
Subsidies for the arts
Highway safety and beautification
Preservation of historic sites.

Some programs ran into criticism: ESEA did not improve academic performance, Medicare and Medicaid led to huge increases in health-care costs because physicians, hospitals, and drug companies raised fees and prices without fear of losing business. The Job Corps had no measurable effect on the unemployment rate and few trainees completed the courses.

**War in Vietnam**

Opposition to the once politically invincible Johnson grew steadily after the president committed the nation to fighting communism in Southeast Asia. In 1954, American military advisers had been sent to train a South Vietnamese army, and more American aid was dispatched to assist the government of President Ngo Dinh Diem. Diem could not suppress the communist forces known as the Vietcong.

Kennedy had indicated that he would reduce the size of the American military in Vietnam, but whether he would have done so has been debated among historians. In any case, shortly before Kennedy's death, a group of South Vietnamese generals assassinated Diem and took over the government.

In the summer of 1964, President Johnson announced that North Vietnamese gunboats had fired on American destroyers in the Gulf of Tonkin. He obtained authorization from Congress to repel any such future attacks, subsequently dispatched combat troops to South Vietnam, and directed air attacks against targets in Vietnam. The American commitment escalated from 184,000 troops at the end of 1965 to a peak of 538,000 in mid-1968. The United States was hence engaged in a full-scale war based on the Tonkin Gulf Resolution.

**Hawks and Doves**

The war sharply divided the American public. Hawks, who accepted Eisenhower's "domino theory" toward the spread of communism, emphasized the need to resist aggression. They contended that the United States was not an aggressor because it was willing to negotiate a general withdrawal of all forces.

Doves viewed the struggle as a civil war between the Vietcong and the South Vietnamese government, which they viewed as repressive and undemocratic. They objected to aerial bombings, the use of napalm and defoliants, the killing of civilians by American troops, and complained about costs and casualties of the war.

President Johnson believed that he was defending freedom and democracy: "If I got out of Vietnam, I'd be doing exactly what Chamberlain did in World War II. I'd be giving a big fat reward for aggression."

**The Election of 1968**

Resentment against Johnson's war policies grew steadily, and in November 1967 Eugene J. McCarthy, a relatively obscure Minnesota senator, announced that he would challenge the president's renomination in order to put the Vietnam question before voters.

Suddenly, early in 1968, North Vietnam and the Vietcong launched the Tet offensive, in which 39 of 44 provincial capitals were attacked. They held the former capital of Hue and threatened Saigon. Though the communists suffered huge losses, the offensive had a devastating psychological effect in the United States. When it was learned that the administration planned to send an additional 206,000 troops to South Vietnam, McCarthy became a formidable figure and polled 42 percent of the Democratic vote in the New Hampshire primary, which Johnson won in a write-in vote.

McCarthy's strength prompted New York Senator Robert Kennedy, brother of the slain president, to enter the race. When Johnson removed himself from the race on March 31, Vice-President Hubert H. Humphrey announced his candidacy—too late to enter any primaries. In the California primary, Kennedy scored a narrow win over McCarthy. He was assassinated after delivering his victory speech in a Los Angeles hotel. Kennedy's death ensured Humphrey's nomination, as professional politicians distrusted the aloof McCarthy.

The Republicans gave Richard Nixon a second nomination, despite his defeat by Kennedy in 1960 and his failure to win the California governorship in 1962. To placate the South, Nixon chose as his runningmate Maryland Governor Spiro T. Agnew, who had criticized black radicalism.

Many southerners, meanwhile, flocked to the independent candidacy of former Alabama Governor George C. Wallace, who hoped to prevent either Humphrey or Nixon from obtaining an electoral majority. Wallace opposed civil rights laws, attacked intellectuals, and denounced the coddling of criminals.

Humphrey's nomination came amidst rioting by activists at the convention in Chicago, where Mayor Richard J. Daley ringed the convention with barricades and police to protect it from disruption. The violence played into the hands of Nixon, who in making relatively few public appearances relied on television interviews and taped commercials prepared by an advertising agency. Nixon pledged national unity and firm enforcement of the law.

Humphrey closed the gap when Johnson suspended air attacks on North Vietnam. Moreover, blacks and the urban poor backed Humphrey, who trailed Nixon by about 500,000 popular votes. Nixon carried the electoral vote, 301 to 191 for Humphrey and 46 for Wallace. Despite Nixon's triumph, Democrats easily retained control of Congress.


**Nixon as President: "Vietnamizing" the War**

Nixon proposed a phased withdrawal of all non-South Vietnamese troops, with internationally-supervised elections to follow. North Vietnam rejected the plan and called on the United States to withdraw unconditionally. As the war dragged on, Nixon tried to build up the South Vietnamese forces so that the Americans could leave. "Vietnamization" had actually been underway for 15 years, as America tried to assist South Vietnam to defend itself against aggression.

Nixon announced the withdrawal of 60,000 troops by the end of 1969, but protestors declared "Vietnam Moratorium Days." Vice-President Agnew verbally assailed demonstrators, and Nixon appealed to the "silent majority" to argue that the war could only be lost in America itself. Troop withdrawals continued in an orderly fashion. A new lottery system for drafting men for military service eliminated some inequities in the selective service law, but the war continued.

Meanwhile, it was learned that in 1968 an American unit massacred civilians, including women and children, in the Vietnamese hamlet of My lai, a tragedy that accented debate over the purposes of the war and its effects on the soldiers.

## The Cambodian "Incursion"

In April 1970, Nixon announced that Vietnamization was proceeding so well that another 150,000 American soldiers would be withdrawn. A week later he ordered thousands of troops to destroy communist "sanctuaries" in neutral Cambodia. He also resumed bombing targets in North Vietnam.

Thousands of students opposed the Cambodian incursion. At Kent State University students clashed for several days with police. When the governor of Ohio called out the National Guard, some students pelted the soldiers with stones. During a noontime protest, Guardsmen, who were poorly trained in crowd control, suddenly opened fire, and four students were killed, two of them women passing by on their way to class.

The condemnation of the invasion led Nixon to remove ground forces from Cambodia, but he stepped up air attacks. In March 1972, Nixon ordered heavy bombing when North Vietnam mounted assaults throughout South Vietnam, and he authorized the mining of Haiphong and other northern ports to stop supplies from reaching the communists.

## Détente

As the war continued, Nixon and his principal foreign policy adviser, Henry A. Kissinger, drafted new diplomatic strategies toward China and the Soviet Union. In February 1972, Nixon and Kissinger flew to Beijing; the United States agreed to support the admission of China to the United Nations and to develop economic and cultural exchanges. The visit ended 20 years of American refusal to acknowledge the communist conquest of China.

In May, Nixon and Kissinger flew to Moscow, where the United States agreed to the first Strategic Arms Limitation Treaty. Nixon permitted large sales of grain to the Soviets. Nixon and Kissinger called the new policy *détente,* a French word meaning "relaxation of tensions." The Chinese and Soviet agreements may have prompted North Vietnam to make diplomatic concessions to get the United States out of the war. Shortly before the 1972 presidential election Kissinger declared peace to be "at hand."

## Nixon in Triumph

President Nixon defeated South Dakota Senator George S. McGovern in a landslide popular and electoral vote. McGovern's campaign had been damaged by divisions within the Democratic party and by the candidate's scheme for funneling more money directly to the poor.

Nixon interpreted his reelection as a mandate, for he had secured the votes of millions of traditional Democrats. Moreover, his "southern strategy" shattered precedent by bringing the entire former Confederacy in to the Republican column.

In January 1973, a settlement was signed in Vietnam, and prisoners of war began returning to America. Still the North Vietnamese retained control of large sections of the South. More than 57,000 Americans had died in the long war, which cost $150 billion.

## The Economy under Nixon

Nixon inherited an inflationary economy caused primarily by the military expenditures and "easy money" policies of the Johnson administration. He balanced the 1969 budget, the last time that national spending failed to outstrip expenditures. The Federal Reserve Board forced up interest rates to slow the expansion of the money supply in an effort to reduce the rate of economic growth without causing unemployment or recession. But prices continued to rise, and unions made large wage demands.

In 1971, Nixon, employing power granted to him the previous year by Congress, announced a 90-day price and wage freeze. He then established a commission to limit wage and price increases when the freeze ended. These controls did not check inflation completely and angered unions, but they did slow the upward spiral.

In other domestic matters, Nixon proposed a "minimum income" for poor families, a plan which got nowhere in Congress. He sought to shore up southern support with the appointment of "strict constructionists" to the Supreme Court. In June 1969, Nixon nominated Warren E. Burger of Minnesota as chief justice to succeed Earl Warren. After the Senate rejected two southern nominees, Nixon named another Minnesotan, the liberal Harry Blackmun, as associate justice. Thereafter, Nixon named conservative William H. Rehnquist to the Court; in 1986, President Reagan elevated Rehnquist as chief justice to succeed Burger.

At the peak of success, Nixon offered proposals to strengthen the presidency in relation to Congress. In 1973, he replaced wage and price controls with voluntary "restraints." Prices thereafter soared, the most rapid rate of inflation since the Korean War. Nixon limited federal expenditures, halted programs, reduced grants, and refused to spend money appropriated by Congress for purposes he opposed, a procedure known as impoundment. Nixon's staff claimed "executive privilege" when challenged about administration actions.

## The Watergate Break-in

On June 17, 1972, five men affilated with the Committee to Re-elect the President broke into the Democratic headquarters in the Watergate apartment house and office building in Washington. The burglars were part of an unofficial surveillance group known as "the plumbers," which was established to halt leaks to the press. Nixon denied that he or the Republican party was behind "this very bizarre incident," and the matter did not affect the 1972 election.

One burglar, James W. McCord, wrote Judge John Sirica that high officials had known about the burglary in advance and had persuaded the other defendants to keep their connection secret. McCord's charges were confirmed by the head of CREEP, Jeb Stuart Magruder, and Nixon's counsel, John W. Dean III. Dean claimed in testimony before a special 1973 Senate Watergate committee that Nixon participated in efforts to cover up the affair.

The committee uncovered other damaging disclosures:

Hush money was paid to insure the silence of the burglars
CREEP officials disrupted Democratic campaigns
Corporations made illegal contributions to Nixon
Acting FBI Director Patrick Gray destroyed documents related to the case
Nixon agents burglarized the office of a psychiatrist seeking evidence against Daniel Ellsberg in the Pentagon papers case
Nixon agents placed wiretaps on telephones of some of their own officials as well as journalists

Still many found it difficult to believe that a president could lie to the entire country. The disclosure that Nixon's office conversations and telephone calls had been taped prompted the Senate committee to demand access to the evidence to determine the extent of Nixon's involvement.

As Nixon's poll standings declined, he named an independent special prosecutor to investigate Watergate. When the prosecutor, Archibald Cox, sought access to White House records, Nixon ordered his dismissal in what was called the "Saturday Night Massacre." Cox's dismissal prompted the House Judiciary Committee to consider impeachment of the president.

Then Nixon named a new special prosecutor, Leon Jaworski, and promised him access to pertinent documents. Nixon surrendered tapes to the judge with the understanding that the evidence would be presented to the grand jury, not the public. Some tapes were missing, and an important section of one had been erased.

## More Troubles

Along with the Watergate affair, other morale-shattering crises developed. The nation faced a serious grain shortage, which caused wheat prices to more than triple.

Vice-President Agnew resigned after admitting to evading taxes on bribes received while he was the executive of Baltimore County and governor of Maryland. He paid a $10,000 fine and was placed on three years' probation. Under the six-year-old Twenty-fifth Amendment, Nixon nominated House Republican Leader Gerald R. Ford of Michigan to succeed Agnew.

After Agnew's exodus, it was disclosed that Nixon had paid only about $1,600 in income taxes during two years in which his earnings had exceeded half a million dollars. Nixon claimed that his returns had been legal because he had taken a deduction for the gift of his vice-presidential papers to the National Archives.

## The Oil Crisis

Another disaster followed when the Yom Kippur War broke out in the Middle East in October 1973. In an attempt to force Western nations to compel Israeli withdrawal from the lands held since the Six-Day War of 1967, the Arabs cut off oil shipments to the United States, Japan, and western Europe.

After Henry Kissinger obtained the withdrawal of Israel from some of the territory taken in 1967, the Arab nations lifted the boycott. America at the time imported more than a third of its oil.

In 1960, the principal oil exporters—Venezuela, Saudi Arabia, Kuwait, Iraq, and Iran—had formed a cartel, OPEC, which had begun to affect world prices by the time of the 1973 war. The days of cheap gasoline ended, and double-digit inflation became a part of the American vocabulary.


### The Judgment: "Expletive Deleted"

Special prosecutor Jaworski continued the investigation of Watergate. In March 1974, a grand jury indicted Haldeman, Ehrlichman, former attorney general John N. Mitchell, and four other White House aides for conspiring to block the Watergate investigation. The jurors named Nixon an "unindicted co-conspirator" because they lacked the power to indict a president. Meanwhile, the IRS announced that Nixon's deductions on his income taxes had been unjustified, and he agreed to pay nearly half a million dollars in taxes and interest.

Transcripts of the Nixon tapes convinced the public that Nixon had abused his office. His foul language prompted the phrase "expletive deleted" to become an overnight catchphrase. When Jaworski subpoenaed 64 additional tapes in search of a "smoking gun," Nixon refused to obey the subpoena. In *United States v. Nixon* the Supreme Court forbade the use of executive privilege for purposes of withholding evidence "demonstrably relevant in a criminal trial." Faced with likely impeachment and conviction, Nixon complied with the subpoena.

On August 5, a tape revealed that Nixon had tried to obstruct justice by engaging the CIA to persuade the FBI not to follow up leads about Watergate on grounds of national security. With that disclosure, Nixon's remaining congressional support crumbled.


### The Meaning of Watergate

Nixon announced his resignation on August 8, 1974; Ford was sworn in as his successor at noon the next day. Some question whether Nixon could have permanently altered the political system had he weathered Watergate. His exaggerated view of executive privilege may have reflected his need for reassurance that he was an effective leader. Out of office, Nixon became a prolific writer of books focusing on his experiences with world leaders, his philosophy of life, and public and foreign policy matters. He moreover undertook a 20-year quest to embrace the role of "elder statesman," the only position left for him to pursue. When Nixon died of a stroke at the age of eighty-one in a New York hospital on April 22, 1994, his passing symbolized the closing of an era.

# People, Places, and Things

*Identify the following concepts:*

sit-in _____

_____

freedom rides _____

_____

work-study program _____

_____

Medicare _____

_____

Medicaid _____

_____

hawks _____

_____

domino theory _____

_____

doves _____

_____

wage-and-price controls _____

_____

"southern strategy" _____

_____

- Vietnamization _____
_____

- moratorium _____
_____

- détente _____
_____

- impoundment _____
_____

- executive privilege _____
_____

*Describe the following*:

New Frontier _Kennedy promised to bring change_
_and send the country in a new direction_

- Bay of Pigs _____
_____

- Nuclear Test Ban Treaty _____
_____

- Warren Commission _____
_____

- Montgomery bus boycott _____
_____

- "Letter from Birmingham Jail" _____

- Great Society _____

- Job Corps _____

- Head Start _____

831 Tonkin Gulf Resolution _____

833 Tet offensive _____

- Cambodian incursion _____

- My lai _____

- Kent State University _____

839 SALT _____

- CREEP _____

"Saturday Night Massacre" _____

OPEC _____

*United States v. Nixon* _____

*Identify the following people*:

John H. Glenn, Jr. _____

Lee Harvey Oswald _____

Jack Ruby _____

Martin Luther King, Jr. _____

Malcolm X _____

Barry M. Goldwater _____

Ngo Dinh Diem _____

Eugene J. McCarthy _____

_____

William Westmoreland _____

_____

Robert F. Kennedy _____

_____

Hubert H. Humphrey _____

_____

George C. Wallace _____

_____

Spiro T. Agnew _____

_____

Richard J. Daley _____

_____

Henry A. Kissinger _____

_____

George S. McGovern _____

_____

James McCord _____

_____

John Dean _____

_____

H. R. "Bob" Haldeman _____

_____

John D. Ehrlichman _____

_____

Archibald Cox _____

_____

Gerald R. Ford _____

_____

John N. Mitchell _____

_____


## Map Exercise

Refer to the Southeast Asian map on the following page. Place the correct letter that corresponds with the location of the following:

____ 1. Bangkok

____ 2. Burma

____ 3. Cambodia

____ 4. Camranh Bay

____ 5. China

____ 6. Danang

____ 7. Hainan

____ 8. Haiphong

____ 9. Hanoi

____ 10. Hue

____ 11. Laos

____ 12. My lai

____ 13. North Vietnam

____ 14. Phnom Penh

____ 15. Saigon

____ 16. South Vietnam

____ 17. Thailand

____ 18. Vientiane

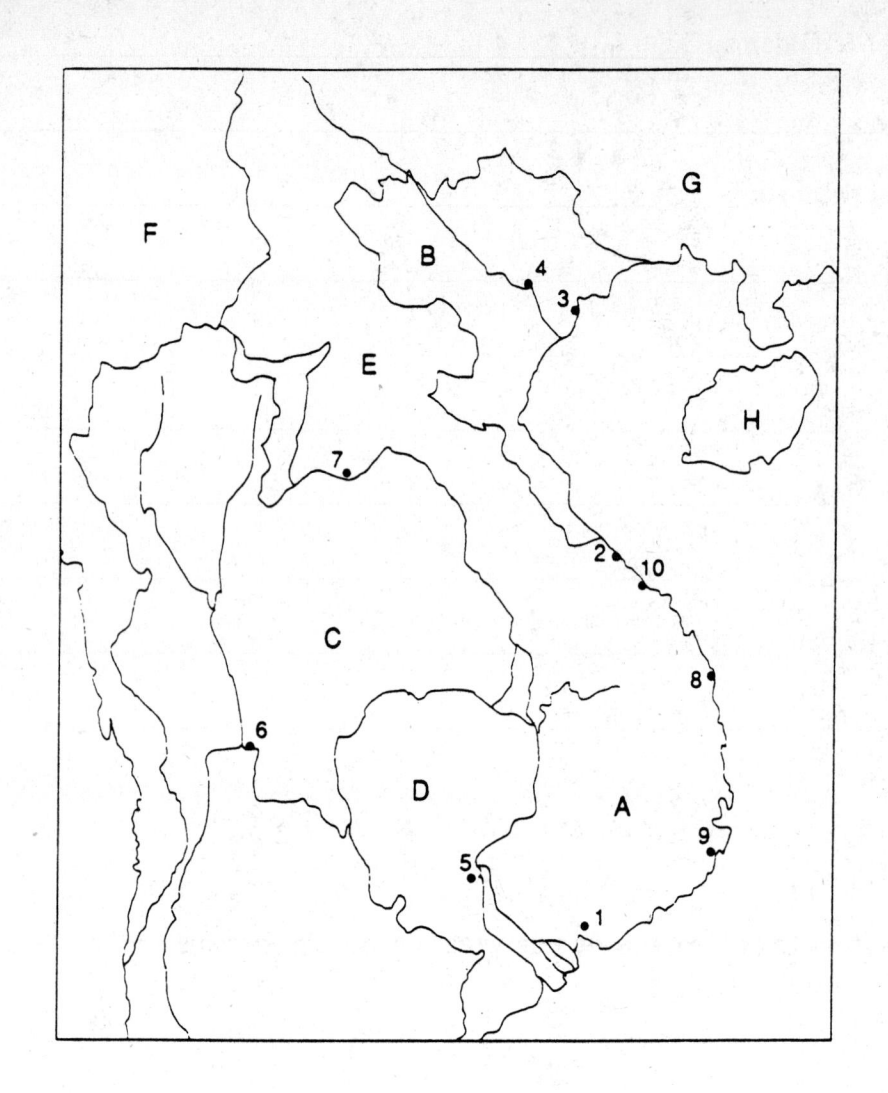

## Self-Test

### Multiple-Choice Questions

1. Which of these was *not* a Democrat?
   A. Eugene McCarthy
   B. John Mitchell   *Attorney Gen (Creep*
   C. George S. McGovern
   D. Robert F. Kennedy

2. The Gulf of Tonkin Resolution led to American involvement in:
   A. The Middle East
   B. Latin America
   C. Southeast Asia
   D. The Near East

3. In the Vietnam War a "hawk" wanted:
   A. A negotiated settlement
   B. A military victory
   C. Immediate American withdrawal
   D. To employ nuclear weapons

4. How many American servicemen were killed in the Vietnam War?
   A. 12,000
   B. 30,000
   C. 57,000
   D. 99,000

5. The heaviest American bombing in Vietnam occurred in:
   A. 1965
   B. 1967
   C. 1969
   D. 1972

6. All of the following Nixon associates were involved in scandals *except*:
   A. John Sirica
   B. John D. Ehrlichman
   C. John W. Dean, III
   D. Spiro T. Agnew

7. In the 1968 election George C. Wallace:
   A. Reluctantly endorsed Nixon
   B. Urged the renomination of President Johnson
   C. Stumped for Hubert Humphrey
   D. Ran as the American Independent nominee

8. Which of these is *not* a member of OPEC?
   A. Japan
   B. Venezuela
   C. Saudi Arabia
   D. Iraq

9. In 1971, Nixon employed what program in an unsuccessful bid to combat inflation?
   A. "Jawboning" business to keep prices down
   B. Free-market economics
   C. "Whip Inflation Now"
   D. Wage and price guidelines

10. The Kent State demonstrations were staged to protest:
    A. The draft lottery
    B. Racial discrimination
    C. The incursion into Cambodia
    D. Chinese intervention in the Vietnam War

11. By 1974, America faced all of the following *except*:
    A. Political scandals
    B. Inflation
    C. High fuel prices
    D. Demonstrations against the draft

12. The "domino theory" was first suggested by:
    A. Henry Kissinger
    B. Dwight D. Eisenhower
    C. Robert F. Kennedy
    D. Barry M. Goldwater

13. Which of these losing presidential candidates polled the strongest *popular* and *electoral* vote?
    A. Hubert Humphrey
    B. George Wallace
    C. George McGovern
    D. Barry Goldwater

14. Which of these statements is *false* regarding the Tet offensive?
    A. It resulted in a sweeping communist military victory
    B. It coincided with the Lunar New Year
    C. For a time the communists successfully occupied part of Saigon
    D. It discredited the American military because of its psychological impact in the United States

15. "Vietnamization" refers to:
    A. Calls for an American military victory in the war
    B. Nixon's plan to turn over most of the fighting to the Army of the Republic of Vietnam
    C. Congressional approval of the military spending bills
    D. Encroachment of the communists into South Vietnam

16. Nixon's resignation resulted when:
    A. He lost the support of 34 senators needed to avoid conviction in Watergate-related matters
    B. The House voted overwhelmingly to impeach him
    C. The Supreme Court ordered him to step down due to obstruction of justice
    D. His aides revealed Nixon's complicity in Watergate

17. The case *United States v. Nixon* placed limits upon:
    A. School desegregation
    B. Military spending
    C. Impoundment
    D. Executive privilege

18. The "Saturday Night Massacre" led to the sacking of:
    A. Robert Bork
    B. Leon Jaworski
    C. H.R. Haldeman
    D. Archibald Cox

19. During the Vietnam War, "doves" objected to all of the following *except*:
    A. Use of defoliants in the Vietnamese jungles
    B. American attacks on Vietnamese civilians
    C. Detente in foreign policy
    D. Massive aerial bombings

20. The official version of the Kennedy assassination concluded that:
    A. There was a conspiracy to set up a military regime to replace Kennedy
    B. The real story of the assassination must be withheld because of national security
    C. Lee Harvey Oswald, a communist sympathizer with ties to Fidel Castro, acted alone in planning and executing the crime
    D. The assassination was arranged by South Vietnamese agents angry about the murder of President Diem

## Essay Questions

1. Discuss the election of 1968 in reference to parties, primaries, nominees, strategies, tactics, issues, outcome, and long-range significance.

2. Evaluate President Nixon's Vietnam policies and show how they eventually led to the removal of American forces from Southeast Asia.

3. Show how the interests of the civil rights movement and the Great Society coincided in the middle and late 1960s.

4. Show how the Watergate affair forced Richard Nixon from office and crushed his standing in history.

5. Discuss the promises, shortcomings, and long-term significance of the New Frontier.

## Critical Thinking Exercise

The terms "liberal" and "conservative" are used in history and political science to refer to opposite shades of opinion on the issues. Identify each of the following points of view, referring to issues between 1963 and 1974, as "L" for liberal, or "C" for conservative.

\_\_\_\_1. Considered the limited use of atomic weapons in Vietnam but insisted such weapons would not be needed if the nation were fully committed to a military victory

\_\_\_\_2. Placed considerable faith in the Strategic Arms Limitation Treaty that reduced antiballistic missiles

\_\_\_\_3. Opposed Nixon's wage and price guidelines on principle as well as practicality

\_\_\_\_4. Stressed personal responsibility in formulating social programs to assist the poor

\_\_\_\_5. Felt that many poor persons lacked motivation and had become alienated from society because of their own shortcomings, not the lack of opportunity

\_\_\_\_6. Urged an emphasis on "butter" over "guns" in the allocation of national resources

\_\_\_\_7. Considered a "minimum income" for the poor to be an unwise repudiation of supply and demand

\_\_\_\_8. Stressed desegregation of public schools more than integration

\_\_\_\_9. Was partial to Nixon-Kissinger detente strategy

\_\_\_\_10. Considered George McGovern's plan to funnel money directly to the poor to be sensible policy

\_\_\_\_11. Backed the appointment of "strict constructionists" to the Supreme Court

\_\_\_\_12. Would have instituted the heaviest bombing of the Vietnam War the month that the United States entered the war

____13. Felt that a nation as affluent as the United States could handily fund "Great Society" programs for the downtrodden

____14. Somewhat receptive to arguments raised by George Wallace though he may have voted for Nixon

____15. Repudiated suggestions that the Clean Air Act of 1965 would cost jobs in certain vital industries without bringing much improvement in the environment

____16. Believed that the Vietcong were "nationalists" who wanted a better life and independence for South Vietnam

____17. Denounced the bombing of civilian targets in Vietnam

____18. Emphasized that the regime of Mao Tse-tung was responsible for the deaths of 30 to 60 million people

____19. Initially considered Fidel Castro too undisciplined and too unpredictable to be a member of the Communist party

____20. Believed that the media misled the public about the military progress made by American troops in Vietnam.

CHAPTER 31

# Society in Flux

## Learning Objectives

*After reading Chapter 31, you should be able to:*

1. Discuss the social mobility of the postwar years.
2. Explain the significance of television to American culture.
3. Show how religion sought to meet changes in American life.
4. Account for the uniqueness of postwar American art and literature.
5. Discuss racial turmoil of the 1960s and 1970s and show how minorities sought to improve their lives.
6. Evaluate educational developments of the postwar years.
7. Show how the student revolt led to the counterculture of the 1960s.
8. Discuss the sexual revolution and women's liberation.

## Overview

**Society in Flux**

Population growth soared from 131 million in 1940 to 200 million in 1960 to 250 million in the late 1980s. Alaska and Hawaii were admitted as states, and an economically exploding "sun belt" stretching from Florida to Texas and California became a national phenomenon. In 1963, California passed New York as the most populous state, and Nevada and Arizona grew at an even greater rate. By 1994, Texas had replaced New York as the second most populous state.

Advances in transportation and communication added to geographic mobility. More Americans owned heavier and more powerful automobiles, and gasoline consumption surpassed new records. The motel industry arose to serve auto travelers. The interstate highway system begun in 1956 was a stimulus to mobility; so was the Seattle-built Boeing 707 jetliner, which began service in 1958.

**Television**

By 1961, some 55 million television sets were in operation. Moreover, government and commercial satellites were relaying pictures from one continent to another instantly. Television became the prime medium for advertising and news broadcasts. Its coverage of the Kennedy assassination made history come alive for tens of millions. Though some excellent programs were aired, most offerings were vulgar serials, variety shows, quiz programs, and reruns of old movies. In time, television became the principal means for politicians with access to large sums of money to reach voters.

By the 1980s, the importance of the three television networks was modified by the growth of cable companies. In addition, the introduction of video tape recorders increased the utility of television sets, which could be programmed to record programs for viewing at convenient times or used to air old and recent movies in private homes.


## "A Nation of Sheep"

Families with middle-class incomes increased rapidly during the postwar years, and the percentage of immigrants in the population declined to less than 5 percent of all Americans. This trend contributed to social and cultural uniformity. The incomes of industrial workers rose and more fringe benefits became available. Blue-collar workers steadily climbed into the ranks of the middle class and moved to suburbs previously reserved for junior executives and shopkeepers.


## Religion in Changing Times

Organized religion, though traditionally concerned with eternal values, was influenced by the social, cultural, and economic developments of the postwar years. The Catholic Church built new schools, hospitals, and churches. Southern Baptists, who emerged as the largest single denomination among Protestants, built 500 new churches to accommodate some 300,000 new members. Jews spent a billion dollars building 1,000 synagogues.

Surveys showed that nearly all Americans believed in God, but many were ignorant of religious history and doctrine. The New Deal had placed upon government a large share of the burden for charity previously borne by churches. The expansion of higher education introduced young adults to new ideas and made people more tolerant of the religious beliefs of others.

Many churches became involved in the civil rights movement and the antiwar demonstrations of the 1960s and 1970s. The sweeping social changes had religious ramifications, as feminists demanded female ministers and priests. Practices such as cohabitation, homosexuality, pornography, and legalized abortion caused shock waves within the religious community.

More conservative denominations rejected Darwinism and advocated the teaching of "creation theory" in the schools. By the 1970s, a new wave of television ministers was preaching religious, political, social, and moral conservatism. The best known of the postwar revivalists, the Reverend Billy Graham, stressed interdenominational cooperation.

## Literature and Art

Leading books in the postwar years included Norman Mailer's *The Naked and the Dead* and James Jones's *From Here to Eternity*, both based on wartime experiences of the authors. The more talented younger writers, such as Jack Kerouac of the beatific school, rejected materialist values but seemed obsessed with violence, perversion, and madness. The most popular novels among college students were J. D. Salinger's *The Catcher in the Rye* and Joseph Heller's *Catch-22*, an indignant denunciation of warfare. Despite the popularity of television, interest in reading continued, particularly in the sale of paperbacks.

Postwar artists like Jackson Pollock were influenced by the subjective school of abstract expressionism, which stressed the "unconscious" in art. Individuals may interpret abstract paintings in different ways. The painter Andy Warhol created portraits of mundane objects such as flags, comic strips, soup cans, and packing cases.

## Two Dilemmas

By the 1960s the nation seemed to face two dilemmas. One was that progress was often self-defeating. Products such as DDT, which killed insects, had an adverse impact on birds, fish, and people. Foreign policies geared to prevent war sometimes led to new wars. Parents who tried to transmit the accumulated wisdom of the years to their offspring found the youngsters rejected their advice.

The second dilemma was that the modern industrial society placed too much emphasis on social cooperation and undermined the individual. These dilemmas produced a paradox. Though the United States was the most powerful nation in the world, it seemed unable to mobilize its resources to confront challenges. The so-called "me generation" hence failed to produce a consensus, as society remained fragmented.

## The Costs of Prosperity

While GNP surpassed $1 trillion, inflation put workers under pressure to demand raises, which drove up prices even more. Workers put their individual interests above those of the whole.

Technological improvements stimulated such new industries as plastics and electronics. In the 1950s, scientists manufactured electricity from nuclear fuels. Computers revolutionized the collection and storage of records, solved mathematical problems, and accelerated the work of bank tellers, librarians, and tax collectors. The benefits of technology produced unpredictable side effects. Petroleum needed for fuel released pollutants into the air. The increased use of paper and plastics threatened to bury the nation in trash. Fertilizers washed into streams and destroyed acquatic life.

**New Racial Turmoil**

Great Society programs did not produce racial peace and social harmony. Some disenchanted blacks, such as Stokely Carmichael of the Student Nonviolent Coordinating Committee, adopted the slogan "Black Power" and refused to cooperate with whites in the civil rights movement. "If we are to proceed toward true liberation, we must set ourselves off from white people," Carmichael said. Groups like the Black Panthers collected weapons to resist the police.

Black anger engulfed Watts, Los Angeles (1965), New York and Chicago (1966), and Newark, New Jersey, and Detroit (1967). The Detroit riot, perhaps the worst since the Civil War erupted, cost 43 lives.

In April 1968, when King was assassinated by James Earl Ray in Memphis, Tennessee, blacks in more than a hundred cities unleashed their anger by burning and looting. A commission headed by Governor Otto Kerner of Illinois, which President Johnson appointed after the 1967 riots, blamed "white racism" for having deprived blacks of jobs, crowded them into slums, and eroded their hopes of future success. To escape urban tensions, millions of middle-class whites moved to the suburbs or called on police to "maintain law and order." The riots tended to polarize society along racial lines.

In 1992, another Watts riot took more than 50 lives and caused heavy property damage, amid a renewed national debate over the federal role in the support of inner cities.

**Native Born Ethnics**

As blacks struggled for equality, so did millions of Mexican-Americans in the Southwest. After World War II, federal legislation encouraged the importation of *braceros* or temporary farm workers. Moreover, other Mexicans and other Spanish-speaking peoples called *mojados* entered the country illegally, settling in city *barrios*, where low-paying but steady work could be found. Some Spanish-speaking "Chicanos" demanded political, social, economic, and educational improvements. In 1965, Cesar Chavez, the most visible Chicano and the organizer of migrant farm workers, launched a national boycott of grapes.

Meanwhile, the American Indian Movement demanded self-determination, the return of lands taken from their ancestors, and the revival of tribal culture. In 1973, radicals occupied the town of Wounded Knee, South Dakota, site of an 1890 Sioux massacre, and held it at gunpoint for weeks. In 1975, Congress passed the Indian Self-determination Act to give tribes more control over education, welfare programs, and law enforcement.

Despite the hurdles, many minorities made striking gains. In 1965, Robert Weaver became the first black to serve in the Cabinet. Two years later, Thurgood Marshall, attorney for the plaintiffs in the *Brown* decision, became the first black appointed to the Supreme Court. In 1966, Edward Brooke, a Massachusetts Republican, was elected the first black senator since Reconstruction. Many cities elected blacks as mayor. Blacks also broke the color line in sports. The boxers Joe Louis and Muhammad Ali attracted fans in both races.

## Rethinking Public Education

After decades of "progressive education" in the John Dewey tradition and emphasis on "adjustment," "self-esteem," and emotional development of youngsters, it became clear that the educational system was producing poor work habits, fuzzy thinking, and plain ignorance of basic knowledge. Former Harvard president James B. Conant in *The American High School Today* flayed the schools for neglecting foreign languages, ignoring the needs of the brightest and the dullest students, and for not effectively teaching English grammar and composition. He argued that teachers colleges should emphasize subject matter over educational methodology in their curricula.

The success of the Soviet *Sputnik* spurred a renewed interest in math and science through passage of the National Defense Education Act in 1958. However, the needs of disadvantaged minority students who lived in slums, often in broken homes, and who lacked the incentives and training of middle-class children, put pressures on schools in a different direction.

Population growth and demand for specialized skills contributed to an increase in college enrollment. To bridge the gap between high school and universities, more than 1,300 junior colleges and community colleges were serving 6.4 million students by the early 1990s.

## Students in Revolt

By the 1960s many students, trained by teachers of New Deal leanings, revolted against established trends in politics, economics, and education. These students felt guilty when they thought about the millions of Americans without the material comforts and advantages they had enjoyed and increasingly regarded poverty, atomic weapons, and racial prejudice as intolerable.

In the Port Huron Statement, Students for a Democratic Society advocated numerous social reforms popular with the political left: making corporations "publicly responsible," allocating national resources on the basis of "social needs," and establishment of "participatory democracy," or getting people involved in small groups where individuals could exert an impact. The SDS grew with the acceleration of the Vietnam War, when students faced possible conscription.

In 1964, a student outburst known as the "Free Speech movement" convulsed the University of California at Berkeley, leading to the resignation of school president Clark Kerr. At Columbia University in 1968, SDS and black students occupied university buildings and made "nonnegotiable" demands concerning military research and the needs of minority groups. When police came to clear the buildings, rioting caused injuries to dozens of students. The unrest led to the resignation of university president Grayson Kirk.

Critics of the radical students found them infantile because they refused to tolerate delay, unwise because their ideas had been refuted by earlier philosophers and scientists, and authoritarian because they rejected majority rule.

Some black students withdrew to themselves, rejected the "white" curriculum, and demanded "black studies" programs taught and administered by blacks.

## The Counterculture

Young people known generally as Hippies retreated from the modern world in a counterculture of communes, drugs, and mystical religions. The poet Allen Ginsberg in his poem *Howl* wrote that the "best minds" of his generation had been destroyed by the "madness" of modern society. The hippie counterculture stressed feelings over thought, natural things over anything manufactured, and love over money or influence. Male hippies wore their hair long and grew beards; female hippies avoided make up, bras, and other devices to make themselves attractive to men.

Hippies held similar beliefs with the radicals, especially in regard to the Vietnam War, but avoided political involvement undertaken by the radical "Yippies." Some Hippies used hallucinogenic drugs, which they claimed increased their "awareness." In time, most hippies left the counterculture to return to the traditional ways of living they once scorned.

## The Sexual Revolution

In the 1960s, conventional ideas about premarital sex, contraception, abortion, homosexuality, and pornography were openly challenged. Alfred C. Kinsey, in *Sexual Behavior in the Human Male* and *Sexual Behavior in the Human Female*, argued that premarital sex, marital infidelity, and homosexuality were more common than many had suspected. Kinsey's research made it possible to view sex in physical terms, a fact liberating to some and frightening to others. The "sexual freedom" had profound psychological results for many and fueled rampant illegitimacy, an explosion of such venereal diseases as gonorrhea and syphilis, and the lethal acquired immune deficiency syndrome (AIDS).

## Women's Liberation

The sexual revolution and the civil rights movement contributed to a revival of feminism, which advocated more job opportunities for women, "equal pay for equal work," and daycare centers. Between 1940 and 1960, the proportion of women workers doubled. Married women entered the work force to counter the ravages of inflation and/or to seek satisfaction outside the home. In the immediate postwar years women often found that they were paid less than men who did the same work, and some occupations were closed to them.

Many feminists who demanded equality with men were spurred by Betty Friedan, whose *The Feminine Mystique* argued that "the only way for a woman ... to know herself as a person is by creative work of her own."

The National Organization of Women copied the tactics of black activists to demand employment opportunities, an equal rights amendment to the Constitution, changes in divorce laws, and the legalization of abortion.

In 1970, Kate Millett's *Sexual Politics* denounced male supremacy and argued that biological distinctions between the sexes need not create gender differences. Other feminists read

*Ms.* magazine, organized "women's studies" programs in colleges, and advocated the rearing of children in communal centers and the abolition of marriage.

Some conservative women activists rallied behind the Illinois lawyer Phyllis Schlafly to defeat the ERA, which passed Congress in 1972 but fell three states short of ratification. Others joined the right-to-life movement in hopes of overturning the Supreme Court's *Roe v. Wade* decision, which declared in 1973 that women have a constitutional right to obtain an abortion and that states may not intervene in the matter.

## People, Places, and Things

*Identify the following concepts:*

"sun belt" _____

_____

interstate highways _____

_____

FCC _____

_____

"creation theory" _____

_____

beatific school _____

_____

abstract expressionism _____

_____

"me generation" _____

_____

black power _____

_____

"white racism" _____

_____

*barrios* _____

_____

*braceros* _____

_____

peyote _____

_____

Hippies _____

_____

Yippies _____

_____

Chicanos _____

_____

equal rights amendment _____

_____

*Describe the following*:

The Lonely Crowd _____

_____

*The Catcher in the Rye* _____

_____

SNCC _____

_____

American Indian Movement _____

_____

Indian Self-determination Act _____

_____

Watts _____

_____

NDEA _____

_____

Kerner Commission _____

_____

Port Huron Statement _____

_____

"Free Speech" movement _____

_____

AIDS _____

_____

*Soul on Ice* _____

_____

*The Feminine Mystique* _____

_____

NOW _____

_____

*Roe v. Wade* _____

_____

*Identify the following people*:

Norman Mailer _____

_____

Jack Kerouac _____

_____

Joseph Heller _____

_____

Jackson Pollock _____

_____

Andy Warhol _____

_____

Stokely Carmichael _____

_____

James Earl Ray _____

_____

César Chávez _____

_____

Muhammad Ali _____

_____

James Conant _____

_____

Allen Ginsberg _____

_____

Kate Millett _____

_____

Phyllis Schlafly _____

_____

# Self-Test

## Multiple-Choice Questions

1. The feminist who wrote that women could find satisfaction only from "creative work" of their own was:
   A. Kate Millett,
   B. Phyllis Schlafly
   C. Betty Friedan
   D. Gloria Steinem

2. Who assassinated Martin Luther King, Jr.?
   A. Eldridge Cleaver
   B. Stokely Carmichael
   C. James Earl Ray
   D. Sirhan B. Sirhan

3. Where was Martin Luther King, Jr. assassinated?
   A. Dallas
   B. Memphis
   C. Los Angeles
   D. Detroit

4. Which part of the United States grew the most rapidly after World War II?
   A. Northeast
   B. Northwest
   C. Middle West
   D. Sun belt

5. The first jetliner was built by:
   A. General Dynamics
   B. Lockheed
   C. Boeing
   D. General Motors

6. Which of these statements regarding organized religion in the postwar years is *false*?
   A. Polls revealed that most Americans believed in God but lacked knowledge about the Bible.
   B. From 1945 to 1965, American Jews spent a billion dollars building synagogues.
   C. There was little relationship between mainline churches and the civil rights movement.
   D. The Catholic Church built more than 1,000 schools and a hundred hospitals in the postwar years.

7. Which of the following was *not* a black athlete?
   A. Jack Johnson
   B. Joe Lewis
   C. Muhammad Ali
   D. Robert Weaver

8. A leading advocate of abstract expressionism was:
   A. J. D. Salinger
   B. Joseph Heller
   C. Jackson Pollock
   D. Norman Mailer

9. Spanish-speaking Americans who resisted their traditional ways of living were known as:
   A. *Braceros*
   B. *Barrios*
   C. Chicanos
   D. *Mojados*

10. César Chávez:
    A. Was the first Mexican-American elected to the United States Senate
    B. Led a national consumer boycott of California grapes and lettuce in the middle 1960s
    C. Founded the Hispanic Crusade for Justice
    D. Urged Hispanics to desert the Democratic party

11. Edward Brooke was the first black to serve as:
    A. State governor
    B. United States senator
    C. Big-city mayor
    D. Supreme Court justice

12. Educators came under challenge in the 1960s for:
    A. Overemphasis on technical subjects
    B. Producing students with poor work habits and academic ignorance
    C. Opposing school desegregation
    D. Emphasizing subject matter to the exclusion of educational methodology

13. The "Free Speech" movement began at:
    A. Columbia University
    B. Harvard
    C. Kent State University
    D. University of California at Berkeley

14. Hippies were the *least* influenced by:
    A. Drugs
    B. Conventional societal mores
    C. Opposition to the Vietnam War
    D. Conformity with the counterculture

15. Alfred Kinsey's studies of sexuality revealed that:
    A. Promiscuity would lead to an increase in illegitimacy
    B. American men engaged in sexual activity outside marriage more often than had been presumed
    C. The relaxation of sexual taboos would wipe out venereal diseases
    D. Sex could not be divorced from religious values

**Essay Questions**

1. Discuss demographic changes caused by the population growth in the post-World War II years.

2. Explain how television has exerted enormous impact on American thought and culture in the postwar years.

3. Evaluate the success of organized religion in its attempt to meet the changing needs of Americans in the postwar era.

4. Explain how racial tension marred the late 1960s just as Great Society programs were being implemented.

5. Evaluate the successes and shortcomings of the women's liberation movement.

6. Discuss the impact of the Conant study on American education in the late 1950s and early 1960s. Explain how the status of education had changed by the 1990s.

# CRITICAL THINKING EXERCISE

Few issues were the subject of more debate in the 1970s and 1980s than women's liberation. Analyze these statements and place an "F" before those that represent a *feminist* viewpoint and a "T" before those that reflect the more *traditional* role of women.

_____ 1. People should not think of the adjectives *strong* and *efficient* as male characteristics and *passive* and *tender* as female traits.

_____2. "The hand that rocks the cradle rules the world."

_____3. Government childcare centers are essential to the preservation of family life into the 21st century.

_____4. "Help wanted" advertisements should be segregated by sex so that job seekers will know whether employers prefer men or women for open positions.

_____5. "I'm not saying that women leaders would eliminate violence. We are not more moral than men; we are only uncorrupted by power so far."

_____6. Abortions should be funded at taxpayer expense because poor women might not otherwise be able to limit their family sizes.

_____7. Reproductive freedom and the "right to privacy" are inherent in interpretation of the Constitution.

_____8. The loosening of sexual mores in the 1960s and 1970s produced side effects its proponents did not expect; namely, rampant illegitimacy and abortion, venereal diseases, and grave psychological effects for many.

_____9. An ERA is superfluous; the 1964 Civil Rights Act already guarantees "equal pay for equal work."

_____10. A woman can best judge her success by maintaining a happy, peaceful home amid an uncertain world of tension and heartache.

_____11. Government should address recurring problems of "latchkey" and other neglected children because families have been unable to do so.

_____12. "The institution of the patriarch" is outmoded and is headed into the dustbin of history.

_____13. A parental leave program mandated by Congress would ignore the realities of the workplace and the varying needs of workers by mandating a plan that, while desirable for some, would work to the detriment of others.

_____14. "At twenty-three I believed that woman was the enemy of man. At forty-three I now know that woman is his completer."

_____15. Men and women really are different and will never be satisfied until they fulfill the roles God ordained for them.

CHAPTER 32

# Our Times

## Learning Objectives

*After reading Chapter 32, you should be able to:*

1. Evaluate the Ford, Carter, Reagan, and Bush administrations.
2. Discuss the winding down of the Cold War from the aftermath of the communist acquisition of Vietnam to the rise of democratic governments in Eastern Europe.
3. Explain how economic problems, particularly inflation, unemployment, recession, and deficits, have persisted since 1974.
4. Understand how the 1979 Iranian hostage crisis developed and how the matter was resolved.
5. Evaluate the elections of 1976, 1980, 1984, 1988, and 1992.
6. Show how the "Reagan Revolution" changed America after the Carter years in reference to foreign and domestic policy.
7. Evaluate the Iran-Contra affair.
8. Reflect on the policies of the Bush and Clinton administrations.

## Overview

**Ford As President**

Gerald Ford's brief presidential tenure was untouched by the scandal that had been the undoing of his predecessor. The decision to pardon Richard Nixon before the former president had been charged with any offense evoked rumors of a "corrupt bargain" and helped cause Ford's defeat in 1976. Ford's "Whip Inflation Now" program did not prevent an economic slump, as unemployment exceeded 9 percent.

When communists launched a new offensive in Vietnam, months after the Americans had left, Ford asked Congress to send arms to help South Vietnam stem the advance. The Democratic Congress refused to send the aid, and in April 1975 Saigon fell, to be renamed Ho Chi Minh City. Meanwhile, communists had seized an American merchant ship, the *Mayaguez,* with a crew of 39, in the Gulf of Siam. Frustrated over the communist takeover of South Vietnam and Cambodia, Ford sent marines to force the release of the ship. Thirty-eight marines died in the operation, which could have been avoided since the Cambodians had already released the ship before the marines struck.

Ford was challenged in the Republican primaries by former California Governor Ronald Reagan, the favorite of the party's right wing, and the president just barely gained nomination at the national convention in Kansas City.

Meanwhile, Democrats chose the largely unknown Jimmy Carter, former governor of Georgia, to challenge Ford. Carter effectively utilized television and mastered the intricate delegate-selection process. He stressed his lack of connection with the Washington establishment and vowed, "I'll never lie to you."

Carter's initially large lead evaporated, but he still won, 297 to 241 electoral votes, with support from organized labor and a coalition of white southerners and blacks.

## The Carter Presidency

Carter set a tone of democratic simplicity and moral fervor. He submitted complicated proposals to Congress but failed to follow up. Carter varied his approach on economic policies, at times seeming to wish to stem inflation, on other occasions aiming his fire at unemployment. He tended to blame others for his political woes, including the public as a whole. In the summer of 1979, he described a national "malaise" that had sapped the nation's energies and undermined civic pride. The speech served to make Carter appear ineffective and petulant.

## Cold War or Détente?

In foreign affairs Carter announced that "basic human rights" would receive highest priority. He cut off aid to Chile and Argentina but took no such action against repressive communist regimes. He successfully negotiated treaties with Panama that provided for the gradual transfer of the isthmian canal to that country by December 1999. He extended diplomatic ties to Communist China.

Carter's Soviet policy fluctuated between the divergent approaches of Secretary of State Cyrus Vance, a conciliator, and National Security Advisor Zbigniew Brzezinski, considered a "cold warrior." He signed a new Strategic Arms Limitation Treaty with the Soviets in 1979. When the Soviets invaded Afghanistan, Carter withdrew the SALT agreement, halted the shipment of American grain and technology to Moscow, and refused to allow American athletes to compete in the Olympic games, which were held in the summer of 1980 in Moscow.

Carter's main diplomatic achievement was the Camp David Agreement, by which Israel and Egypt negotiated a treaty ending the state of war that had existed between them since 1948. Egypt in effect became the first Arab country to recognize Israel. In 1994, the Palestine Liberation Organization signed a similar treaty with Israel.

## A Time of Troubles

The Carter presidency coincided with an era in which the United States had lost much of its international prestige due to the failure to prevent the communists from overrunning South Vietnam. The nation seemed unable to manage its economic and energy policies. The inner sections of the great cities, such as the South Bronx, seemed beyond repair, crime in urban areas soared, and discipline and academic achievement of the public schools fell to abysmal levels.

## Double-digit Inflation

The 5 percent inflationary rate of 1971 would have seemed rather uneventful by 1979, when the rate reached 13 percent. Such inflation had devastating effects on the retired, the poor, and others living on fixed incomes. Inflation discouraged long-term investment and caused some to stop saving. To escape the ravages of inflation, some transferred their assets from cash to houses, land, gold, art, or jewelry. Interest rates rose as lenders demanded higher returns to compensate for inflation.

Congress approved a cost of living index in Social Security to protect retirees, an action that made balancing the budget politically infeasible. When wages and salaries rose, taxes automatically increased because larger dollar incomes thrust people into "bracket creep." Taxpayer revolts such as California's Proposition 13 in 1978 caused some to turn against expensive government programs.

## The Carter Recession

Carter appointed the monetarist Paul Volcker to head the Federal Reserve Board. Volcker claimed that the way to check inflation was to limit growth of the money supply. Under Volcker's direction, the board adopted a tight-money policy, which caused already high interest rates to soar. Such rates were devastating to the housing and automobile industries and to businesses seeking to expand. Savings and loan institutions were hard-hit because they were saddled with mortgages made when rates were 4 and 5 percent.

## The Iran Crisis: Origins

On November 4, 1979, some 400 armed Moslem militants broke into the American Embassy in Teheran, Iran, and took captives. The militants opposed the rule of the shah, Muhammad Reza Pahlavi, who had been kept in power by an American-supplied army.

In 1979, popular uprisings forced the shah to flee the country. A revolutionary government headed by the Ayatollah Khomeini, who returned to Iran after a exile in France, assumed power. Khomeini denounced the United States as the "Great Satan." The revolutionists seized the embassy when President Carter allowed the shah to come to the United States for medical treatment.

## The Iran Crisis: Carter's Dilemma

The Iranian militants said they would hold the hostages until the United States returned the shah for trial as a traitor. They also demanded the shah's wealth. Carter froze Iranian assets and banned trade with Iran until the hostages were freed. Carter wanted to rescue the hostages but feared going to war would mean their execution. Months passed, and the shah, terminally ill with cancer, left the United States for Panama.

Before the seizure of the hostages, Massachusetts Senator Edward M. Kennedy announced he would challenge Carter for renomination. Despite the 1969 Chappaquiddick affair, Kennedy appeared to be a formidable opponent until the taking of the hostages seemed to revive Carter's fortunes. In April 1980, Carter ordered a team of marine commandos flown into Iran by helicopters to try to free the hostages. The raid was a fiasco, as several helicopters broke down, and eight commandos were killed in a crash.

## The Election of 1980

Carter beat Kennedy decisively in the Democratic primaries and had more than enough delegates to be renominated on the first ballot at the party convention in New York City. The Republicans turned to Ronald Reagan, who at 69 was the oldest person ever nominated for president by a major party. A former liberal Democrat, Reagan had been twice elected governor of California. One of Reagan's opponents for the Republican nomination, liberal Illinois Congressman John Anderson, bolted the GOP and ran in the general election as an independent.

Reagan's defense of patriotism, religion, family life, and old-fashioned virtues won him the backing of conservative groups. He promised to cut spending and taxes, contending that the budget could be balanced while inflation was simultaneously reduced.

In a television debate, Reagan gained the upper hand by posing a question Carter had posed to Ford in 1976: "Are you better off now than you were four years ago?" Reagan won a popular majority and an electoral landslide. The Republicans gained control of the Senate for the first time since the elections of 1952 and cut into the Democratic majority in the House.

Carter devoted his last weeks in office to the continuing hostage crisis. Just as Reagan was being inaugurated in 1981, the hostages were released after 444 days in captivity. In return, the United States agreed to release the Iranian assets.

## Reagan As President

With his amiable, unaggressive style, Reagan tried to change the direction of the nation. He urged the return of some federal functions to the states and called for decreased government regulations. He proposed increasing military expenditures on grounds that the Soviets had taken unfair advantage of détente.

Congress adopted Reagan's "supply-side" proposal to reduce income taxes by 25 percent over three years. Updating the philosophy of Andrew Mellon, Reagan reasoned that a tax cut would spur investment, increase production, create more jobs and prosperity, and bring more income to government despite the lower tax rates. While Congress went along with the tax cuts, it rebuffed Reagan's proposals to slash domestic programs impacting the poor and disadvantaged. The impasse between the president and Congress failed to produce a balanced budget, and deficits continued to accumulate.

Reagan acquired organized labor's wrath by breaking an illegal strike of air traffic controllers. Some 11,400 controllers were not rehired even after the strike collapsed.

By 1982 the nation faced a recession of relatively short duration, as unemployment topped 10 percent. The Reagan "recovery" that began in early 1983 reduced inflation and unemployment and spurred prosperity and economic expansion in much of the country.

The continuing turmoil in the Middle East prompted Reagan to send troops to Beirut, Lebanon, as part of an international peacekeeping force. Tragedy resulted in October 1983 when a fanatical Moslem crashed a truck loaded with explosives into an airport building housing the American marines. The structure collapsed, killing 239 marines. Early in 1984, Reagan removed the troops.

Meanwhile, Reagan pursued a military buildup and attempted to overthrow the communist Sandinistas in Nicaragua by arming "Contra" rebel troops. In 1983, he used American troops to overthrow a Cuban-backed regime on the island of Grenada in the Lesser Antilles.


## Four More Years

Reagan was renominated in 1984 without opposition, while the Democrats chose Walter Mondale, Carter's vice-president. Mondale selected New York Representative Geraldine Ferraro as his runningmate, the first woman ever given such a nomination.

Reagan consolidated the support of social conservatives, the group that Nixon had termed the "silent majority." A Reagan supporter, the Reverend Jerry Falwell of Lynchburg, Virginia, formed the Moral Majority (1979-1989) to lobby against drugs, communism, homosexuality, abortion, and "coddling" criminals. Reagan also won the support of blue-collar workers, white southerners who had long been Democratic, and some northern Democrats as well. Reagan benefited from voter tendency to support a sitting president when the economy seemed strong. Mondale dampened his chances when he vowed in his acceptance speech to raise taxes if elected.

Reagan lost only in Mondale's Minnesota and in the District of Columbia. The Democratic tactic of nominating a woman for vice-president failed, as a majority of women supported Reagan. Reagan's triumph was largely personal, as the GOP made only minimal gains in the House and lost two Senate seats.


## "The Reagan Revolution"

When Mikhail S. Gorbachev became head of the Soviet government in 1985, he seemed to encourage political debate in his country, a policy called *glasnost*. He sought to stimulate the Soviet economy by rewarding individual achievement (*perestroika*). In 1986, Reagan, having gradually abandoned his earlier comments about a Soviet "evil empire," met with Gorbachev in Reykjavik, Iceland, to discuss arms control. The summit deadlocked when Reagan stood behind the strategic defense initiative, a proposal to prevent a nuclear first strike against the United States. At another summit in 1988, Reagan and Gorbachev signed a treaty eliminating medium-range nuclear missiles.

Reagan's presidency corresponded with the launching of the first space shuttle, the *Columbia*, in 1981. In 1986, another shuttle, the *Challenger*, exploded shortly after takeoff, killing its seven-member crew, a disaster that curtailed flights until 1989.

In 1985, four Arabs seized control of an Italian cruise ship, the *Achille Lauro*, in the Mediterranean and killed an elderly American tourist. After Libyan-supported terrorists bombed a West German club frequented by American servicemen, Reagan retaliated by ordering an air strike against Libya, a popular move at home.

The Income Tax Act of 1986 reduced the top levy on personal incomes from 50 to 28 percent and the tax on corporate profits from 46 to 34 percent. The law abolished numerous tax shelters and established the principle of tax indexing to avoid "bracket creep." It provided only two basic rates: 15 percent on incomes below $29,750 and 28 percent on incomes above this limit.

Reagan—like Nixon earlier—attempted to move the Supreme Court in a more conservative direction. He appointed Sandra Day O'Connor of Arizona as the first woman justice and elevated Associate Justice William Rehnquist as chief justice. His other appointees were Antonin Scalia, the first Italian-American on the Court, and Anthony Kennedy of California. Kennedy assumed the seat Reagan had initially planned to fill with Judge Robert Bork, the man who as Nixon's solicitor general had discharged Watergate special prosecutor Archibald Cox. Bork was rejected by the Senate after liberal groups mobilized nationally against him on ideological grounds.

## Change and Uncertainty

By the 1960s, many immigrants poured into the United States from Asia and Latin America. Some were refugees fleeing repressive regimes in Vietnam, Cuba, Haiti, and Central America. Others came illegally across the Mexican border. The Simpson-Mazzoli Immigaration Act of 1986 granted amnesty to some illegal immigrants and imposed civil sanctions on employers who hired "undocumented" aliens in the future.

Family life underwent drastic change by the 1970s and 1980s, as the "breadwinner father" and "housewife and mother" ceased to be the norm. The number of single-parent families living in poverty increased by 46 percent between 1979 and 1987. More than a million marriages ended in divorce, and cohabitation and illegitimacy rose steadily. The number of abortions rose from 763,000 in 1974 to an average of 1.3 million a year in the 1980s.

The crime rate continued to soar, and a national campaign was launched against illegal drugs with mixed results. Cocaine became available in a cheap, smokeable form known as "crack." AIDS, uniformly fatal, wreaked havoc on promiscuous homosexuals and intravenous drug users who shared needles. The spread of AIDS led to a new emphasis on the use of condoms, which by 1990 were being distributed free in many high schools.

The unionized work force declined to 19 percent in 1985, a situation that stemmed from the difficulty of organizing white-collar workers. Furthermore, many "multinational" manufacturing companies relocated to Asia and Latin America in order to take advantage of low labor costs.

## The Merger Movement

The Reagan administration's abandonment of strict enforcement of antitrust laws encouraged a new trend toward mergers in which unrelated companies swallowed up one another. In 1989, Time Inc. borrowed $13.9 billion to purchase Warner Communications, thus forming one of the world's largest publishing concerns.

Corporate raiders raised cash by issuing high-interest bonds secured by the assets of the company purchased. The broker Michael Milkin of Drexel Burnham Lambert, emerged as the "king" of the "junk bond" business. The system enabled a small company or an individual to buy a corporation. One deal often led to another. In 1985, the R. J. Reynolds Tobacco Company bought Nabisco for $4.9 billion. Three years later, RJR Nabisco was itself consumed by Kohlberg, Kravis, Roberts, and Company for $24.9 billion.

The fluctuating price of petroleum created problems for OPEC, whose members had to cut back on their imports of manufactured goods when cheaper oil devastated their economies. A similar situation developed in the agricultural heartland, as the value of wheat exports decreased 50 percent, causing bankruptcy for some farmers.

## The Iran-Contra Arms Deal

President Reagan sought to aid the Nicaraguan Contras in their fight against the communist Sandinistas and to free a number of remaining hostages being held in Lebanon. In 1985, he approved the delivery of arms to Iran by way of Israel in hopes of getting the release of hostages. He subsequently ordered the secret sale of American weapons to Iran, a transaction arranged by Marine Colonel Oliver North, the aide to Reagan's national security adviser, Admiral John Poindexter. With Poindexter's knowledge, North used $12 million of the profits from the Iranian sales to provide weapons for the Contras, a violation of a Congressional ban on such aid. When news of the sales to Iran and the diversion of profits to supply the Contras came to light, Poindexter resigned, North was fired, and a special prosecutor was appointed by Reagan to investigate.

Reagan said that he knew nothing about the diversion of aid to the Contras, but polls showed that a majority of Americans did not believe him. Iran-Contra undermined Reagan's influence with Congress and dampened his political reputation.

## The Election of 1988

Vice-President George Bush easily won the Republican nomination to succeed Reagan, while the Democrats turned to Massachusetts Governor Michael S. Dukakis, who brushed aside a spirited challenge waged by the Reverend Jesse Jackson. Dukakis, who stressed "competence" over ideology began the race with a lead in the polls, but Bush closed the gap after criticizing a Massachusetts law granting furloughs to prisoners serving life sentences for murder. Bush also challenged Governor Dukakis's veto of a bill requiring teachers to lead students in the recitation of the pledge of allegiance.

Much attention was focused on the vice-presidential nominees in 1988. Dukakis tapped Lloyd M. Bentsen to challenge Bush on his home turf. (In 1970, Bentsen had defeated Bush for the Senate seat from Texas.) Bush chose the 41-year-old Senator Dan Quayle, heir to an Indianapolis publishing family. Quayle appeared slow witted in his debate with Bentsen, and Bush seemed unable to explain why he had selected Quayle in the first place.

Bush nevertheless carried the Electoral College, 426 to 112, but the Democrats maintained firm control of Congress, the governorships, and state legislatures.

### The End of the Cold War

President Bush softened his campaign rhetoric and promised a "kinder and gentler" nation. He maintained opposition to abortion and gun control and endorsed constitutional amendments to prohibit the burning of the American flag and to enforce a balanced budget.

The Cold War finally ended not so much in an outright victory for the United States as a defeat for the Soviet Union. Poland, Hungary, Czechoslovakia, Bulgaria, Romania, and East Germany overthrew repressive regimes that had ruled throughout the postwar era and moved toward democratic reforms. Except in Yugoslavia and Romania, where the dictator Nicolae Ceausescu was executed, the changes occurred in a peaceful manner. Nearly overnight the international political climate changed, as Soviet-style communism fell in disfavor.

Bush sent American forces into Panama in December 1989 to overthrow the regime of General Manuel Noriega, under indictment in the United States for drug trafficking. Noriega was taken to the United States, tried, found guilty, and given a long prison sentence.

President Bush also benefited from the ending of the conflict between the Sandinistas and the Contras in Nicaragua. For the first time in that nation's history, a free presidential election was held; it resulted in a victory for middle-of-the-road democratic forces.

### Domestic Problems and Possibilities

In the 1988 campaign, Bush pledged ("Read my lips") not to raise taxes. Once in office, he endorsed reducing taxes on capital gains to spur investment. As deficits soared, Bush said that the government needed new tax revenues. In October 1990, despite opposition within his party, Bush signed into law a bill that raised income taxes on higher-income families from 28 percent to 31 percent and increased levies on gasoline, liquor, expensive automobiles, and certain other luxuries. Within six months, the economy was headed into a recession.

Government continued to spend heavily on a plethora of programs though Congress moved to cut defense spending in hopes of a vanishing "peace dividend" from the end of the Cold War. Especially costly was the bailout of the savings and loan institutions, some of which had lent money recklessly and invested in "junk bonds." Costs of the bailout plus interest were estimated at $500 billion.

## The War in the Persian Gulf

In August 1990, Bush dispatched a large force to Saudi Arabia to prevent a threatened invasion from Iraq's Saddam Hussein, who overran Kuwait and jeopardized Western petroleum needs. For five months the United Nations (United States, Great Britain, France, Italy, Egypt, and Syria) bolstered its forces in the Saudi desert. Public opinion divided over whether Saddam could be starved into submission through sanctions or whether full-scale war was required.

When Saddam refused to vacate Kuwait, the United States on January 17, 1991, launched "Operation Desert Storm," an enormous air attack directed by General Norman Schwartzkopf. This month-long assault reduced much of Iraq to rubble. Iraq fired a number of Scud missiles at Israel and Saudi Arabia, but otherwise simply endured the onslaught. In liberating Kuwait, the UN forces killed tens of thousands of Iraqis. Bush ordered an end to the attack, and Saddam, who remain entrenched in Baghdad, agreed to pay reparations to Kuwait. In the aftermath of the war, Bush received the highest presidential approval ratings ever, and his reelection seemed assured.

## Things Go Wrong

President Bush's popularity began to wane. When Saddam used remnants of his army to crush the Kurds in northern Iraq and the pro-Iranian Moslems in southern Iraq, critics argued that Bush should not have stopped the fighting until Baghdad, the Iraqi capital, had been captured and Saddam's army totally crushed.

Moreover, the American economy continued sluggishly. Because uncertain times made many feel insecure, Bush could not capitalize on the fact that inflation remained in check and mortgage interest rates had dipped to twenty-year lows.

In addition, political and economic conditions in eastern Europe and the Soviet Union continued to deteriorate. Civil war broke out in Yugoslavia as Croatia and Slovenia sought independence from the Serbian dominated government. The conflict turned into a religious war pitting Serb and Croatia Christians against Bosnian Moslems. In August 1991, a coup toppled Gorbachev in the Soviet Union. Within hours, Gorbachev was back in charge, but by the end of the year, Boris Yeltsin, the anticommunist president of the Russian Republic, had emerged as the dominant figure in Moscow. The 74-year-old Soviet Union was disbanded in favor of a federation of states.

## The Election of 1992

Bush's political fortunes and approval ratings declined sharply by the winter of 1991-92. Conservative columnist Patrick J. Buchanan challenged Bush in the early primaries, and billionaire Texas industrialist H. Ross Perot mounted an independent presidential challenge. When major Democratic prospects declined to enter the race on the theory that Bush would be reelected, Arkansas Governor Bill Clinton swept the primaries and had a solid majority of the delegates at the Democratic convention. He chose Tennessee Senator Albert Gore, Jr., an environmentalist, as his runningmate.

In the campaign Clinton accused Bush of failing to deal effectively with the recession, vowed to undertake public works projects and to encourage private investment, and pledged to reform the nation's health care and educational systems. Bush discounted the seriousness of the recession and emphasized the need to reduce the national deficit and balance the budget.

On election day, Clinton won only 43 percent of the popular vote but swept the Electoral College, 370-168. Bush carried only eighteen states, mostly in the South and West. Although Perot polled nearly 20 percent of the popular vote, he garnered no electoral votes.

## A New Start

Clinton's knowledge of governmental detail created a general impression of mastery and self-confidence that voters found reassuring. Though Clinton set out to reverse the policies of the Reagan-Bush era, circumstances often forced him to back down. He had promised to end the ban on homosexuals in the armed services, but when the Joint Chiefs of Staff and a number of important congressmen objected, he settled for a policy known as "don't ask, don't tell," which allowed persons to enlist only if they did not openly proclaim their sexual preferences.

Clinton used his executive authority to reverse certain Reagan-Bush policies that had limited access to abortion. He named Ruth Bader Ginsburg, a strong advocate of legalized abortion, to the Supreme Court seat vacated by Byron White, who had cast one of the two votes against *Roe v. Wade* in 1973. He also reversed Bush policies by signing a revived family leave bill into law.

Clinton's economic program, packaged as a deficit-reduction plan, passed Congress in the summer of 1993 by the narrowest of margins. The legislation increased income tax rates on families earning more than $140,000 and imposed a 4.3 cent a gallon increase in the federal gasoline tax despite Clinton's campaign pledge not to raise taxes on the middle class.

Meanwhile, Clinton named his wife, Hillary Rodham Clinton, to head a task force on a proposal to reform the nation's health insurance system.

## The Imponderable Future

Although historians may explain how and why events developed, they cannot predict the future. This textbook, rich in events and their causes and results, must end without a conclusion. Moreover, even with later printings, the book will by necessity end inconclusively because not knowing the future is one of the main reasons life is so interesting.

# People, Places, and Things

*Identify the following concepts:*

national malaise _____

_____

human rights policy _____

_____

double-digit inflation _____

_____

"bracket creep" _____

_____

safety net _____

_____

Reaganomics _____

_____

trickle-down theory _____

_____

*glasnost* _____

_____

Strategic Defense Initiative _____

_____

space shuttle _____

_____

undocumented aliens _____

_____

crack _____

_____

seven dwarfs _____

_____

wimp _____

_____

*Describe the following*:

WIN _____

_____

*Mayaguez* _____

_____

SALT II _____

_____

Camp David Agreement _____

_____

Moral Majority _____

_____

*Challenger* _____

_____

Iran-contra affair _____
_____

Sandinistas _____
_____

Contras _____
_____

*Identify the following people*:

Cyrus Vance _____
_____

Anwar Sadat _____
_____

Paul Volcker _____
_____

Muhammad Reza Pahlavi _____
_____

Ayatollah Khomeini _____
_____

Walter Mondale _____
_____

Jesse L. Jackson _____
_____

Geraldine Ferraro _____

_____

Jerry Falwell _____

_____

Mikhail Gorbachev _____

_____

Muammar al-Qaddafi _____

_____

Sandra Day O'Connor _____

_____

Robert Bork _____

_____

Oliver North _____

_____

John Poindexter _____

_____

Michael Dukakis _____

_____

Dan Quayle _____

_____

Manuel Noriega _____

_____

# Map Exercise

Refer to the world map at the top of the following page. Place the correct letter that corresponds with the location of these cities:

____1. Baghdad

____2. Beijing

____3. Beirut

____4. Berlin

____5. Bogota

____6. Buenos Aires

____7. Cairo

____8. Capetown

____9. Caracas

____10. Damascus

____11. Havana

____12. Ho Chi Minh City

____13. Jerusalem

____14. Kabul

____15. London

____16. Managua

____17. Mexico City

____18. Montreal

____19. Moscow

____20. Paris

____21. Reykjavik

____22. Rio de Janeiro

____23. San Salvador

____24. Seoul

____25. Teheran

____26. Tripoli

276

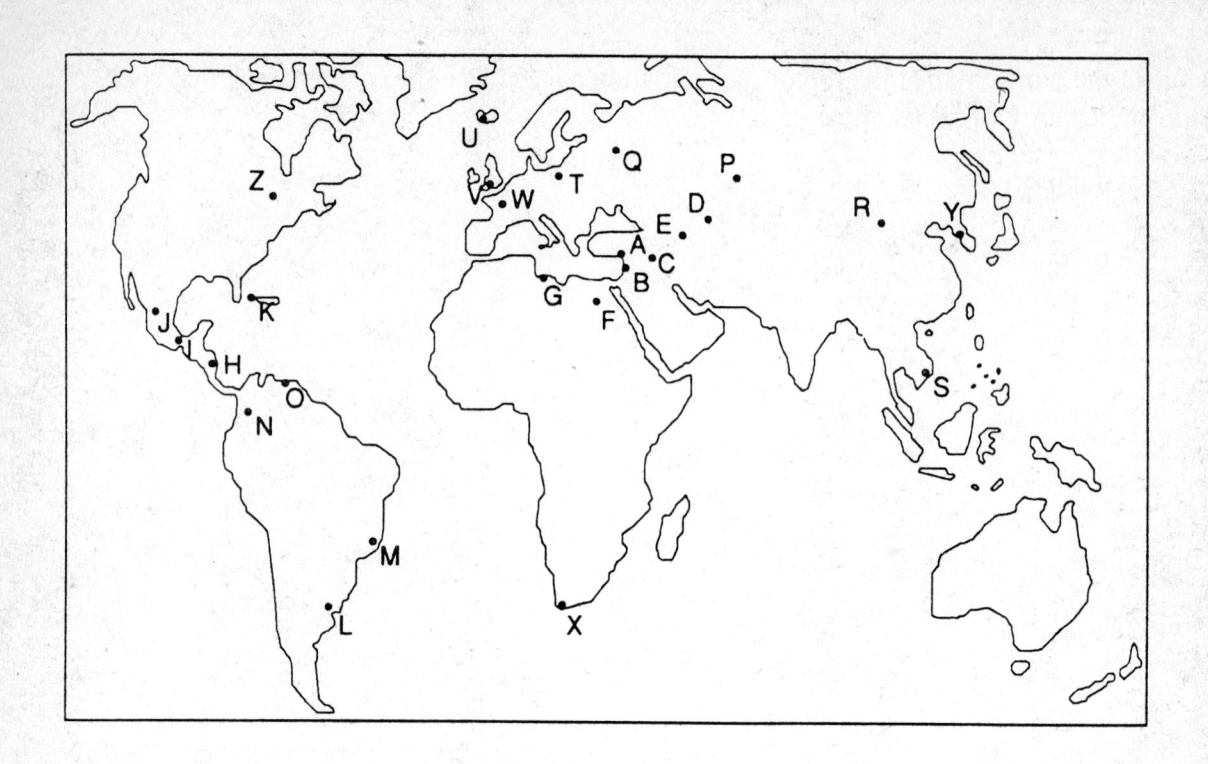

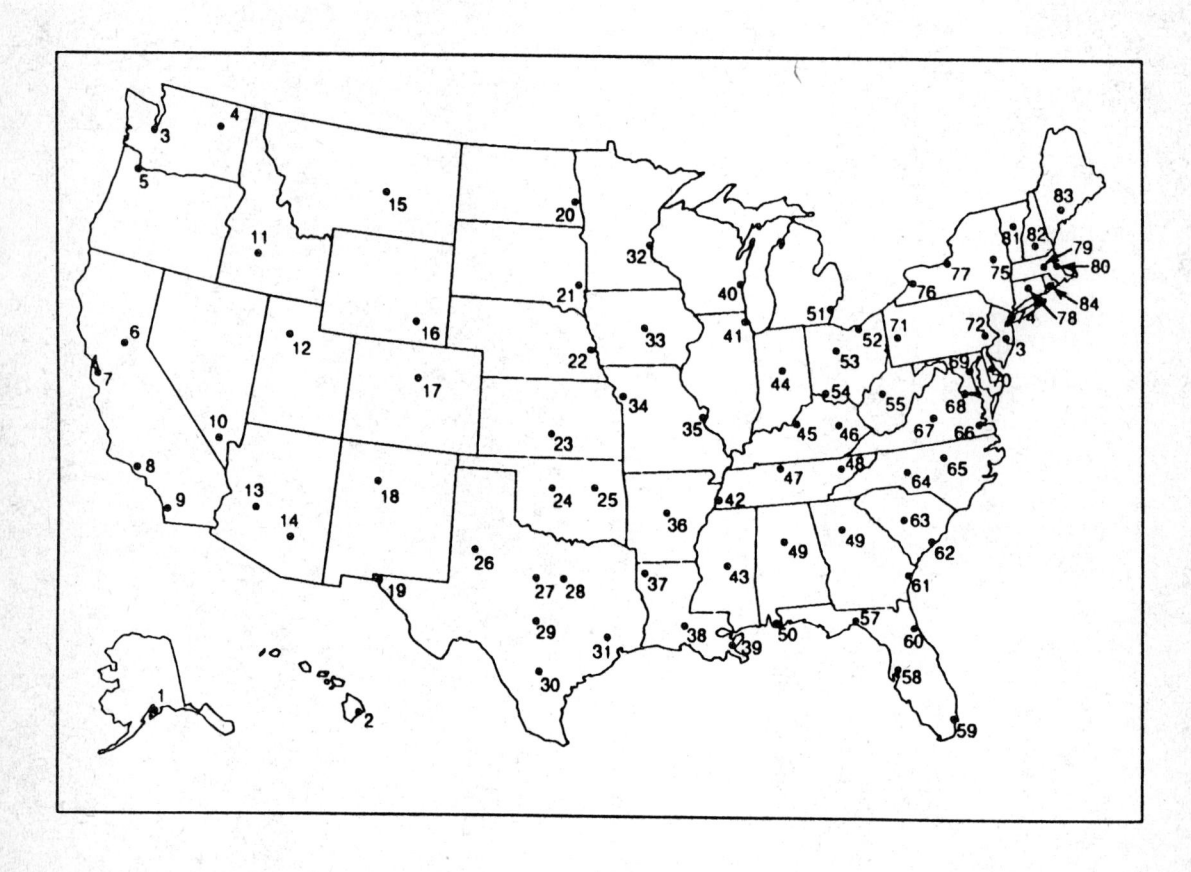

Refer to the United States map on the bottom of the preceding page. Place the number that corresponds with the location of each city beside the proper selection.

| | | | | |
|---|---|---|---|---|
| ____ | 1. Albany | | ____ | 43. Manchester, NH |
| ____ | 2. Albuquerque | | ____ | 44. Memphis |
| ____ | 3. Anchorage | | ____ | 45. Miami |
| ____ | 4. Atlanta | | ____ | 46. Milwaukee |
| ____ | 5. Austin | | ____ | 47. Minneapolis |
| ____ | 6. Baltimore | | ____ | 48. Mobile |
| ____ | 7. Baton Rouge | | ____ | 49. Montpelier |
| ____ | 8. Billings | | ____ | 50. Nashville |
| ____ | 9. Birmingham | | ____ | 51. New Orleans |
| ____ | 10. Boise | | ____ | 52. New York City |
| ____ | 11. Boston | | ____ | 53. Norfolk |
| ____ | 12. Buffalo | | ____ | 54. Oklahoma City |
| ____ | 13. Charleston, SC | | ____ | 55. Omaha |
| ____ | 14. Charleston, WV | | ____ | 56. Philadelphia |
| ____ | 15. Charlotte | | ____ | 57. Phoenix |
| ____ | 16. Cheyenne | | ____ | 58. Pittsburgh |
| ____ | 17. Chicago | | ____ | 59. Portland, ME |
| ____ | 18. Cincinnati | | ____ | 60. Portland, OR |
| ____ | 19. Cleveland | | ____ | 61. Providence |
| ____ | 20. Columbia, SC | | ____ | 62. Raleigh |
| ____ | 21. Columbus, OH | | ____ | 63. Richmond, VA |
| ____ | 22. Dallas | | ____ | 64. Rochester |
| ____ | 23. Denver | | ____ | 65. Sacramento |
| ____ | 24. Des Moines | | ____ | 66. Salt Lake City |
| ____ | 25. Detroit | | ____ | 67. San Antonio |
| ____ | 26. El Paso | | ____ | 68. San Diego |
| ____ | 27. Fargo | | ____ | 69. San Francisco |
| ____ | 28. Fort Worth | | ____ | 70. Savannah |
| ____ | 29. Hartford | | ____ | 71. Seattle |
| ____ | 30. Houston | | ____ | 72. Shreveport |
| ____ | 31. Honolulu | | ____ | 73. Sioux Falls |
| ____ | 32. Indianapolis | | ____ | 74. Spokane |
| ____ | 33. Jackson, MS | | ____ | 75. St. Louis |
| ____ | 34. Jacksonville | | ____ | 76. Tallahassee |
| ____ | 35. Kansas City | | ____ | 77. Tampa |
| ____ | 36. Knoxville | | ____ | 78. Trenton |
| ____ | 37. Las Vegas | | ____ | 79. Tucson |
| ____ | 38. Little Rock | | ____ | 80. Tulsa |
| ____ | 39. Lexington, KY | | ____ | 81. Washington, DC |
| ____ | 40. Los Angeles | | ____ | 82. Wichita |
| ____ | 41. Louisville | | ____ | 83. Wilmington, DE |
| ____ | 42. Lubbock | | ____ | 84. Worcester |

# Self-Test

## Multiple-Choice Questions

1. Diplomatic developments during the Carter administration included all of the following EXCEPT:
   A. Strengthening trade and cultural ties to Taiwan
   B. Israel and Egypt recognize each other
   C. Preparation for turning over Canal Zone to Panama
   D. SALT II

2. All of the following terms deal with economic issues EXCEPT:
   A. Tight money
   B. Reagonomics
   C. Bracket Creep
   D. *Glasnost*

3. Reagan appointed all of the following Supreme Court justices EXCEPT:
   A. Clarence Thomas
   B. Sandra Day O'Connor
   C. Antonin Scalia
   D. Anthony Kennedy

4. The greatest increase in immigration in the past 25 years has come from:
   A. Southern Europe
   B. Southeast Asia and Latin America
   C. Eastern Europe
   D. Africa

5. Republicans tended to credit whom for the winding down of double-digit inflation which ravaged the late 1970s?
   A. Paul Volcker
   B. Alan Greenspan
   C. Ronald Reagan
   D. George Bush

6. In 1985, R. J. Reynolds Tobacco Company purchased:
   A. Drexel Burnham Lambert
   B. Nabisco
   C. Revlon
   D. Time, Inc.

7. Which of the following did NOT occur in Iran-contra?
   A. Colonel Oliver North gained a national following after his testimony before Congress, and his conviction was later tossed out because of improperly obtained evidence
   B. President Reagan's pardon of Admiral John Poindexter prevented the full disclosure of the story
   C. A special prosecutor was appointed to investigate
   D. Reagan insisted that he knew nothing about transferring profits from the arms sale to Iran to assist the contras

8. The Sandinistas:
   A. Cemented their hold over Nicaragua after the Iran-contra affair
   B. Were defeated in the 1990 Nicaraguan elections
   C. Were toppled when the Soviet Union withdrew financial backing to Nicaragua
   D. Hoped to roll back communist forces threatening the government of El Salvador

9. The Reagan administration was involved in all of the following EXCEPT:
   A. Bombing of Tripoli
   B. Negotiating a treaty with the Soviets to limit medium-range missiles
   C. Sending American marines into Beirut
   D. The overthrow of Panamanian leader Manuel Noriega

10. The president who extended diplomatic recognition to Communist China was:
    A. Nixon
    B. Ford
    C. Carter
    D. Reagan

11. SALT II was rejected by the United States Senate in the aftermath of:
    A. The Soviet Union's shooting down of a Korean airliner
    B. Soviet meddling in Southeast Asia
    C. The Soviet invasion of Afghanistan
    D. Terrorist bombings in the Middle East

12. The tight-money policy is associated with:
    A. Ronald Reagan
    B. George Bush
    C. Paul Volcker
    D. Issuance of junk bonds

13. Double-digit interest rates hurt all of the following groups EXCEPT:
    A. Those with investments in high-yield securities
    B. Construction workers
    C. Consumers desiring houses and automobiles
    D. Savings and loan institutions

14. According to the Ayatollah Khomeini, the "Great Satan" was:
    A. The Shah of Iran
    B. Mikahil S. Gorbachev
    C. Ronald Reagan
    D. The United States

15. Jimmy Carter faced a renomination struggle from:
    A. John Anderson
    B. Edward Kennedy
    C. Jesse Jackson
    D. Ronald Reagan

16. Zbigniew Brzezinski and Henry Kissinger once held the same governmental position as:
    A. Cyrus Vance
    B. Lawrence Walsh
    C. John Poindexter
    D. Gerald Ford

17. All of the following occurred during the Ford administration EXCEPT the:
    A. *Mayaguez* affair
    B. Communist conquest of Vietnam and Cambodia
    C. Panama Canal treaty
    D. Continuation of detente

18. In 1983, Reagan proceeded to liberate what island from communist rule?
    A. Taiwan
    B. Indonesia
    C. Grenada
    D. Cuba

19. The president who vowed to "never lie" to the American people was:
    A. Nixon
    B. Ford
    C. Carter
    D. Bush

20. In his 1988 campaign George Bush stressed:
    A. Expanded social programs
    B. "No New Taxes"
    C. Abortion on demand
    D. Military victory in the Cold War

**Essay Questions**

1. What events worked to the advantage of the little-known Jimmy Carter in his remarkable bid for the White House?

2. Show how and why Ronald Reagan was able to turn the tables on the Carter administration in the 1980 election.

3. Discuss Carter's handling of the Iranian hostage crisis over the 444 days of captivity.

4. How and why did the Iran-contra affair work to undermine the effectiveness of the Reagan administration? Explain the roles of Colonel Oliver North and Admiral John Poindexter.

5. Compare and contrast the elections of 1980 and 1988 in reference to parties, nominees, issues, strategies, congressional outcome, and long-term significance.

## Critical Thinking Exercise

Some events and ideas are primarily supported by Democrats; others by Republicans; still others draw the backing of both parties. Place a "D" beside each selection primarily identified with Democrats; an "R" beside each choice identified mostly with Republicans; a "B" beside each selection supported by both parties; and an "N" beside each selection identified with neither party.

_____ 1. Supply-side economics

_____ 2. School desegregation

_____ 3. Reduced federal aid to education

_____ 4. "Tax the rich"

_____ 5. Bombing of Libya, 1985

_____ 6. No new taxes

_____7. Détente

_____8. Wholesale cuts in military spending

_____9. Support for the Boland Amendment

_____10. Urban enterprise zones

_____11. More progressivity in income taxes

_____12. Arms control agreements

_____13. Reinstituting some trade barriers

_____14. Nationalization of natural resources

_____15. Preserving the environment

_____16. Federal subsidies for farmers

_____17. Foreign aid for Israel

_____18. School prayer amendment

_____19. Lowering capital gains taxes

_____20. Minimum wage laws

# ANSWERS

## Chapter 16

*Multiple-Choice Questions*

1. A   2. D   3. B   4. C   5. C   6. C   7. A   8. A   9. B   10. C
11. C   12. B   13. A   14. A   15. A   16. D   17. C   18. B   19. C   20. B

*Critical Thinking*

1. F   2. F   3. F   4. F   5. I   6. F   7. J   8. F   9. F   10. J
11. F   12. I   13. I   14. I   15. J   16. F   17. F

## Chapter 17

*Map Exercise*

1. F   2. I   3. A   4. C   5. G   6. E   7. H   8. B   9. D

*Multiple-Choice Questions*

1. D   2. B   3. A   4. C   5. C   6. B   7. C   8. C   9. B   10. C
11. D   12. A   13. A   14. A   15. A   16. C   17. A   18. C   19. D   20. C

*Critical Thinking*

1. Faro
2. Atchison
3. Citizenship
4. Irrigation
5. Humid
6. Harvest
7. Reservation
8. Miners
9. Cherokee
10. Subsidies

## Chapter 18

*Map Exercise*

1. E   2. K   3. D   4. M   5. G   6. I   7. A   8. L   9. H   10. B
11. J   12. F   13. C

*Multiple-Choice Questions*

1. C   2. D   3. B   4. A   5. D   6. C   7. B   8. B   9. B   10. D
11. C   12. A   13. C   14. C   15. C   16. D   17. A   18. A   19. B   20. B

*Critical Thinking*

1. S   2. R   3. L   4. L   5. S   6. L   7. R   8. L   9. S   10. R

## Chapter 19

*Multiple-Choice Questions*

1. D   2. A   3. B   4. B   5. C   6. C   7. D   8. B   9. C   10. D
11. C   12. A   13. A   14. D   15. B   16. C   17. D   18. C   19. C   20. D

*Critical Thinking*

1. P   2. SG   3. SG   4. SG   5. P   6. SG   7. SG   8. P   9. P   10. P
11. SG   12. P   13. P   14. SG   15. SG

## Chapter 20

*Multiple-Choice Questions*

1. B   2. C   3. D   4. B   5. C   6. D   7. B   8. D   9. A   10. A
11. A   12. C   13. D   14. B   15. A   16. D   17. C   18. A   19. C   20. C

*Critical Thinking*

1. T   2. P   3. P   4. P   5. P   6. P   7. T   8. T   9. P   10. T

## CHAPTER 21

*Map Exercise*

Oklahoma, Arizona, and New Mexico were not yet states. Bryan carried the 11 ex-Confederate states plus Missouri, Kansas, Nebraska, South Dakota, Colorado, Wyoming, Montana, Idaho, Utah, Nevada, and Washington. McKinley carried all other states, including normally Democratic Kentucky, as well as California and Oregon.

*Multiple-Choice Questions*

1. C  2. C  3. A  4. D  5. C  6. A  7. C  8. C  9. A  10. D
11. B  12. D  13. C  14. D  15. B  16. D  17. A  18. B  19. D  20. C

*Critical Thinking*

1. T  2. T  3. F  4. F  5. F  6. T  7. F  8. O  9. O  10. O

## CHAPTER 22

*Map Exercise I*

1. N  2. H  3. F  4. Q  5. M  6. J  7. A  8. C  9. L  10. D
11. K  12. B  13. E  14. G  15. O  16. I  17. P

*Map Exercise II*

1. J  2. E  3. C  4. F  5. H  6. G  7. A  8. D  9. I

*Multiple-Choice Questions*

1. C  2. B  3. C  4. A  5. A  6. B  7. C  8. B  9. A  10. B
11. B  12. C  13. D  14. B  15. C  16. A  17. B  18. D  19. B  20. C

*Critical Thinking*

1. E  2. E  3. I  4. I  5. I  6. E  7. I  8. E  9. E  10. I

# Chapter 23

*Multiple-Choice Questions*

1. A   2. A   3. A   4. A   5. A   6. D   7. B   8. B   9. D   10. D
11. D  12. C  13. D  14. D  15. B  16. A  17. B  18. B  19. D  20. C

*Critical Thinking*

1. Status quo
2. "Old Guard"
3. Monopoly
4. Equality
5. Carter Woodson
6. Bryan
7. Debs
8. Laissez-faire
9. Elbert Gary
10. Abe Ruef

# Chapter 24

*Map Exercise*

1. E   2. H   3. C   4. F   5. D   6. G   7. I   8. K   9. B   10. N
11. A  12. J  13. M  14. L

*Multiple-Choice Questions*

1. B   2. D   3. B   4. C   5. D   6. C   7. D   8. A   9. C   10. D
11. D  12. A  13. B  14. C  15. C  16. C  17. C  18. C  19. B  20. A

*Critical Thinking*

1. F   2. O   3. F   4. I   5. F   6. F   7. O   8. F   9. I   10. O

# Chapter 25

*Multiple-Choice Questions*

1. C   2. A   3. C   4. A   5. D   6. B   7. A   8. D   9. D   10. A
11. C  12. C  13. B  14. A  15. D  16. A  17. B  18. A  19. C  20. C

*Critical Thinking*

1. F. Scott Fitzgerald
2. Fitzgerald
3. Ernest Hemingway
4. H. L. Mencken
5. Sinclair Lewis
6. Robert and Helen Lynd
7. W. E. B. Du Bois
8. Langston Hughes

# CHAPTER 26

*Multiple-Choice Questions*

1. **C**  2. **B**  3. **D**  4. **C**  5. **D**  6. **A**  7. **D**  8. **C**  9. **B**  10. **B**
11. **D**  12. **D**  13. **B**  14. **B**  15. **A**  16. **B**  17. **B**  18. **B**  19. **C**  20. **C**

*Critical Thinking*

1. **T**  2. **T**  3. **O**  4. **O**  5. **F**  6. **T**  7. **F**  8. **O**  9. **T**  10. **O**
11. **O**  12. **F**

# CHAPTER 27

*Map Exercise*

1. **I**  2. **F**  3. **C**  4. **G**  5. **H**  6. **E**  7. **J**  8. **D**  9. **B**  10. **K**
11. **A**

*Multiple-Choice Questions*

1. **D**  2. **A**  3. **D**  4. **A**  5. **B**  6. **A**  7. **A**  8. **D**  9. **A**  10. **C**
11. **B**  12. **A**  13. **A**  14. **C**  15. **A**  16. **B**  17. **A**  18. **B**  19. **B**  20. **B**

*Critical Thinking*

1. **T**  2. **F**  3. **T**  4. **O**  5. **O**  6. **O**  7. **T**  8. **O**  9. **F**  10. **T**
11. **T**  12. **F**

# Chapter 28

*Map Exercise I*

1. I   2. C   3. B   4. F   5. K   6. H   7. A   8. J   9. D   10. E
11. L   12. G

*Map Exercise II*

1. G   2. L   3. D   4. B   5. H   6. F   7. E   8. C   9. A   10. K
11. I   12. J

*Multiple-Choice Questions*

1. D   2. D   3. B   4. B   5. C   6. C   7. B   8. B   9. C   10. D
11. B   12. B   13. D   14. A   15. B

*Critical Thinking*

1. N   2. B   3. I   4. B   5. I   6. II   7. I   8. I
9. B   10. N   11. B   12. NH   13. II   14. B   15. N

# Chapter 29

*Map Exercise*

1. N   2. C   3. L   4. M   5. F   6. G   7. A   8. B   9. H   10. K
11. J   12. E   13. D   14. I

*Multiple-Choice Questions*

1. B   2. B   3. C   4. C   5. C   6. D   7. C   8. D   9. B   10. B
11. A   12. B   13. B   14. D   15. A   16. A   17. B   18. C   19. D   20. B

*Critical Thinking*

1. 14   2. 1   3. 7   4. 13   5. 12   6. 15   7. 3   8. 5   9. 2   10. 11
11. 8   12. 4   13. 9   14. 6   15. 10

# CHAPTER 30

*Map Exercise*

1. **6**   2. **F**   3. **D**   4. **9**   5. **G**   6. **10**   7. **H**   8. **3**   9. **4**   10. **2**
11. **E**   12. **8**   13. **B**   14. **5**   15. **1**   16. **A**   17. **C**   18. **7**

*Multiple-Choice Questions*

1. **B**   2. **C**   3. **B**   4. **C**   5. **D**   6. **A**   7. **D**   8. **A**   9. **D**   10. **C**
11. **D**   12. **B**   13. **A**   14. **A**   15. **B**   16. **A**   17. **D**   18. **D**   19. **C**   20. **C**

*Critical Thinking*

1. **C**   2. **L**   3. **C**   4. **C**   5. **C**   6. **L**   7. **C**   8. **C**   9. **L**   10. **L**
11. **C**   12. **C**   13. **L**   14. **C**   15. **L**   16. **L**   17. **L**   18. **C**   19. **L**   20. **C**

# CHAPTER 31

*Multiple-Choice Questions*

1. **C**   2. **C**   3. **B**   4. **D**   5. **C**   6. **C**   7. **D**   8. **C**   9. **C**   10. **B**
11. **B**   12. **B**   13. **D**   14. **B**   15. **B**

*Critical Thinking*

1. **F**   2. **T**   3. **F**   4. **T**   5. **F**   6. **F**   7. **F**   8. **T**   9. **T**   10. **T**
11. **F**   12. **F**   13. **T**   14. **T**   15. **T**

# CHAPTER 32

*Map Exercise I*

1. **E**   2. **R**   3. **A**   4. **T**   5. **N**   6. **L**   7. **F**   8. **X**   9. **O**   10. **C**
11. **K**   12. **S**   13. **B**   14. **P**   15. **V**   16. **H**   17. **J**   18. **Z**   19. **Q**   20. **W**
21. **U**   22. **M**   23. **I**   24. **Y**   25. **D**   26. **G**

*Map Exercise II*

1. **75**  2. **18**  3. **1**  4. **56**  5. **29**  6. **69**  7. **38**  8. **15**  9. **49**  10. **11**
11. **80**  12. **76**  13. **62**  14. **55**  15. **15**  16. **16**  17. **41**  18. **54**  19. **52**  20. **63**
21. **53**  22. **28**  23. **17**  24. **33**  25. **51**  26. **19**  27. **20**  28. **27**  29. **78**  30. **31**
31. **2**  32. **44**  33. **43**  34. **60**  35. **34**  36. **48**  37. **10**  38. **36**  39. **46**  40. **8**
41. **45**  42. **26**  43. **82**  44. **42**  45. **59**  46. **40**  47. **32**  48. **50**  49. **81**  50. **47**
51. **39**  52. **74**  53. **66**  54. **24**  55. **22**  56. **72**  57. **13**  58. **71**  59. **83**  60. **5**
61. **84**  62. **65**  63. **67**  64. **77**  65. **6**  66. **12**  67. **30**  68. **9**  69. **7**  70. **61**
71. **3**  72. **37**  73. **21**  74. **4**  75. **35**  76. **57**  77. **58**  78. **73**  79. **14**  80. **25**
81. **68**  82. **23**  83. **70**  84. **79**

*Multiple-Choice Questions*

1. **A**  2. **D**  3. **A**  4. **B**  5. **C**  6. **B**  7. **B**  8. **B**  9. **D**  10. **C**
11. **C**  12. **C**  13. **D**  14. **D**  15. **B**  16. **C**  17. **C**  18. **C**  19. **C**  20. **B**

*Critical Thinking*

1. **R**  2. **B**  3. **N**  4. **D**  5. **B**  6. **R**  7. **B**  8. **N**  9. **D**  10. **R**
11. **D**  12. **B**  13. **D**  14. **N**  15. **B**  16. **B**  17. **B**  18. **R**  19. **R**  20. **B**